IMAGES
of America

ROSLYN

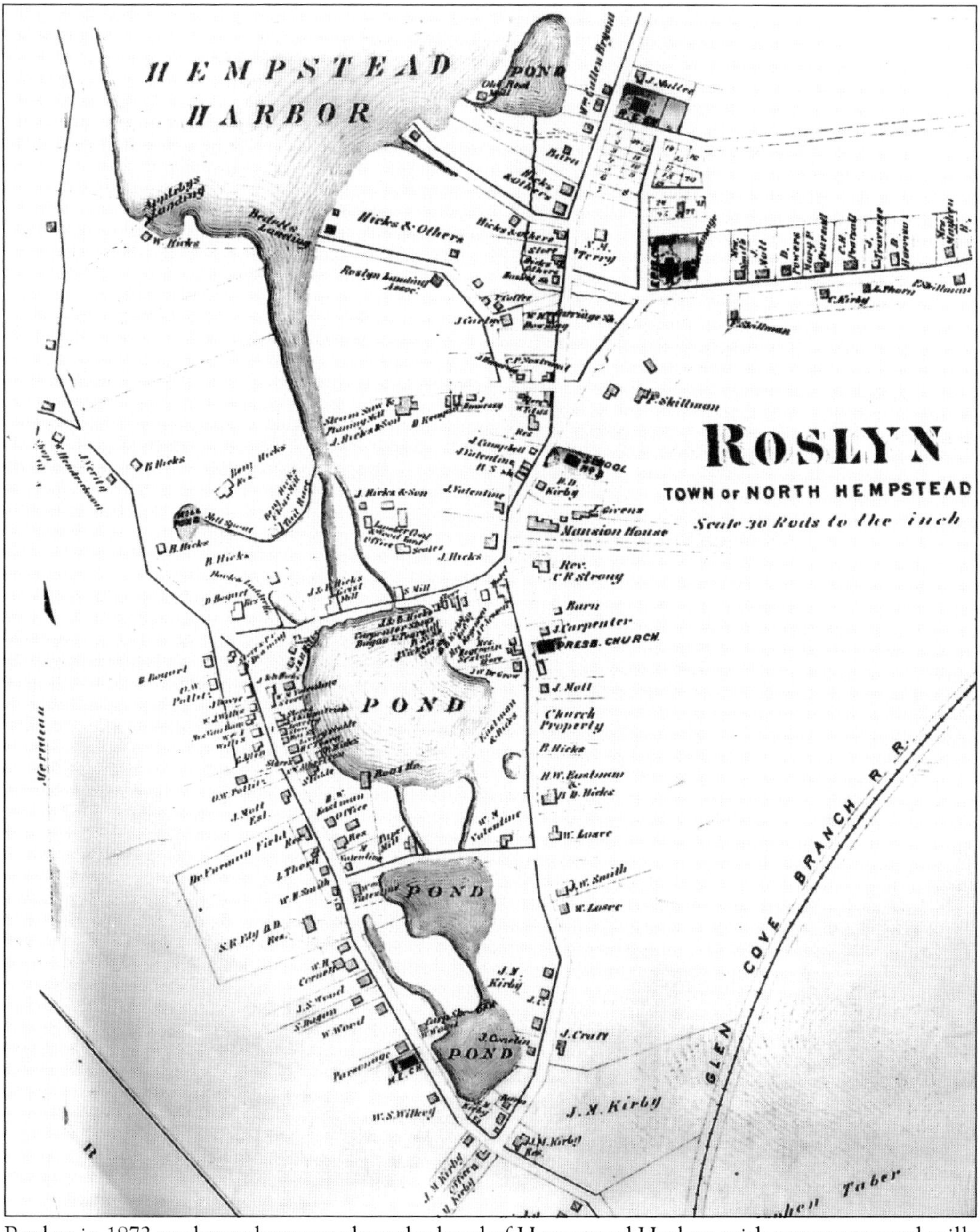

Roslyn in 1873 encloses three ponds at the head of Hempstead Harbor, with water-powered mills and lumberyard owned by the Hicks and Valentine families. It supports two churches. The New York stage stops at the Mansion House hotel. On the east side of the harbor poet William Cullen Bryant dwells at Cedar Mere. This map is from the Beers, Comstock and Cline Atlas of Long Island, 1873. (Courtesy of the Roslyn Landmark Society.)

On the cover: Please see page 36. (Courtesy of the Roslyn Landmark Society.)

IMAGES
of America

ROSLYN

Ellen Fletcher Russell and Sargent Russell
for the Roslyn Landmark Society

ARCADIA
PUBLISHING

ISBN 978-0-7385-6505-7

Published by Arcadia Publishing
Charleston, South Carolina

Printed in the United States of America

Library of Congress Control Number: 2008942609

For all general information contact Arcadia Publishing at:
Telephone 843-853-2070
Fax 843-853-0044
E-mail sales@arcadiapublishing.com
For customer service and orders:
Toll-Free 1-888-313-2665

Visit us on the Internet at www.arcadiapublishing.com

To the late Roger and Peggy Gerry, who gave themselves and their great resources to the preservation of Roslyn; and to the members of the Roslyn Landmark Society and the Roslyn Preservation Corporation who continue the work.

Contents

ACKNOWLEDGMENTS

The authors' first thanks go to Huyler C. Held and Robert B. Mackay of the Gerry Charitable Trust for their support during the writing of this book. Our partner in this work is Florence Westergard; we appreciate her skill and energy in production and organization. Craig Westergard, who grilled for us and lent office space, gets thanks too. Anne Tinder and Catherine Tamis of the Roslyn Landmark Society welcomed us to headquarters, gave us files, and made many arrangements. John and Michelle Santos and Ian Zwerdling opened their collections to us, and Ray Jacobs allowed us to publish his handsome photographs. Special thanks go to Jefferson Mansell, who proposed the book. As always, Mary Ann Brandl, Roslynian par excellence, encouraged us and made sure we were never bored. John and Marion Stevens assisted in this effort.

At Cedarmere, a Nassau County museum, Harrison Hunt enriched our understanding and provided outstanding images. Robert L. Harrison assisted him, and Linda Hunt added previously unknown Roslyn facts and images.

Kathy D'Amato-Smith of Roslyn Heights invited us to experience the ambience of her community and invited us to meet her neighbors, who shared their knowledge with us. Robert Sargent introduced us to Roslyn Estates and lent items from his collection. We were also ably assisted in Roslyn Estates by village clerk Nancy Yoshii.

Myrna Sloam of the Bryant Library Local History Collection provided some of the best images in the book. At the Nassau County Museum Collection, Long Island Studies Institute, we enjoyed working with George Fisher and Dolores Contreras. In Jamaica, Eric Huber, John Hyslop and Judith Todman of the Long Island Division of the Queens Borough Public Library helped us find outstanding images. Judy Estes of the Society for the Preservation of Long Island Antiquities opened the society's collections. Wallace W. Broege and Kathy Then of the Suffolk County Historical Society showed us the work of a fascinating photographer in the Fullerton Collection.

Through everything, we have enjoyed the calm and cheerful support of Rebekah Collinsworth, our capable editor at Arcadia Publishing. Many images in this volume appear courtesy of the Roslyn Landmark Society (RLS).

INTRODUCTION

From settlement in the 1640s through modern times, Roslyn's unique geography determined its character and the ways in which it changed. The first newcomers were both English and Dutch speakers. They found a sheltered, wooded valley opening to Hempstead Harbor. A Native American trail ran east and west, and another one curved south along the edge of a swamp. The settlement was founded as an entry port on Long Island Sound, the great, protected waterway that linked cities and towns from Manhattan to Cape Cod. Through Hempstead Harbor came the goods and supplies people needed for their houses and farms. The lively village attracted farmers, fishermen, sailors, boatbuilders, and merchants. Around 1705, someone built a dam across the swamp to power a gristmill. An ancient mill survives today, an artifact of the past and the reason insiders still call Roslyn's shopping street the milldam. The gristmill fed New York City's triangle trade—flour to the West Indies. From there, sugar and rum went to trade at English ports for manufactured goods and luxuries. As time went on, other industries came: sawmills, paper mills, a fulling mill, and a silk mill.

Hempstead Harbor's leading citizen in the late 1700s was Dutch-speaking merchant Hendrick Onderdonk. Most of Onderdonk's neighbors remained loyal to England during the Revolution, and Long Island was occupied by the British. Tales of the soldiers' raids still flourish here. Some believe that Onderdonk spied for the Americans. After the peace, on a tour of Long Island in 1790, Pres. George Washington stopped at Onderdonk's house. Today that house is the Washington Manor restaurant. Onderdonk's gristmill survives as well, and a replica of his paper mill stands in Roslyn Park.

In the generation after Onderdonk's, the Quaker families of Valentine and Hicks took over and extended milling and commerce. Henry Western Eastman dominated Roslyn's financial and real estate affairs and "Captain" Jacob Kirby the maritime trade. Throughout today's village buildings survive that housed these families and their enterprises.

Before the mid-1800s, most of the town's traffic with the world went by water. In 1818, merchant Daniel Bogart started a weekly stagecoach to Brooklyn over primitive roads. From that time until the railroad, stage lines ran from the Mansion House hotel in Roslyn. In 1835, entrepreneurs incorporated a turnpike company to improve the road to Flushing and operate it as a toll road. That road, which follows a Native American trail, became Route 25A (Northern Boulevard).

In the 1830s, John Willis, a large landowner on the west side of the village, began selling building lots along Main Street. A building boom ensued, resulting in a village shaped like an inverted A. Converging streets bracketed three swampy ponds, and a road ran across the milldam at the top. Soon the village had 250 inhabitants, 2 paper mills, 3 stores, a tavern, a Methodist meetinghouse, a lumberyard, and 40 or 50 dwellings.

Long Island's North Shore has long been a seasonal retreat for New Yorkers—its location, temperate climate, and picturesque scenery made it attractive for country homes. By midcentury, one could take the Long Island Rail Road part of the way. Roslyn is less than 20 miles from Times Square. Poet and newspaper editor William Cullen Bryant was the best known of the early commuters, buying a house and farm here in 1843. Bryant's Cedarmere still stands north of the village overlooking the harbor. The poet's friends, who made long visits and lived in cottages on his land, included such literary figures as Margaret Fuller, John Ordronaux, and Parke Godwin, who married Bryant's oldest daughter. More significantly for Roslyn, Bryant's visiting friends included top architects and landscape designers as well. Frederick Law Olmsted, designer of New York's Central Park, came, as did Gothic Revival architects Calvert Vaux, Jacob Wrey Mould, and Frederick Copley. The high-style local buildings they designed still stand today.

Shortly after Bryant's arrival, the post office insisted that the village's name be changed to avoid confusion with the other "Hempsteads." Residents chose romantic-sounding Roslyn, with its suggestion of Scottish hills and lochs.

During the early 20th century, New York's rich found the North Shore ideal for great estates where they enjoyed social life and outdoor sports. Their Gold Coast paradise stretched from the city line east, past Huntington. Here in Nassau County, the estates absorbed thousands of acres of farmland and villages. Equestrians could ride for miles across their field and woodland paths. Two of the great estates, Clarence and Katherine Mackay's Harbor Hill and Childs and Frances Frick's Clayton, shouldered next to Roslyn, providing benefactions, employment, and gifts of buildings and other lasting improvements. These years were good for Roslyn as they were for its wealthy neighbors. Such civic improvements as a park, a trolley line, libraries, a war memorial that housed a little theater, historic preservation, and an active neighborhood association made the village shine for awhile. But the Great Depression and World War II brought the golden years to a close, and postwar Roslyn fell into desuetude.

Roslyn Estates, East Hills, Flower Hill, Greenvale, and Roslyn Harbor had incorporated in 1931, with Roslyn following in 1932. Unincorporated Roslyn Heights had grown up around the Long Island Rail Road station after the end of the Civil War. Development roared eastward on Long Island during the 1950s, exerting pressures and demands on the little village huddling in its wooded head-of-harbor valley.

Yet postwar Roslyn had a charming quality that had all but disappeared on the Long Island of Robert Moses and Levittown. It looked tired, but its handsome houses and quaint mills seemed more "antique" than "decayed." Roslyn's fine architecture and its strong sense of the past attracted people who would pour great resources of effort, influence, and money into preserving and beautifying the village. Roger and Peggy Gerry, he an oral surgeon retired from the U.S. Navy and she a gifted artist, arrived in 1951. For the next half-century, they organized themselves, their neighbors, and selected experts into a powerful engine of historic preservation and quality-of-life enhancement. The specialized organizations they founded and shaped—the Roslyn Landmark Society and the Roslyn Preservation Corporation—exist to this day. Because of the Gerrys and those who followed them, Roslyn is one of the few places on Long Island that is more attractive today than it was 40 or 50 years ago.

One

Harbor Town

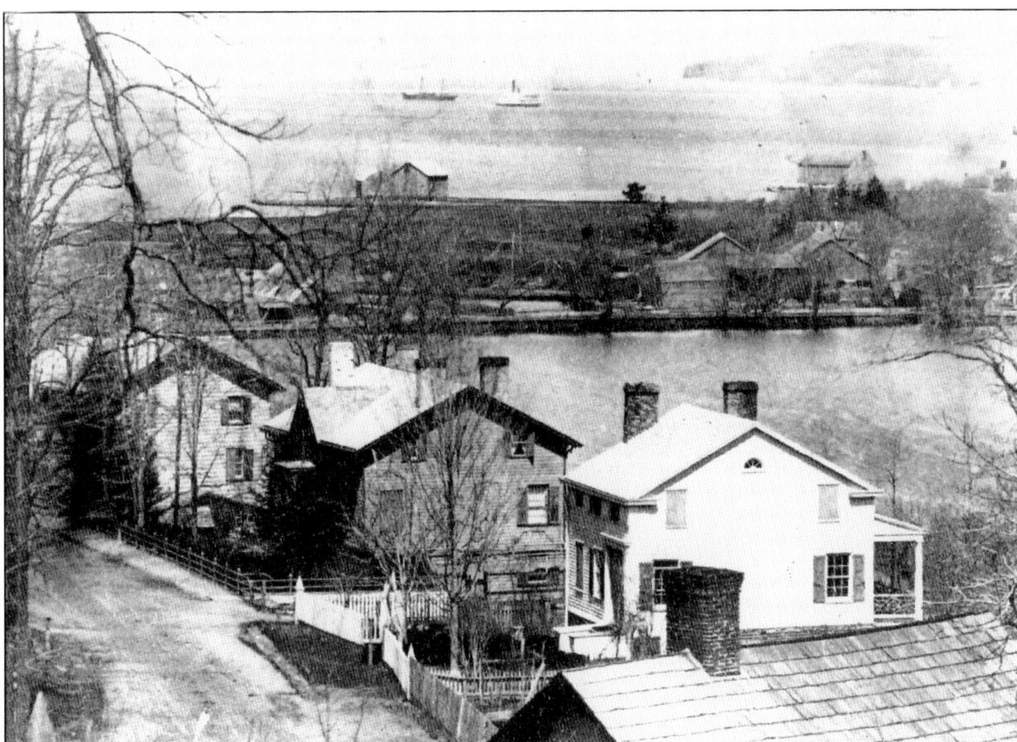

Roslyn was founded as an entry port on Long Island Sound. Until the 20th century, much of its traffic with the world went by water. This *c.* 1880 photograph looks north past Main Street and the milldam out to Hempstead Harbor. The white house, right of center, was built around 1840 for paper mill operator Washington Valentine. The buildings on the milldam include, center, the gristmills and sawmills. (Courtesy of RLS.)

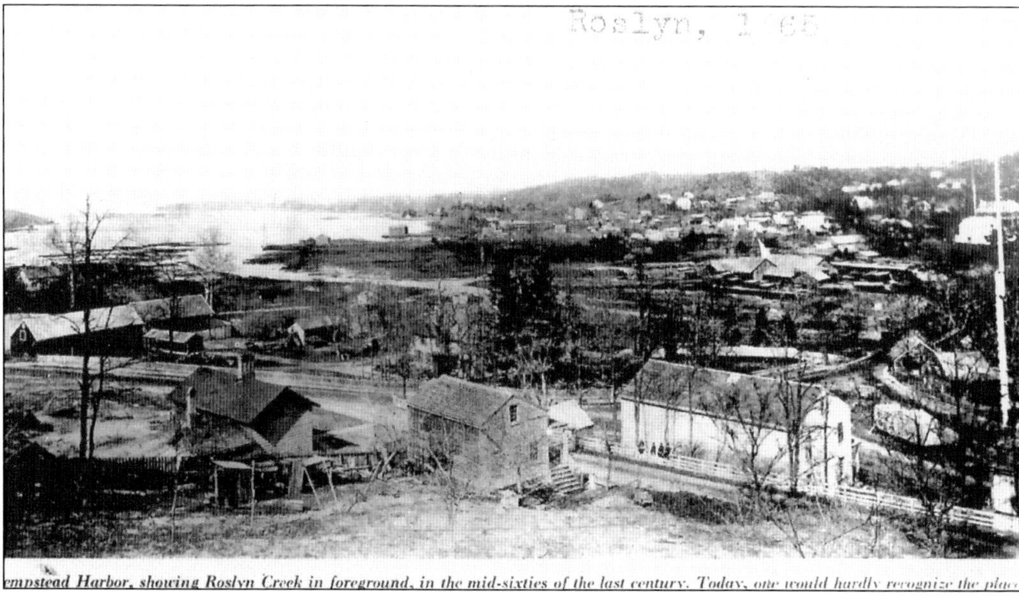

One of the oldest photographs of Roslyn looks northeasterly from the west hillside around 1865. The long white house behind the fence is the George Allen house on Main Street, and the two near houses are on Glen Avenue. In the center stands the house visited by Pres. George Washington; the sheds and barns behind belong to Hicks Lumberyard. (Courtesy of the Nassau County Museum Collection, Long Island Studies Institute.)

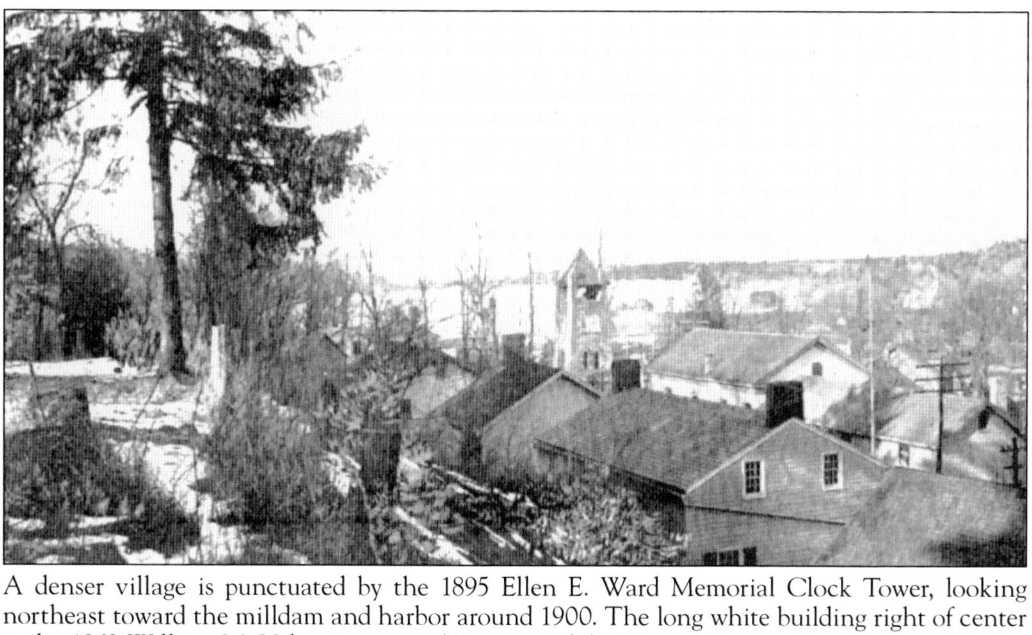

A denser village is punctuated by the 1895 Ellen E. Ward Memorial Clock Tower, looking northeast toward the milldam and harbor around 1900. The long white building right of center is the 1862 William M. Valentine store. (Courtesy of the Nassau County Department of Parks, Recreation and Museums, Cedarmere.)

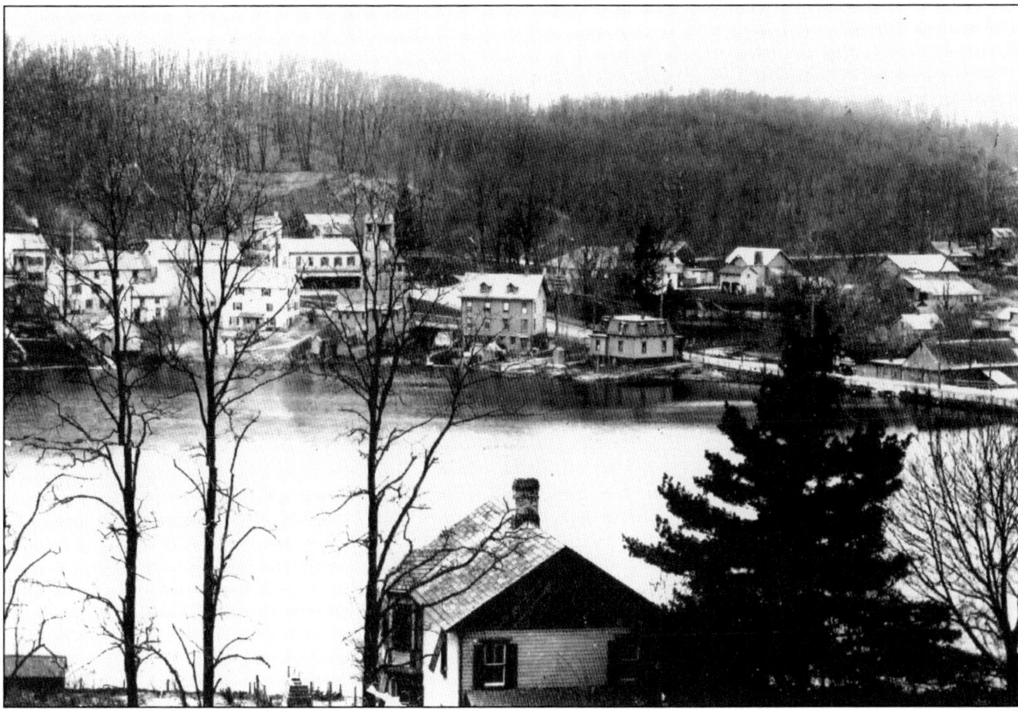

The Edward Ramsauer tinsmith shop on East Broadway is on the near side in this 1895 view west across the gristmill pond. The milldam and gristmill are at center right. Beyond is the roofscape of the Hicks Lumberyard. Right of center stands the mansard-roofed Joshua T. Hicks house, built in 1865, and just up the road stands the new Ellen E. Ward Memorial Clock Tower. (Courtesy of RLS.)

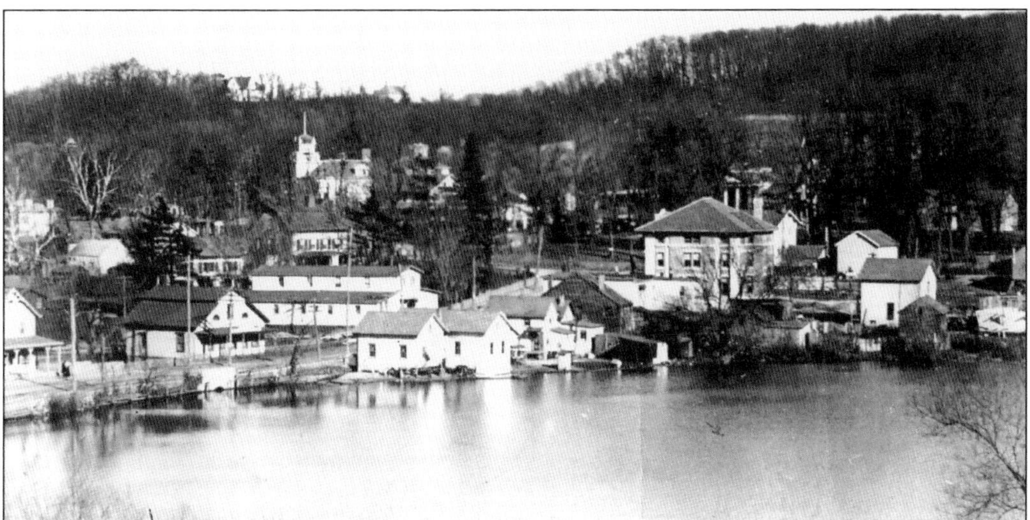

From northern Main Street, around 1915, this view shows the east end of the milldam and upper East Broadway. On the milldam stands, left, one of the two-story Frederick C. Hicks stores, built in 1910; the Hicks sawmill; and the Joshua T. Hicks store. Behind stands the gambrel-roofed Anderis Onderdonk house, built in 1797. Right of center is the 1906 Roslyn Savings Bank. Right of that are East Broadway shops and barns on Silver Lake. (Courtesy of RLS.)

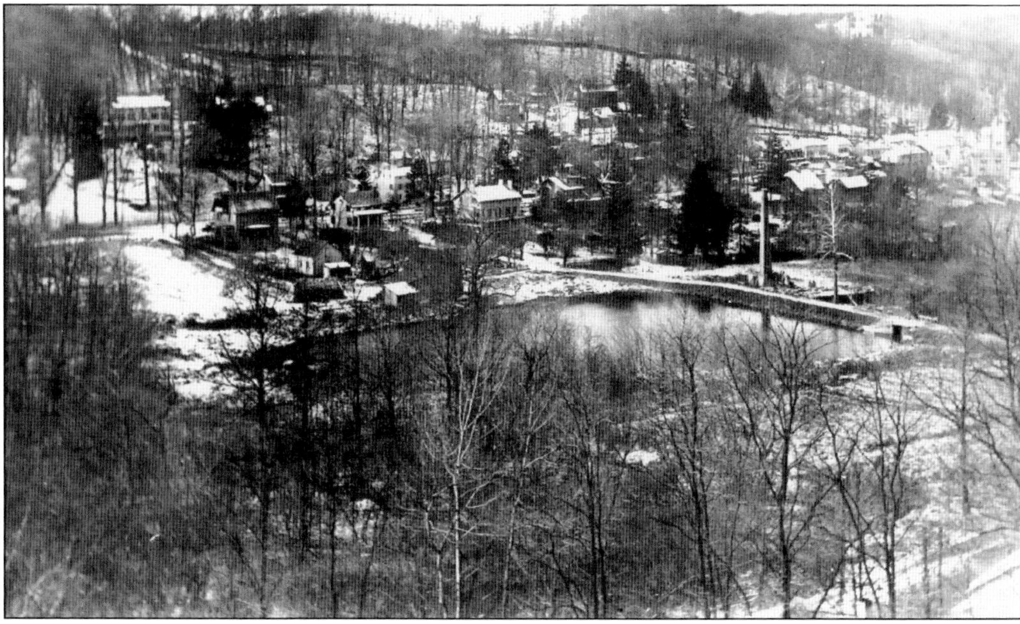

Looking toward Main Street around 1910, the tall chimney at center right is the remnant of the old paper mill, blown down in 1906. The houses left of center stand on the east side of Main Street: the Presbyterian parsonage, then the houses of paper mill operators Washington and Myers Valentine. Across Main Street up the hill stands the 1837 house and school run by Presbyterian minister Samuel Rose Ely. (Courtesy of RLS.)

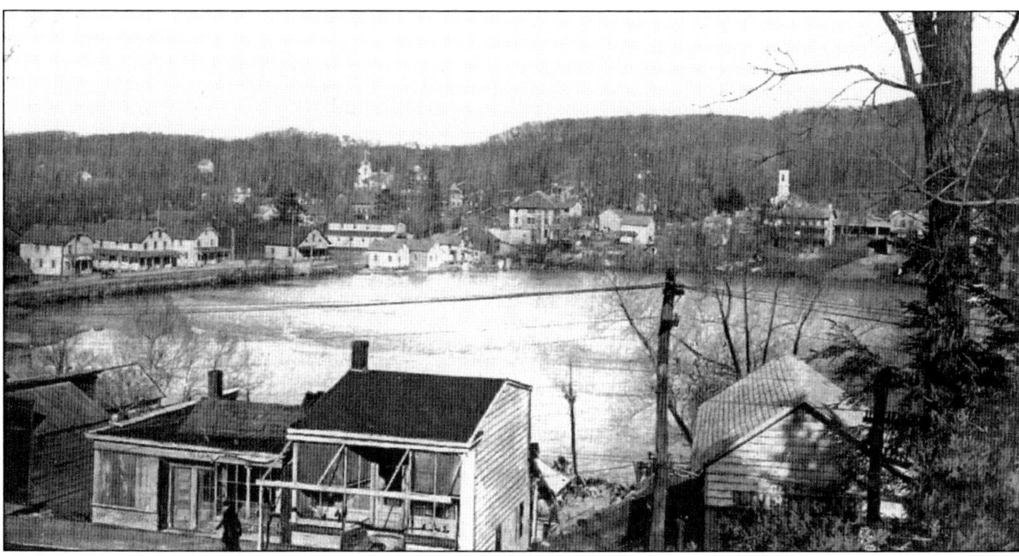

The driveway for the Jolly Fisherman restaurant replaced these small, ramshackle stores near the north end of Main Street. Across the pond, from left to right, stand the Frederick C. Hicks stores, the Hicks sawmill, and the Joshua T. Hicks store. The 1906 Roslyn Savings Bank is on the south side of the milldam; to its right is the Presbyterian church steeple. (Courtesy of Linda Hunt.)

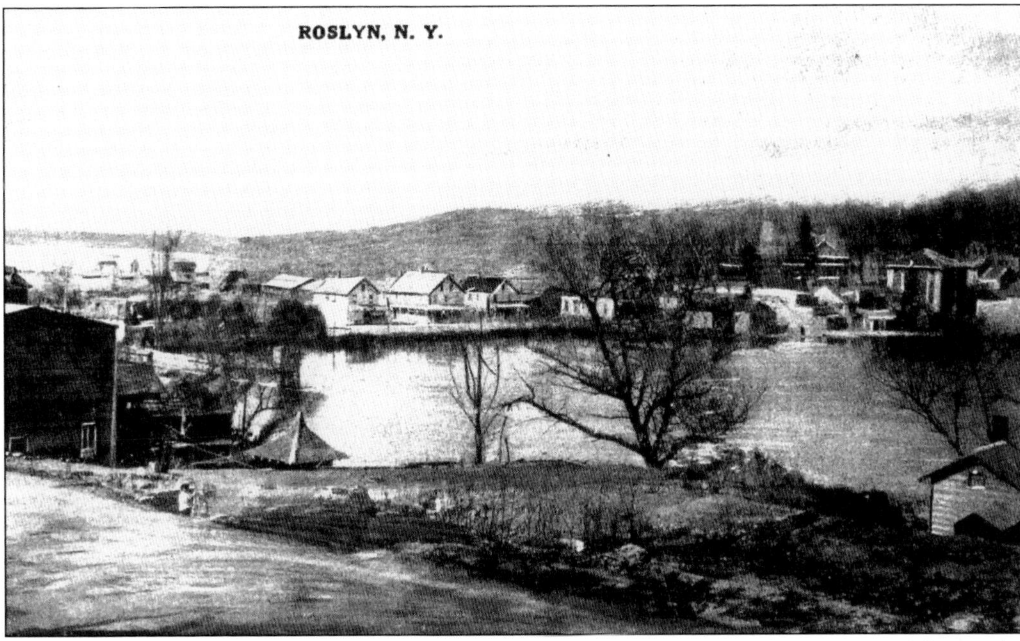

From the west side of Main Street, this *c.* 1915 postcard view looks northeast across Silver Lake. Len Thorne's livery stable stands at the far left, and the milldam crosses the center of the picture. Three Hicks stores, built between 1905 and 1910, stand to the right of the gristmill, with the Roslyn Savings Bank at far right. (Courtesy of Ian Zwerdling.)

Alice Titus, who opened the Grist Mill Tea House in 1919, loved this view. "The Creek was most beautiful at sunset," she wrote. "Blue herons were often seen in the grasses at the edge of the water [and] kingfishers, gulls and ducks were a constant source of entertainment." In 1929, the creek was bulkheaded, and the wildlife all but disappeared. (Courtesy of RLS.)

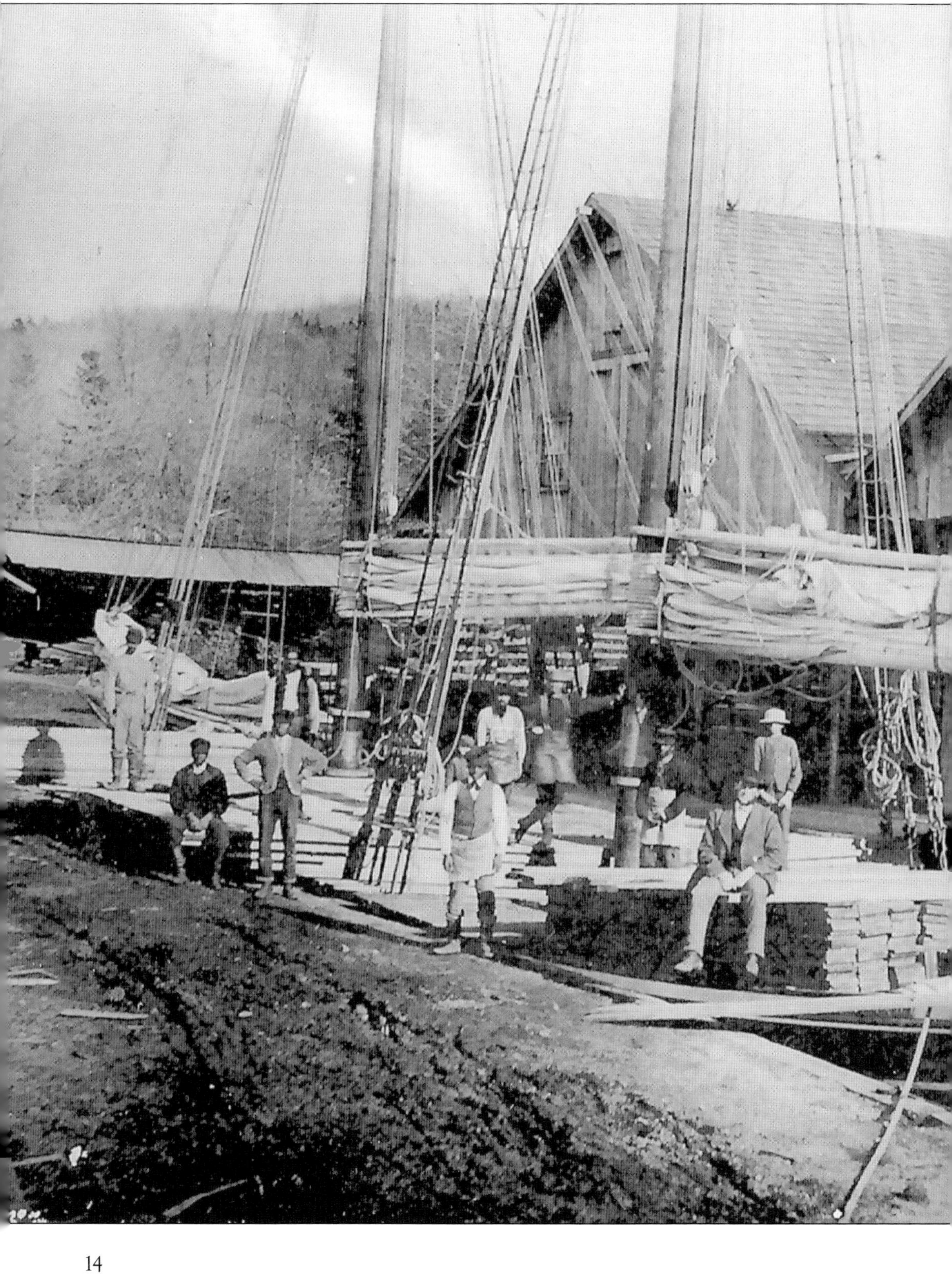

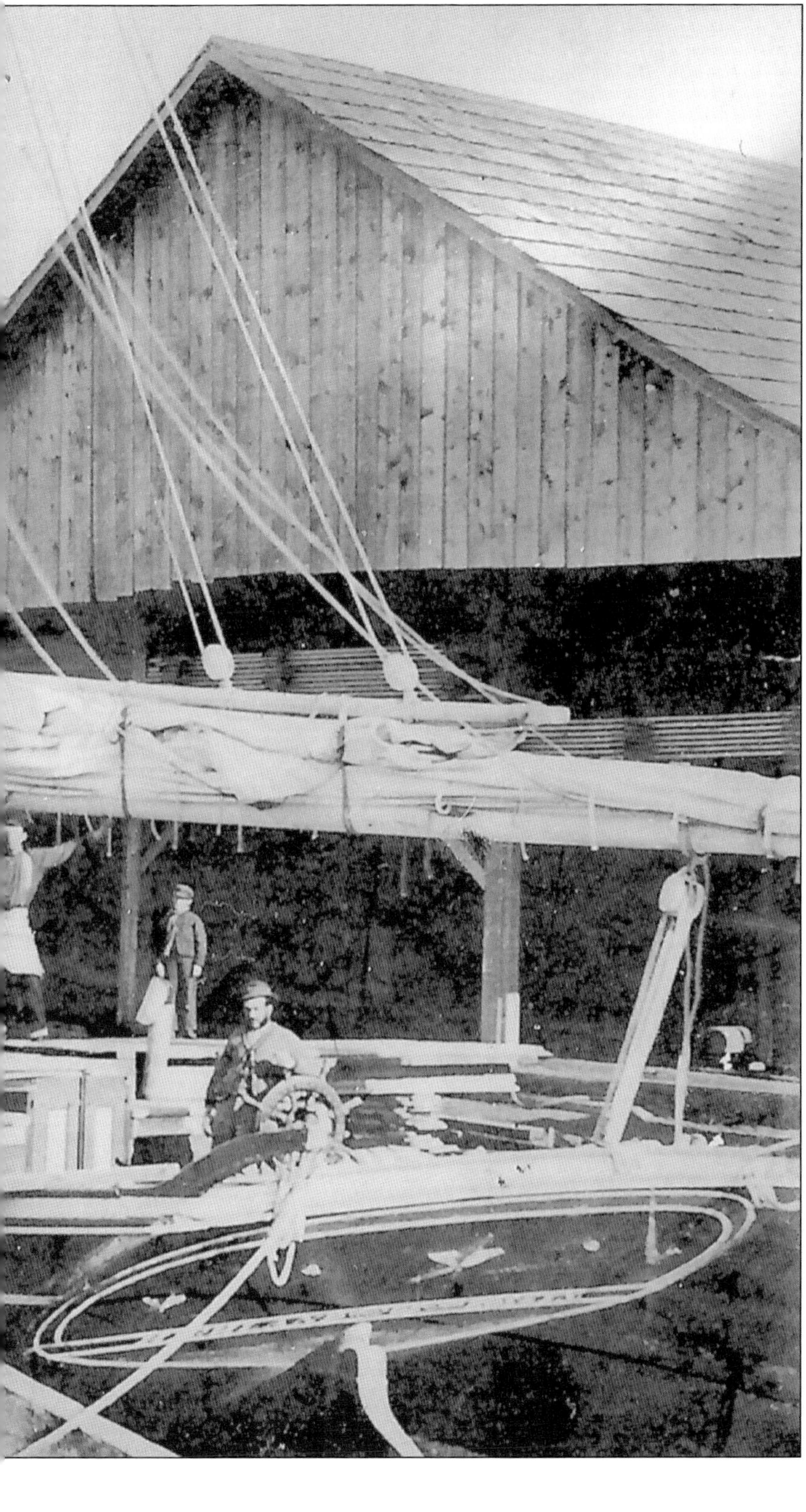

Jacob Kirby sailed schooners to New York from the mid- to late 19th century. They carried hay, firewood, lumber, flour, shellfish, and farm produce to the city, and brought back such staple supplies as coffee, tea, sugar, hardware, coal, pork, and liquors. Here the *Highlander*, with Capt. Peter Lynch at the wheel, lies alongside the Hicks Lumberyard around 1865. (Courtesy of RLS.)

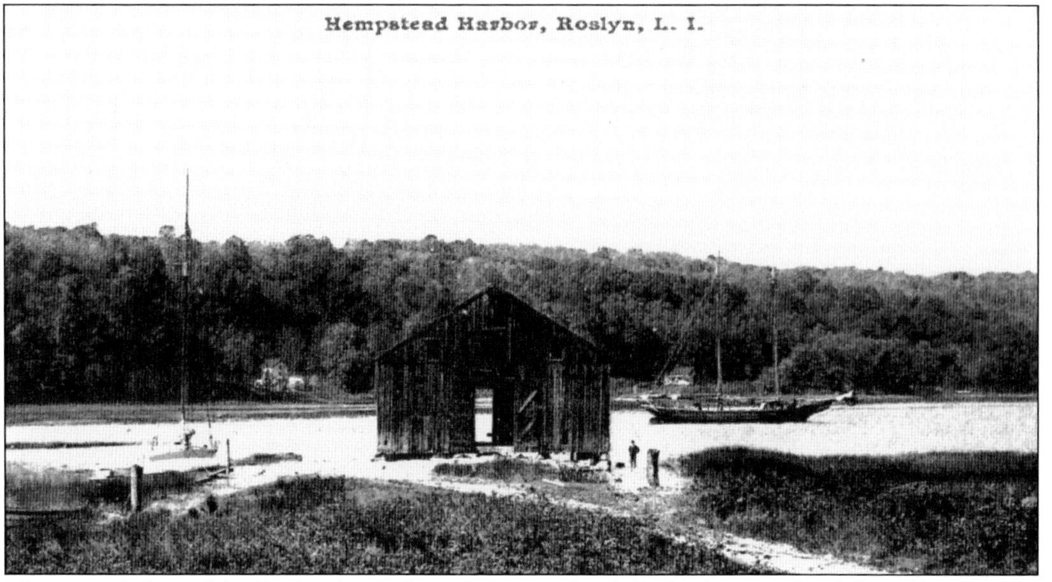

Most vessels bound for Roslyn landed on the east side of the harbor north of the village. Motts Landing, shown here, was the wharf near where William Hicks established his first sawmill in the 1830s. Moored out in the harbor is the kind of two-masted schooner used in the lumber trade. (Courtesy of John and Michelle Santos.)

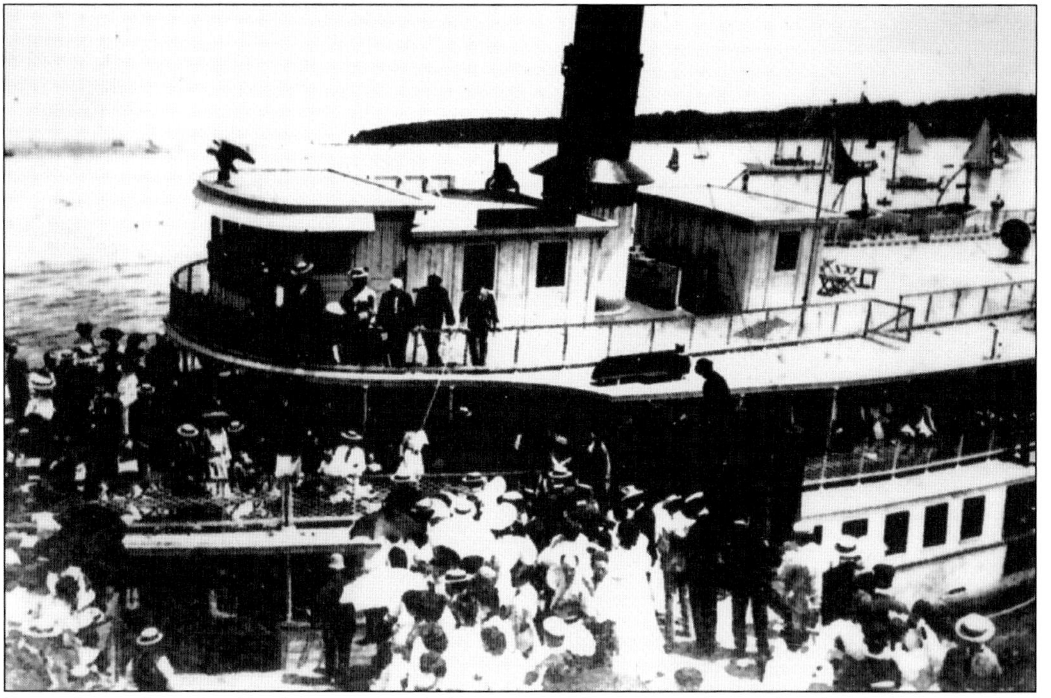

From the early 1860s, Roslynians traveled to New York on steamboats that landed just north of Cedar Mere, William Cullen Bryant's home. The steamboat landing was used until sand mining on the west side of the harbor silted up the ship channel. In 1900, the *Idlewild* was the last vessel to use Roslyn's steamboat landing. Here it takes on passengers at Sea Cliff about that time. (Courtesy of RLS.)

Two

Downtown

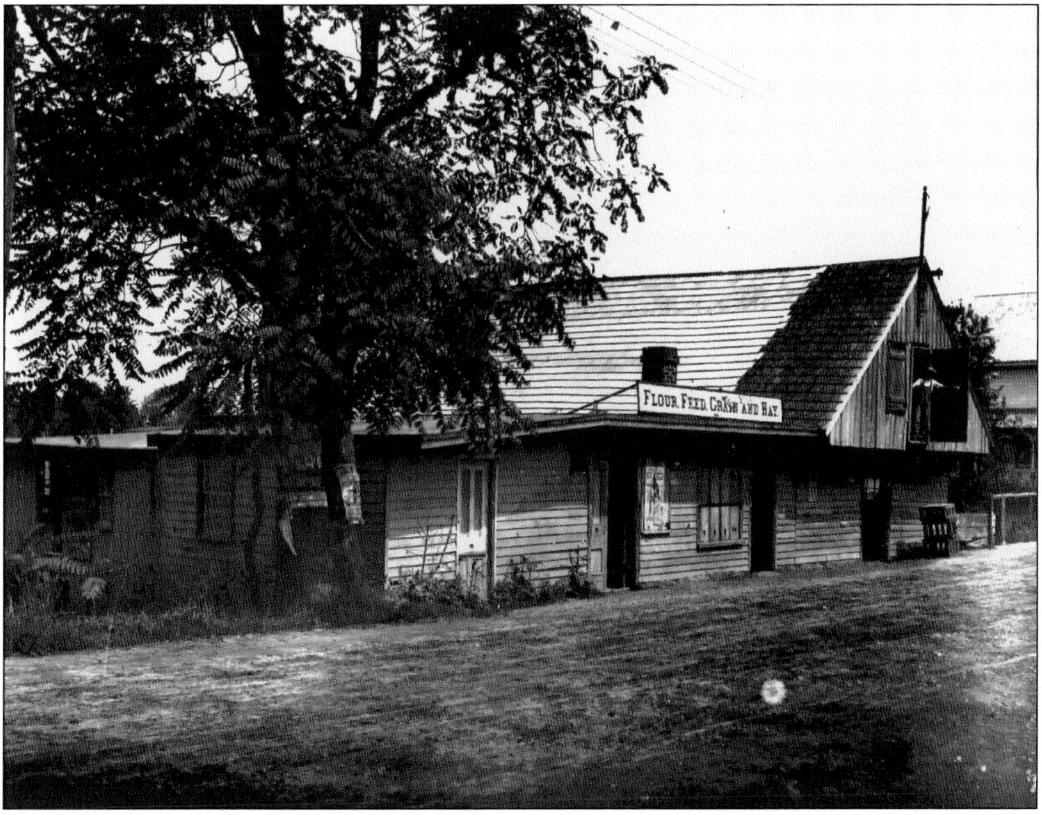

Many Roslyn stores and mills stood on the dam, built around 1705 for this gristmill, shown around 1890. Around 1840, the milldam was improved as the North Hempstead Turnpike, a toll road. The business zone also included a sawmill and the Hicks Lumberyard on both sides of Roslyn Creek. (Courtesy of the Nassau County Department of Department of Parks, Recreation and Muscums, Cedarmere.)

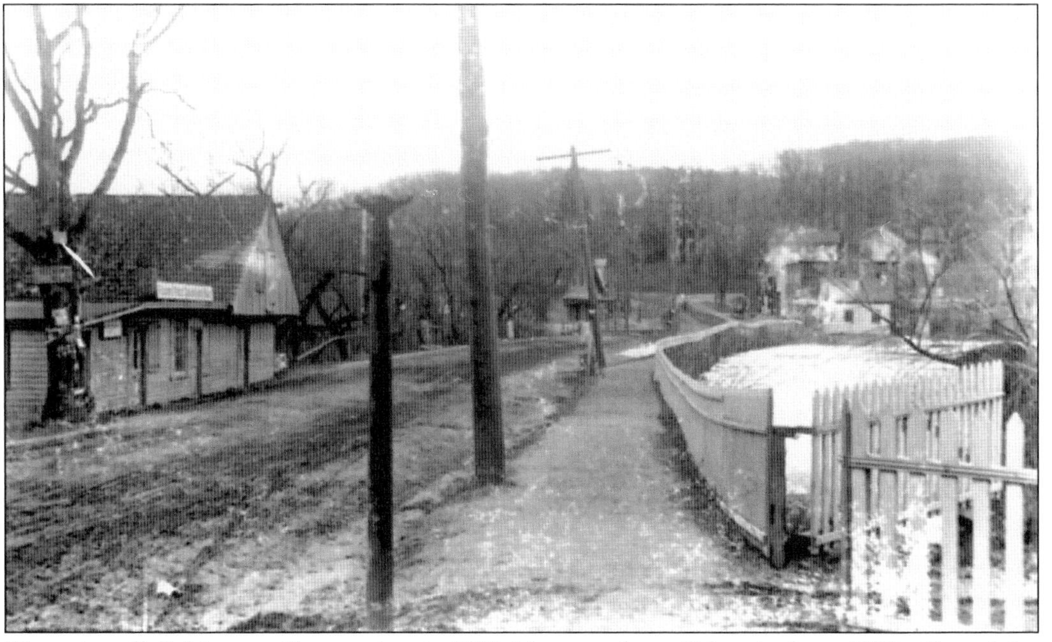

The gristmill (left) was still operating in 1888. Next on the milldam is the *c.* 1880 office of the Conklin-Tubby-Conklin Lumberyard. Both buildings stand today. To the right of the fence is the gristmill pond, later called Silver Lake. The small shops at right housed a carpenter, a harness maker, and a blacksmith. A kerosene lamp stands in the foreground, with a telephone pole beyond. (Courtesy of the Nassau County Museum Collection, Long Island Studies Institute.)

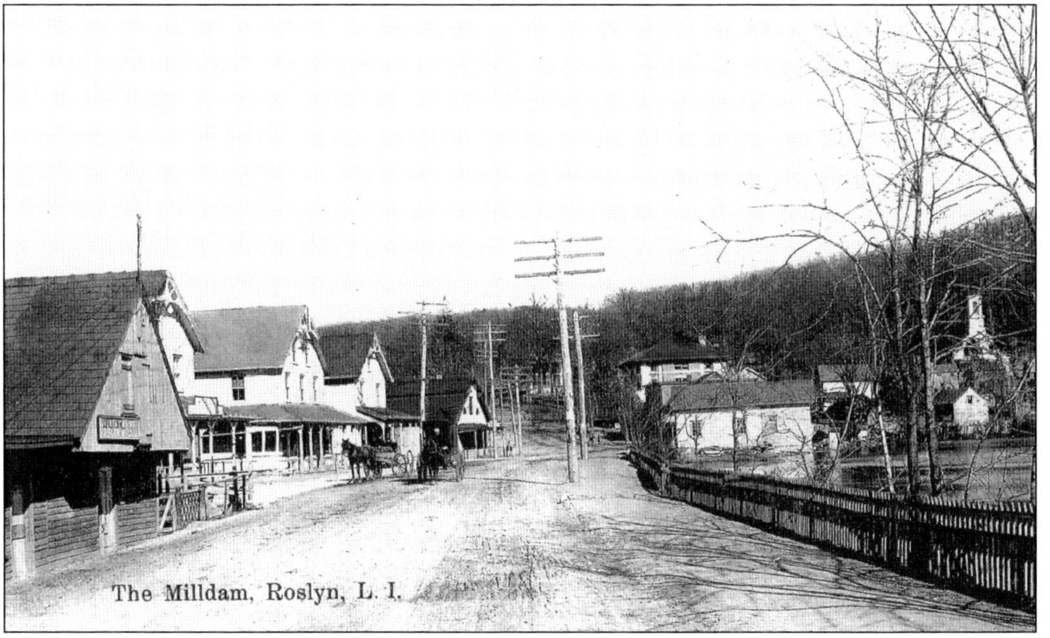

In this *c.* 1910 postcard, three stores have been built by Frederick C. Hicks between the gristmill and the lumber office. The south side of the milldam is unchanged from above, except that the kerosene lamps are gone and the 1906 Roslyn Savings Bank stands at the end of the street. The steeple at the far right belongs to the Presbyterian church. (Courtesy of John and Michelle Santos.)

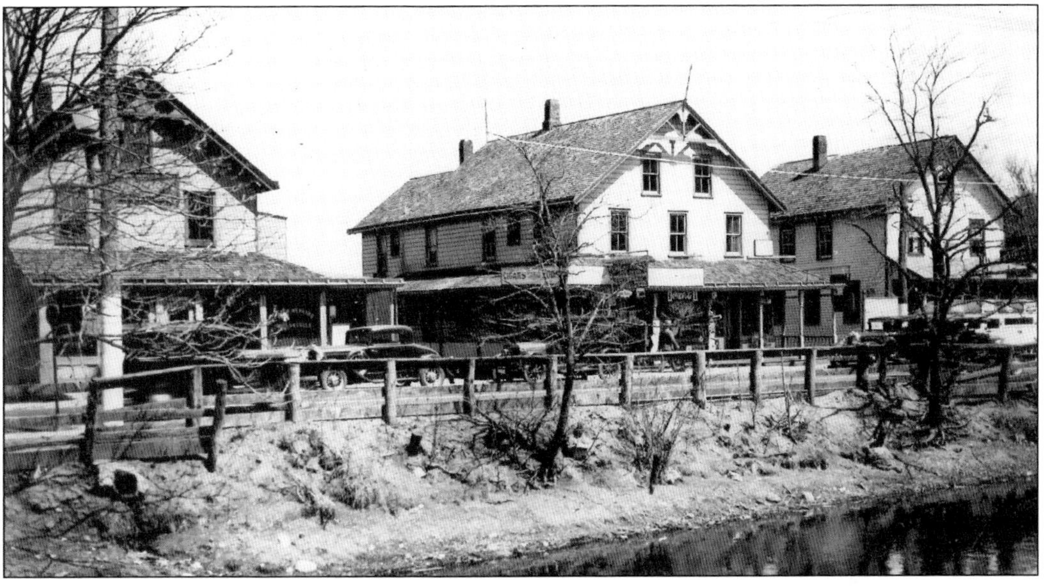

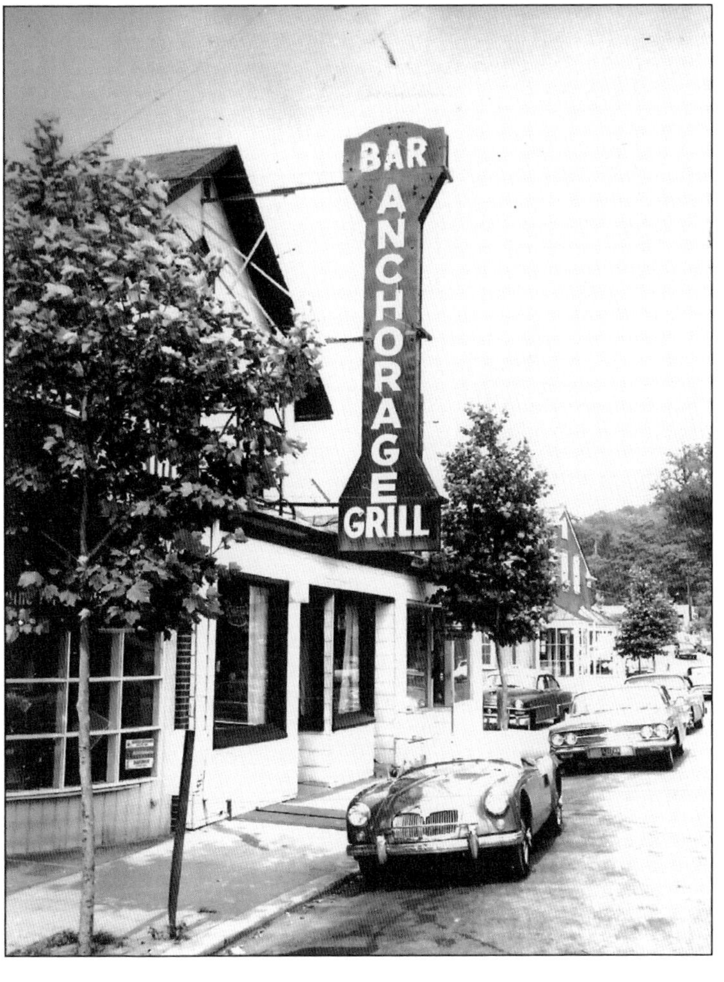

Thirty years separates these views of the Hicks stores on the milldam. During the 1930s, the building on the left was a garage, and later an awning shop. The center building was a paper store, then a lunchroom and soda fountain. The right-hand building, newer than the others, housed the *Roslyn News*. In the foreground, Silver Lake, in the 1930s no longer the gristmill pond, laps the edge of the street. The newest of the buildings appears in the 1963 photograph at right as the Anchorage, a popular watering hole, which, along with My Father's Place on School Street, attracted young people from all over Long Island. All three Hicks stores remain in use today. (Courtesy of RLS.)

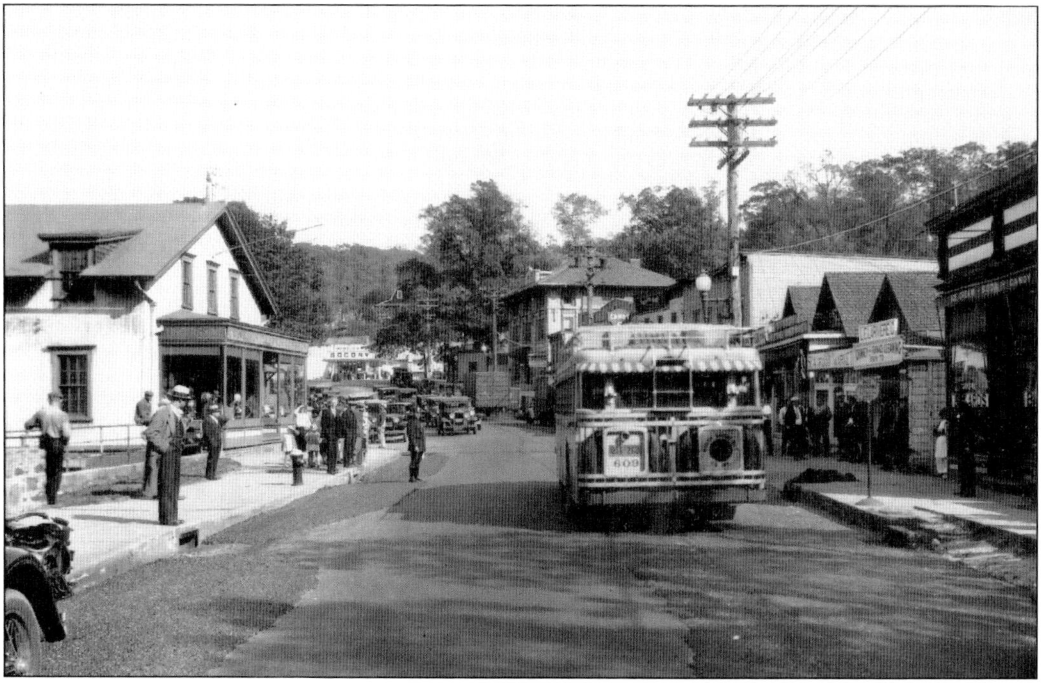

This view looks east on the milldam in the early 1940s and features the Conklin-Tubby-Conklin office (left), which today is a Junior League consignment shop. Far left, a railing surrounds the sluiceway that powered the former Hicks sawmill. In the street, a bus heads west, the hipped roof of the Roslyn Savings Bank is visible above. (Courtesy of the Queens Borough Public Library, Long Island Division, Illustrations Collection, Roslyn.)

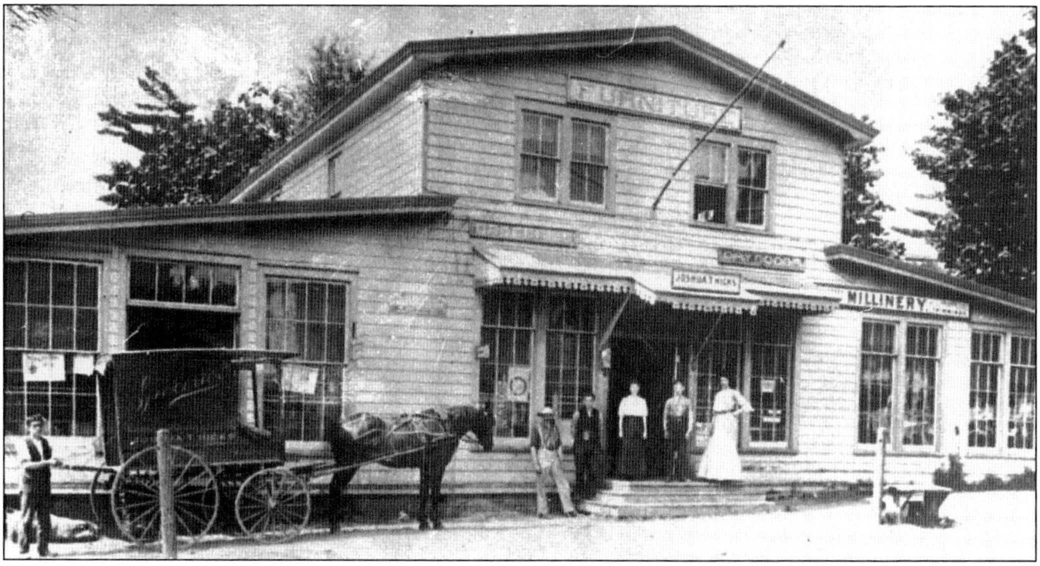

This c. 1850 general store near the east end of the milldam was occupied by Joshua T. Hicks when William Pickering photographed it around 1910. The center held groceries, the east wing (right) millinery and dry goods, and the second floor, furniture. The west wing (left) held barrels of flour, vinegar, cider, and molasses. Today the building is the Roslyn Post Office. (Courtesy of the Nassau County Museum Collection, Long Island Studies Institute.)

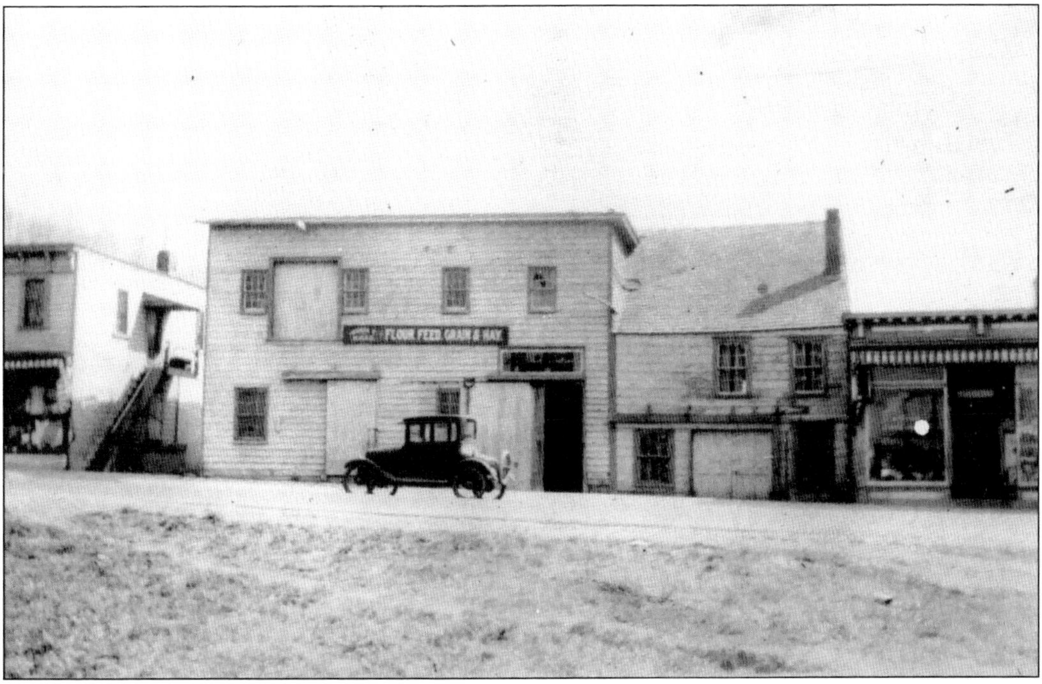

Across the milldam from his store, Joshua T. Hicks's annex, photographed around 1910, held flour and feed, grain, and hay. The very old building to the right had been a blacksmith shop. The building at far left, a harness shop that would become Raymon's Department Store, was demolished in 1983 for an expansion of the Roslyn Savings Bank. A replica was built a little to the west in 1984. (Courtesy of RLS.)

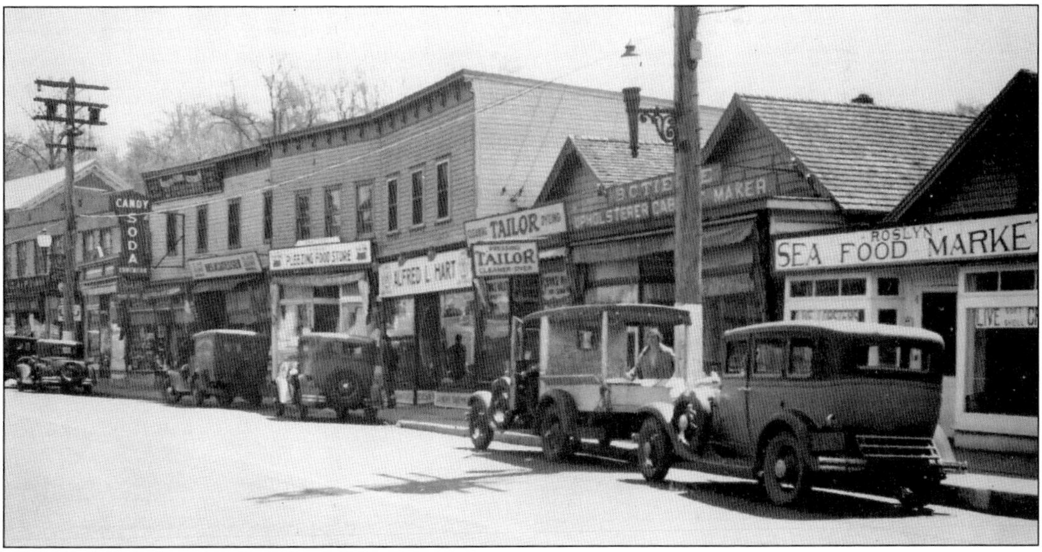

The south side of the milldam developed quickly between 1910, seen in the previous photograph, and 1935, when this photograph was made. The main block of the Hicks feed annex is just visible at the top of the street, with the brand-new Roslyn Savings Bank building looming behind it. Coming toward the foreground, representing the modern business model, are the drugstore, the deli, the Pleezing Food Store, the five-and-dime, and other enterprises. (Courtesy of RLS.)

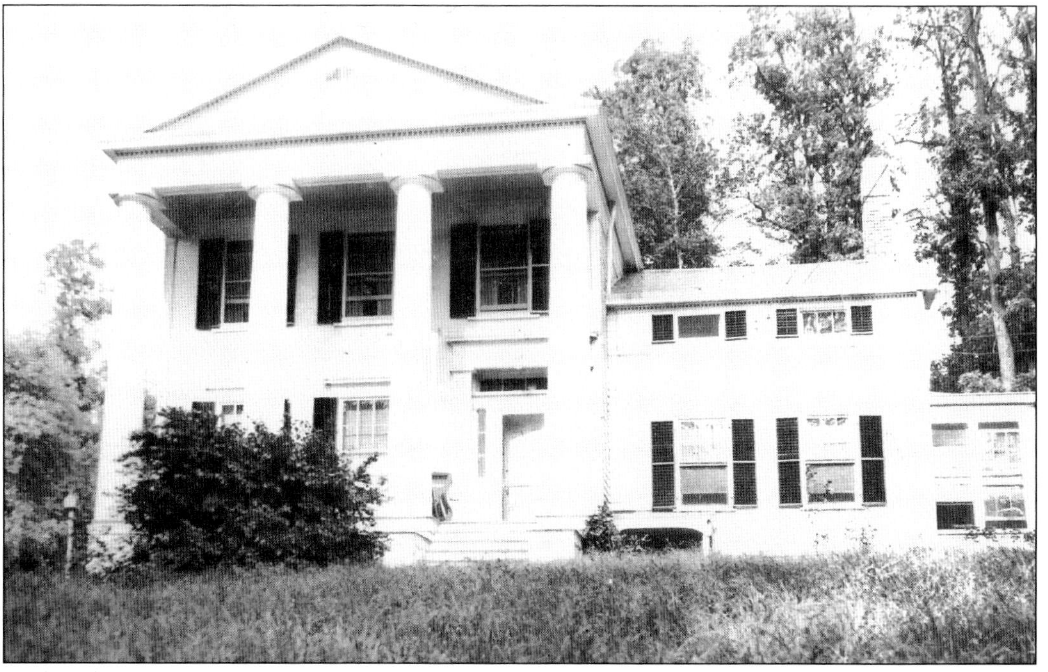

Little is known about this elegant Greek Revival temple-front house, probably built for John R. Schenck around 1835. Known for years as "the mansion," it looked due west across the milldam. It had landscaped grounds, a carriage drive, and a large barn. From the 1960s through around 1980, a gas station stood on the site, which is now vacant with plans in the making for a park. (Courtesy of RLS.)

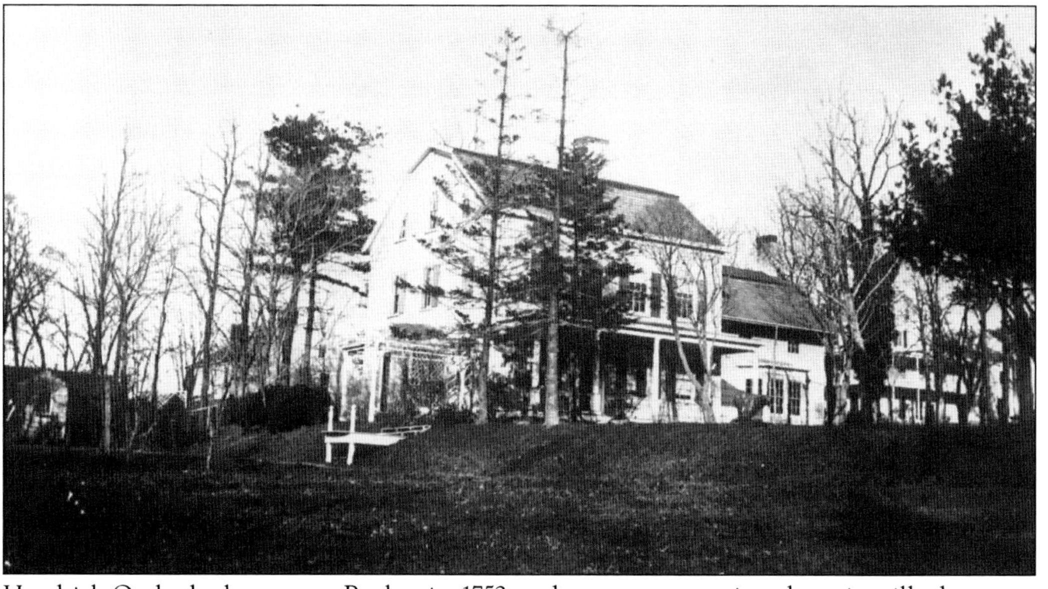

Hendrick Onderdonk came to Roslyn in 1752 and was soon running the gristmill, the paper mill, and the general store. His son Anderis built this Federal-style house in 1797, but died before moving in. Hendrick lived here until his death in 1809. George Brainard photographed it in 1880, when it was part of the lumberyard. Today the house is used for professional offices. (Courtesy of the Nassau County Museum Collection, Long Island Studies Institute.)

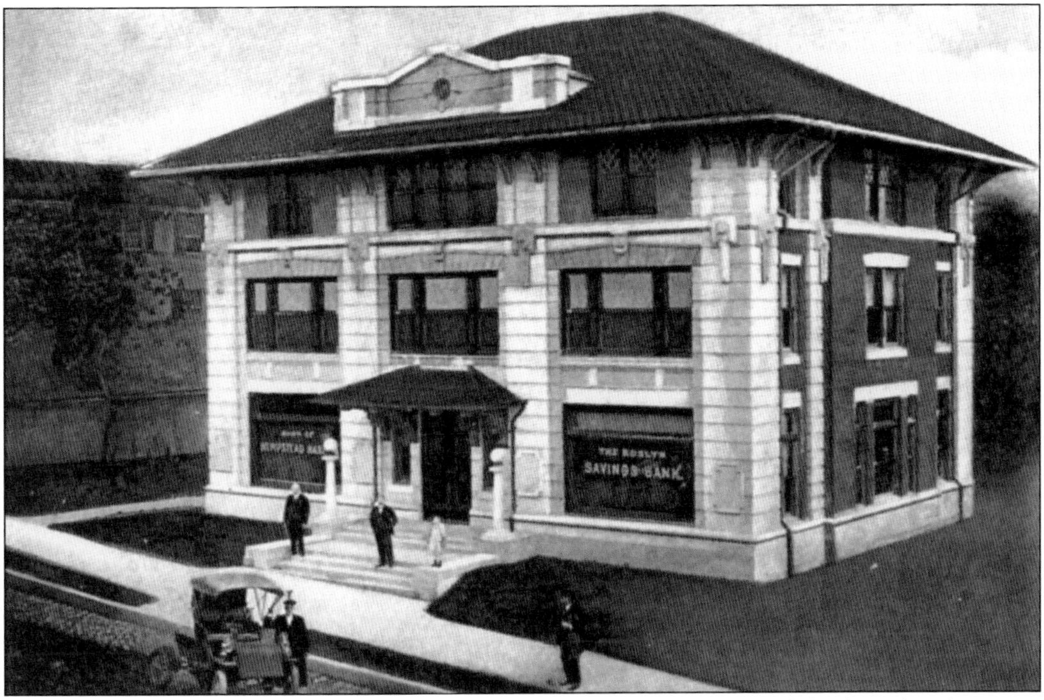

Founded by Henry Western Eastman in 1876, the Roslyn Savings Bank built its headquarters in 1906. William Pickering photographed it after the grand opening on June 11, 1906. Offices occupied the bank's second floor, with the telephone exchange above. By 1930, this building was demolished and replaced in 1932 by the main block of today's Georgian Revival brick building. (Courtesy of the Nassau County Museum Collection, Long Island Studies Institute.)

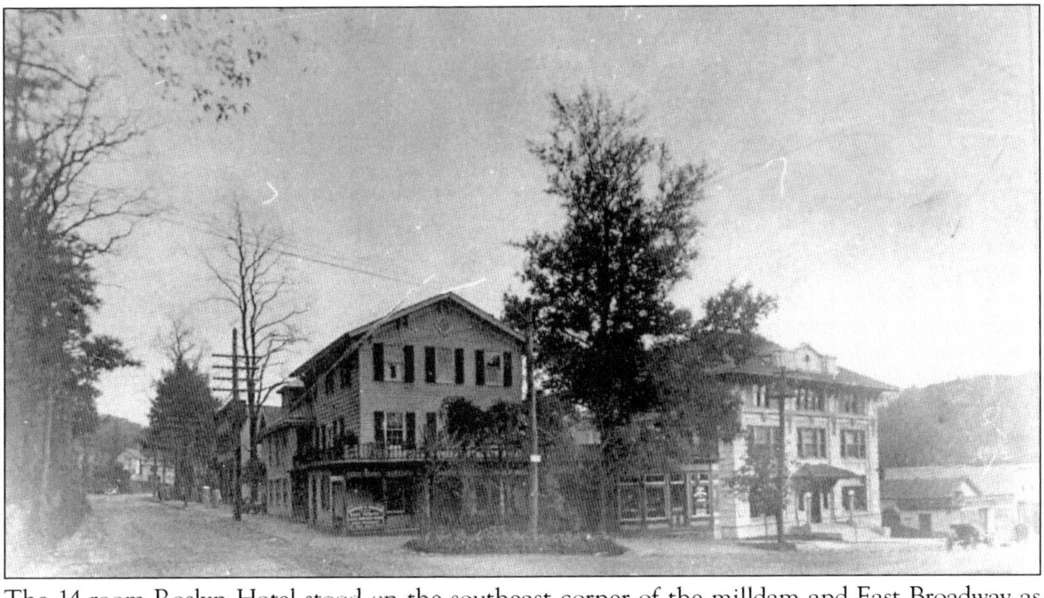

The 14-room Roslyn Hotel stood on the southeast corner of the milldam and East Broadway as early as 1852, when Roslyn Rescue Hook and Ladder Company No. 1 was formed there. It was the last of the old village hotels when the Roslyn Savings Bank bought it in 1960 to demolish it for a parking lot. (Courtesy of the Nassau County Museum Collection, Long Island Studies Institute.)

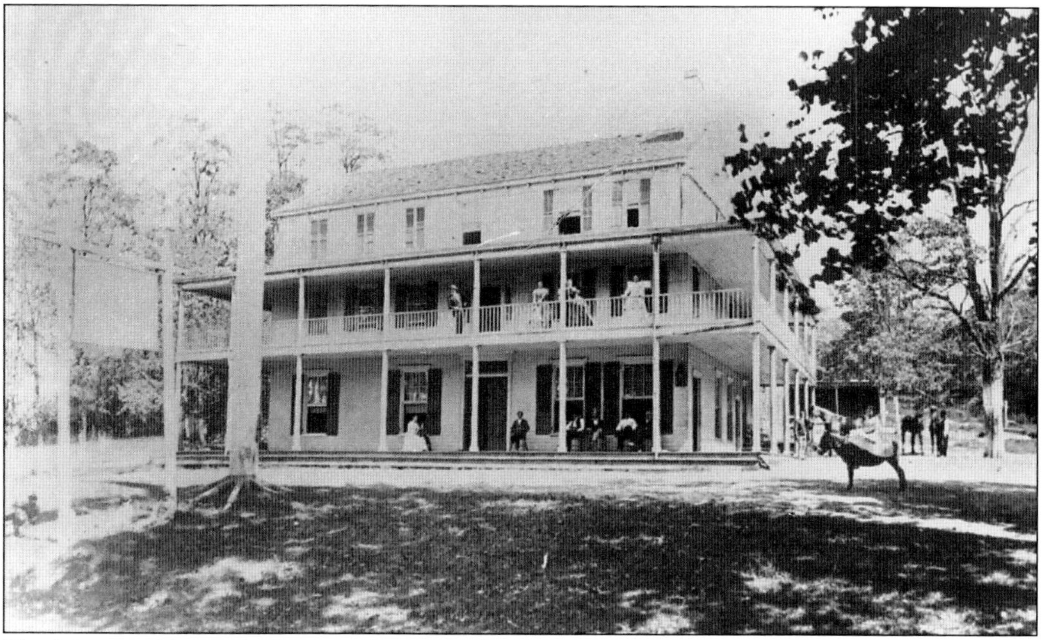

The Mansion House, built around 1810, looks elegant in this *c.* 1860 photograph. In 1890, the *Brooklyn Daily Eagle* listed it as a favorite country retreat for Brooklynites. Remsen Avenue, originally Mansion House Road, led up Harbor Hill to an observatory and picnic grounds, then down the other side of the hill to the Long Island Rail Road station at Roslyn Heights. (Courtesy of the Nassau County Museum Collection, Long Island Studies Institute.)

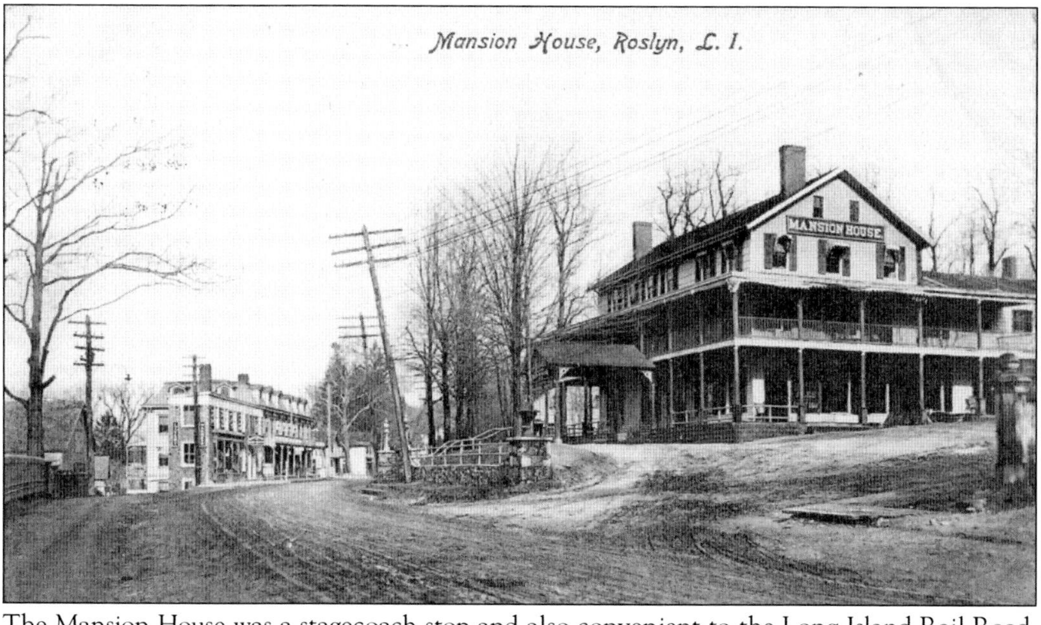

The Mansion House was a stagecoach stop and also convenient to the Long Island Rail Road. It catered to permanent guests, transients, and "drummers" (traveling salesmen). *Ripley's Believe It or Not* cited the elm that grew through its annex roof. The hotel was torn down around 1930 for the Roslyn National Bank and Trust Company. The picturesque commercial buildings across the street are still there. (Courtesy of John and Michelle Santos.)

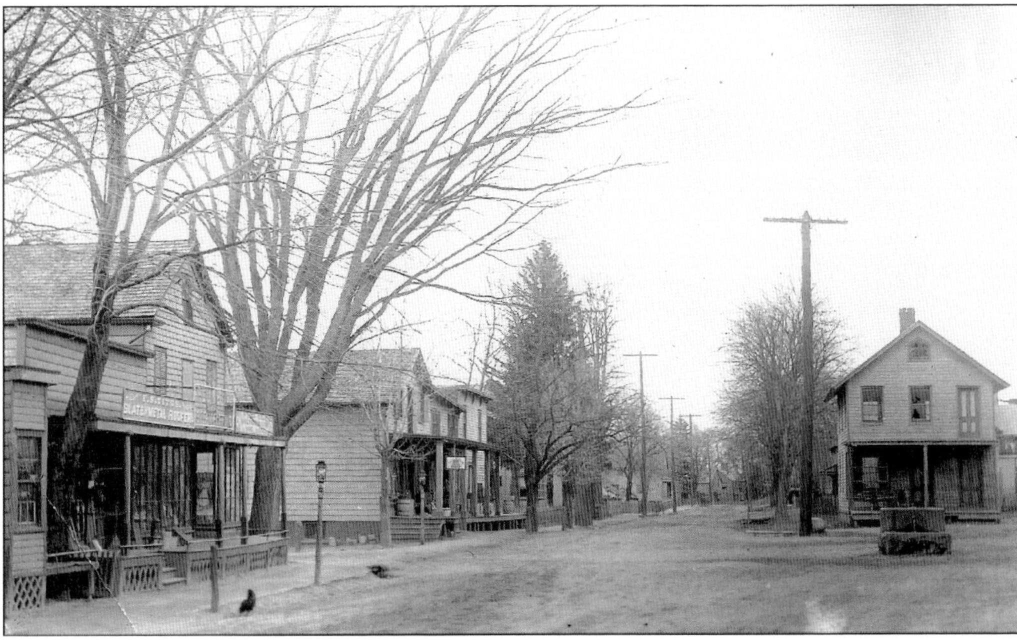

Where School Street meets Bryant Avenue stands Roslyn's then-new horse watering trough. Ellen Ward donated it in 1884 in memory of her husband Elijah, once the advocate general of the United States. Ten years later, the newspaper reported that "not less than 300 horses are watered here daily as well as numerous cattle." Ellen Ward was generous to Roslyn, especially to Trinity Episcopal Church, where for a time she paid the rector's salary. (Courtesy of RLS.)

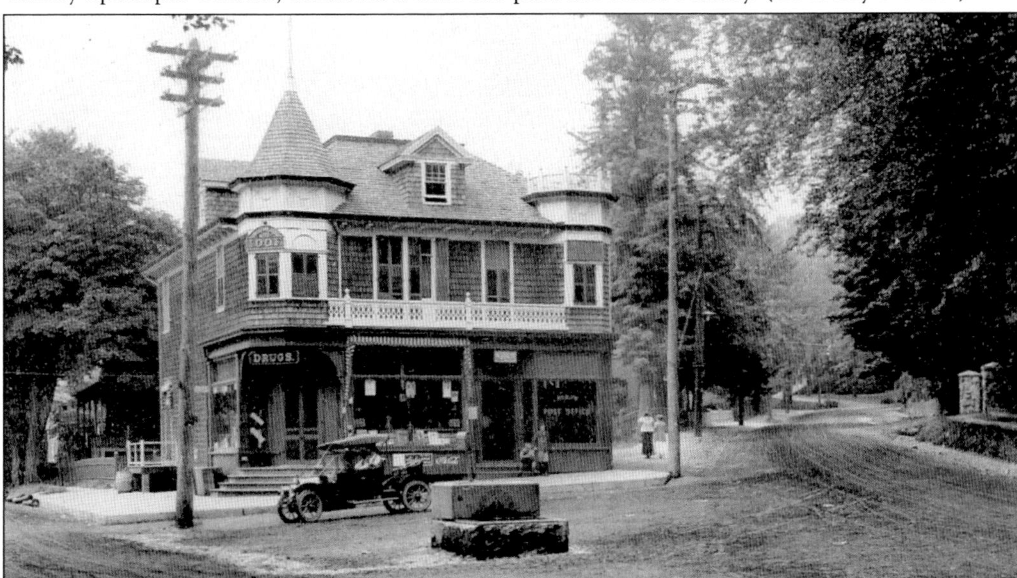

This 1890s building housed Roslyn's post office (right) and A. E. Pickard's drugstore (left). The horse trough stands in front, as it still does today. Roslyn's mail came by train, and an old horse-drawn wagon brought it here. On the building's east side is still to be seen the drive-up window for carriages. The square in front of this building was popular for war bond rallies and other public events. (Courtesy of Ian Zwerdling.)

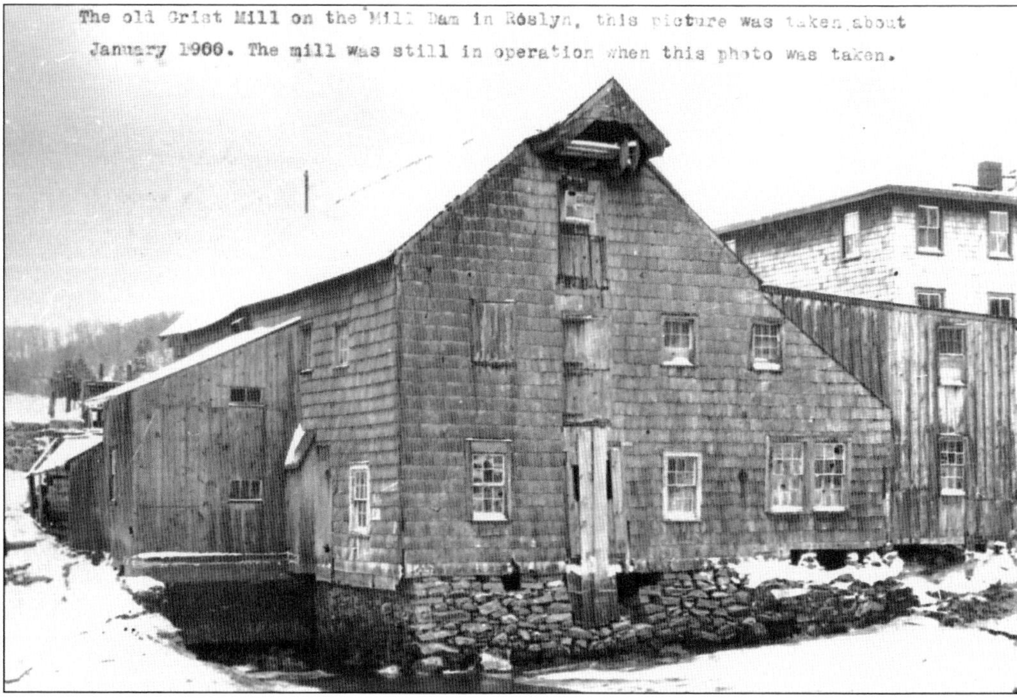

The Roslyn gristmill, shown from the north around 1900, is probably not the first mill at the head of the harbor, but it descends from the earliest, built by John Robeson around 1705 and rebuilt in 1740 by Jeremiah Williams. It is the only commercial building of Dutch origin known to exist in the United States. (Courtesy of the Nassau County Museum Collection, Long Island Studies Institute.)

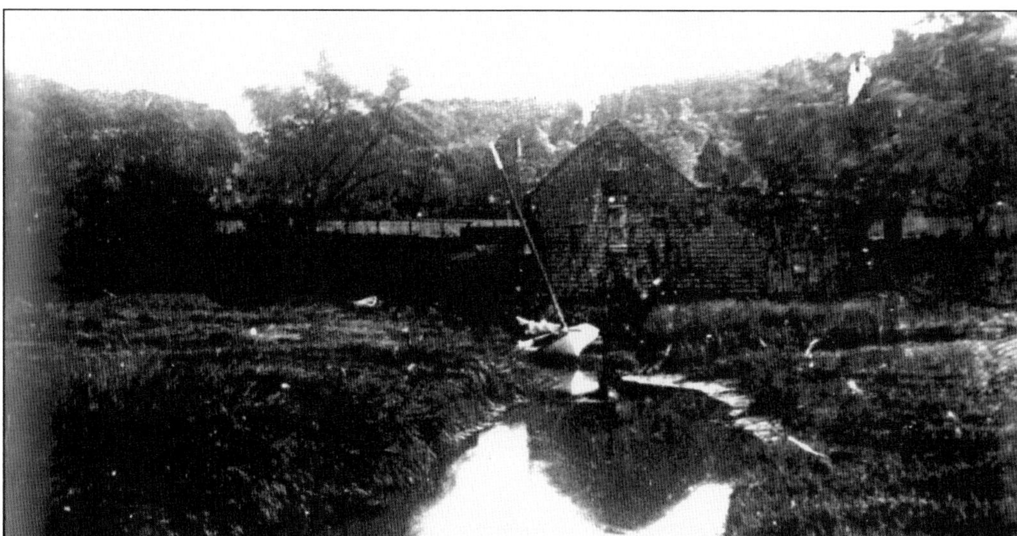

This *c.* 1917 photograph was taken by Harold Godwin, grandson of William Cullen Bryant, who restored the gristmill in 1916. Before 1929, Roslyn Creek meandered freely out to the harbor after it left the millrace (shown at left of the mill). Birds and wildlife abounded, and vessels like the sloop heeled over in the stream came up right behind the mill. (Courtesy of the Nassau County Department of Parks, Recreation and Museums, Cedarmere.)

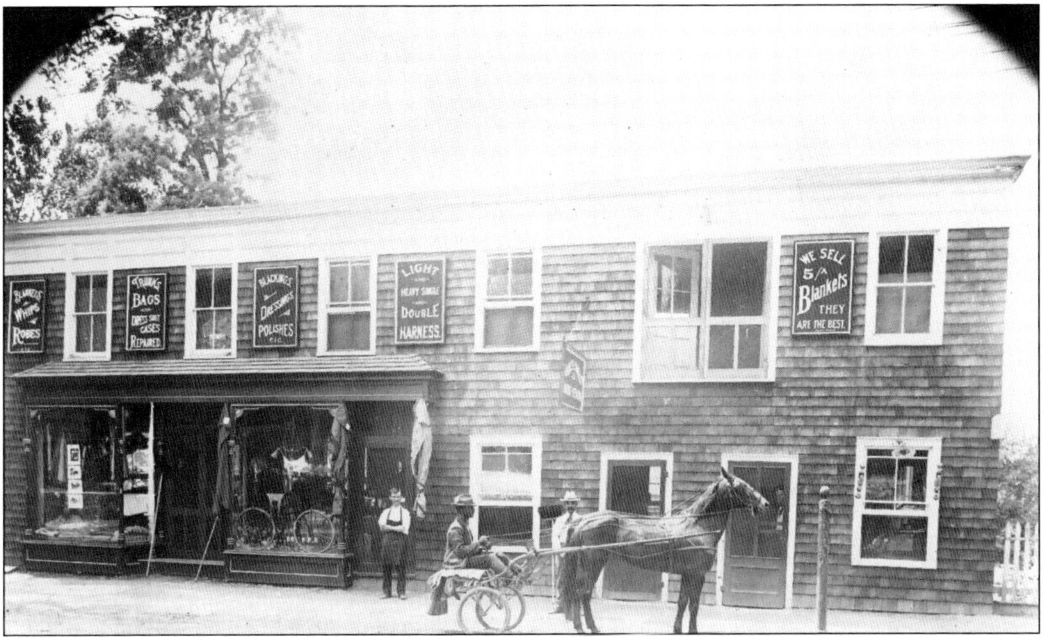

In 1887, John F. Remsen worked leather in his School Street harness shop, shown around 1910. Remsen, who entered the livery business in 1887, stands behind the cart. In his stable in back he kept his horses and his big purple-upholstered funeral carriages. A later proprietor was "Captain" Thomas Fearns, a British veteran of the Boer War. In the 1970s, the restaurant Fern's Harness Shop occupied the building (which survives today). (Courtesy of the Nassau County Museum Collection, Long Island Studies Institute.)

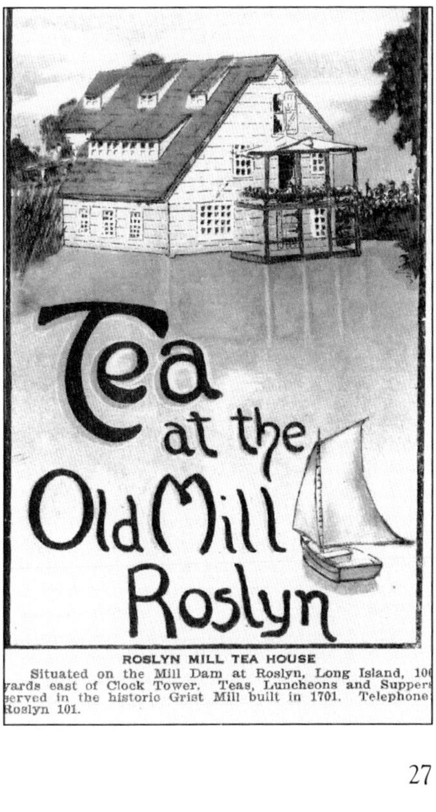

In 1916, the last gristmill operator, Isaac Hicks, gave the gristmill to the village, and Harold Godwin restored it as a museum. In 1919, Alice Titus opened a teahouse there to attract people and earn income. Broadway luminaries and locals savored the chicken salad sandwiches, popovers, and pies served in flickering light powered by the old waterwheel. (Courtesy of the Nassau County Department of Parks, Recreation and Museums, Cedarmere.)

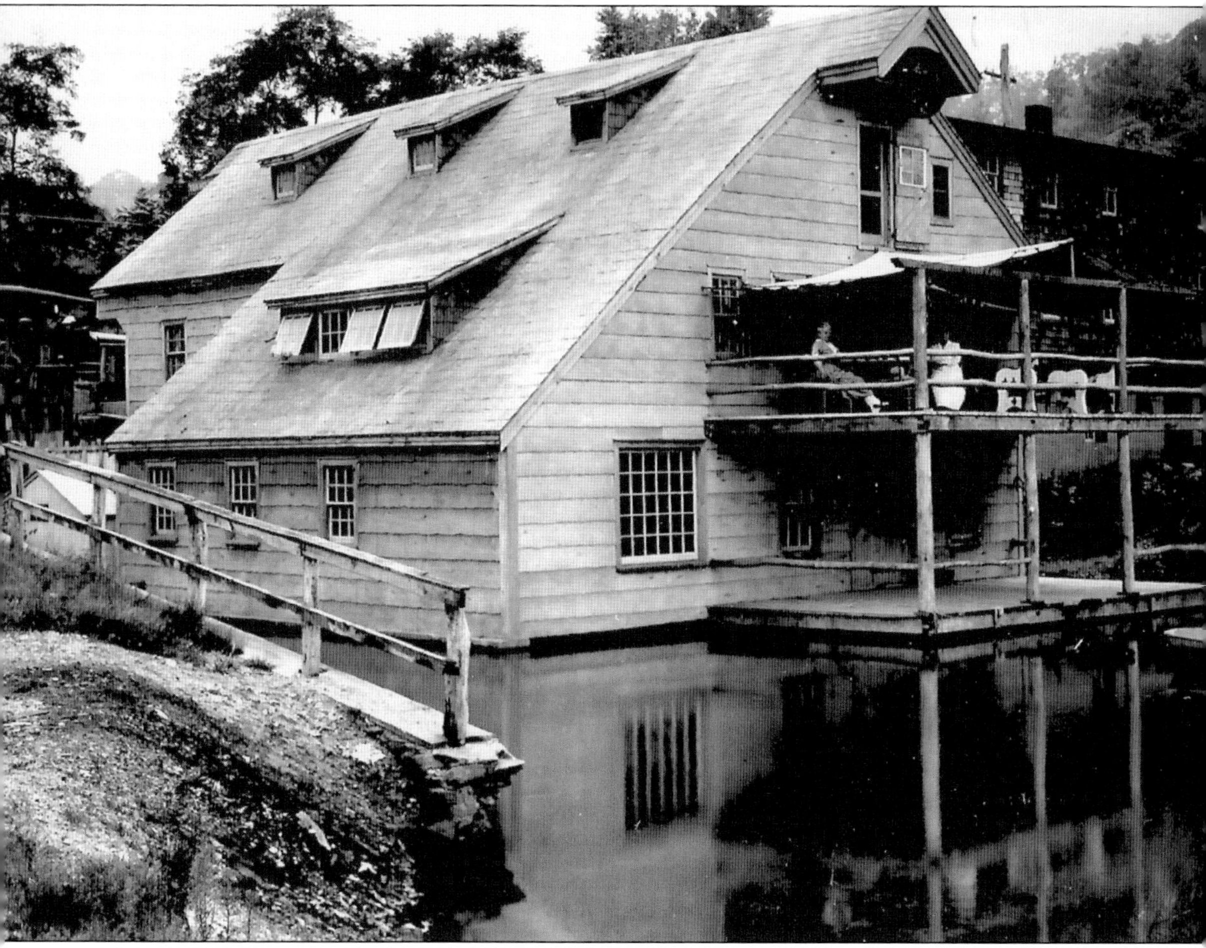

This c. 1919 photograph shows the back of the gristmill teahouse with its new two-story rear porch. Diners could sit outside and enjoy beautiful views over Roslyn Creek. Later the porch was screened in, and in 1975 it was removed as part of a structural evaluation of the building when it was turned over to the county. (Courtesy of RLS.)

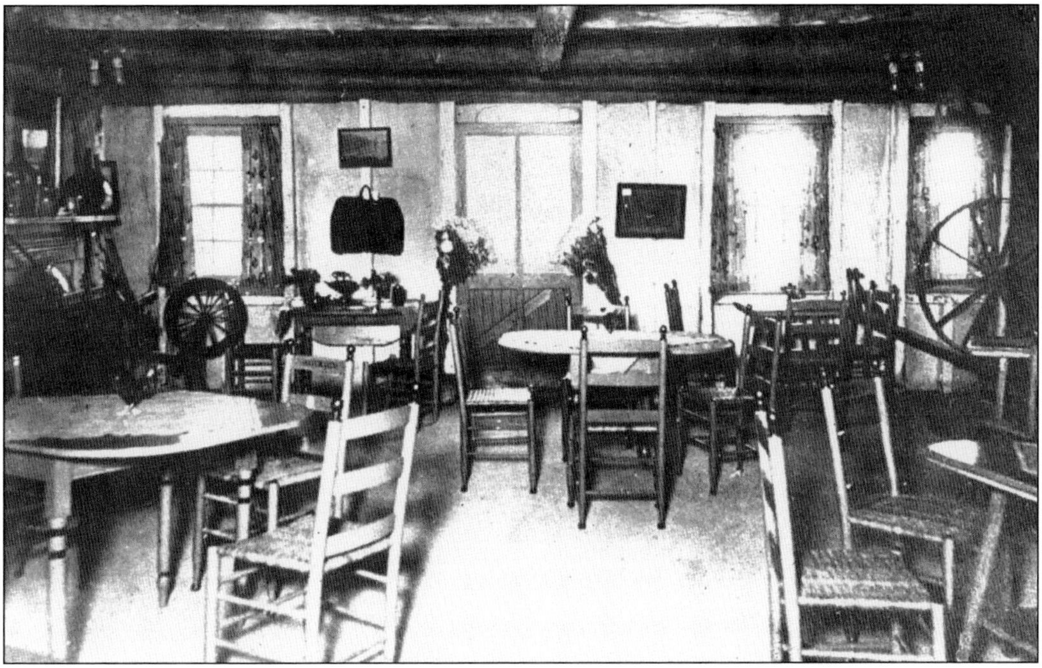

The teahouse interior hardly changed from 1919 through 1975. Spindle-legged tables and rush-seated chairs accommodated diners amid the artifacts collected for the history museum. In the spring the mill was gay with lilacs, forsythia, and pussy willows, while in winter, skaters came in from Silver Lake for popovers and hot chocolate by the fireplace (far left). (Courtesy of the Nassau County Department of Parks, Recreation and Museums, Cedarmere.)

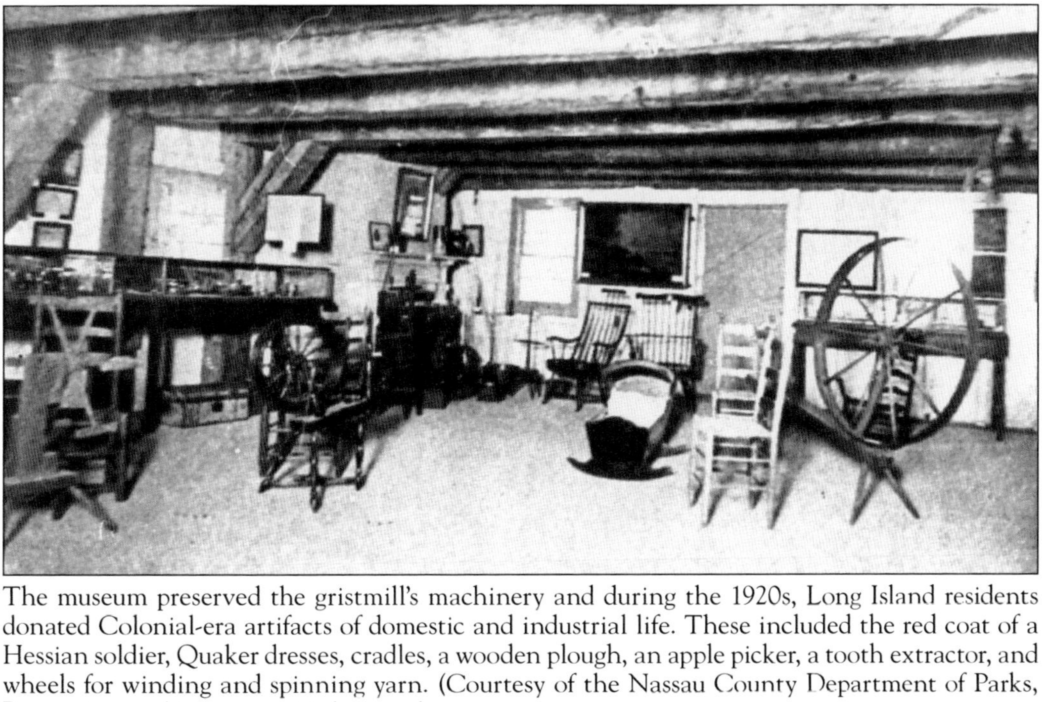

The museum preserved the gristmill's machinery and during the 1920s, Long Island residents donated Colonial-era artifacts of domestic and industrial life. These included the red coat of a Hessian soldier, Quaker dresses, cradles, a wooden plough, an apple picker, a tooth extractor, and wheels for winding and spinning yarn. (Courtesy of the Nassau County Department of Parks, Recreation and Museums, Cedarmere.)

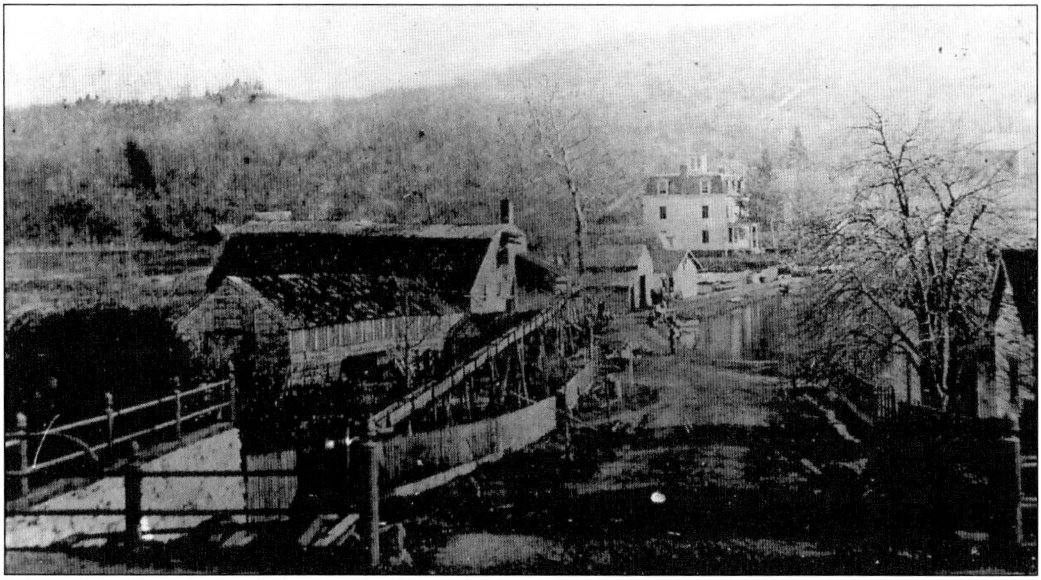

Hendrick Onderdonk established this paper mill in 1773; paper manufacture had been suppressed in the colonies and import duties imposed during the pre–Revolutionary War struggles over taxation. This was the first paper mill in New York State and one of the first in the colonies. Hugh Gaines used its paper for his *New-York Gazette and the Weekly Mercury*. In 1801, Onderdonk sold the mill to Caleb Valentine, whose family operated it until 1896. (Courtesy of RLS.)

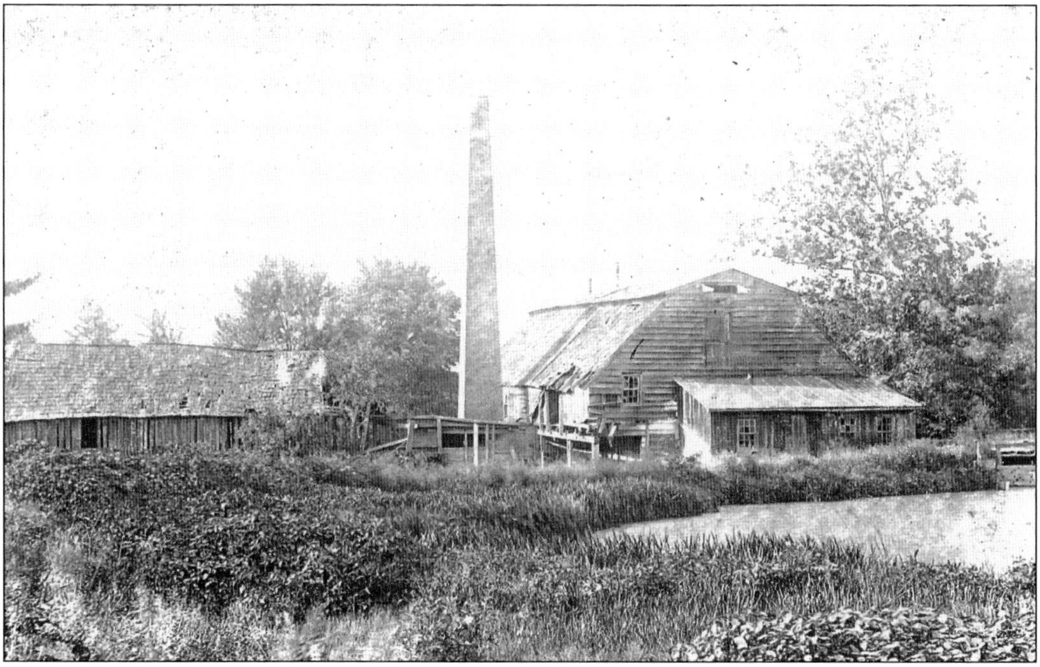

In 1880, the last paper mill operator, Myers Valentine, changed to steam power, adding the tall brick chimney shown here around 1890. Operations ceased in 1896, and 10 years later the mill blew down. One of its late products was a set of pasteboard cake boxes for the June 1886 wedding of Pres. Grover Cleveland. His was the only wedding ever of a sitting American president. (Courtesy of the Nassau County Department of Parks, Recreation and Museums, Cedarmere.)

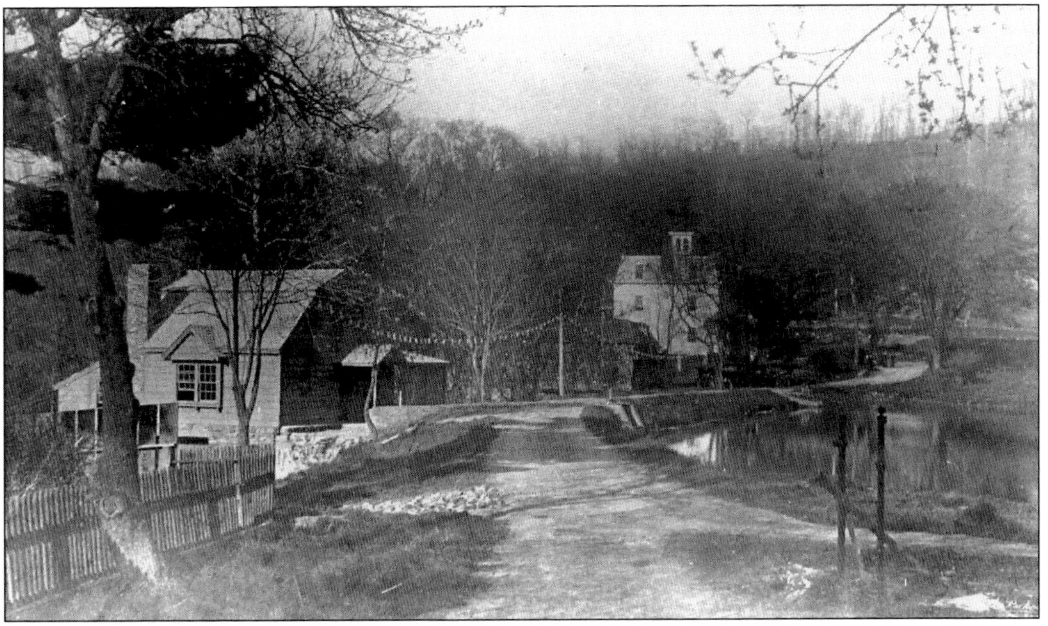

Around 1915, the last remnants of the paper mill were torn down, and the newly formed Roslyn Neighborhood Association built this small replica. The new building housed community meetings and social activities. Its waterwheel provided electricity to the building and park, including the swags of lightbulbs shown along Paper Mill Road. (Photograph by William Pickering, courtesy of the Nassau County Museum Collection, Long Island Studies Institute.)

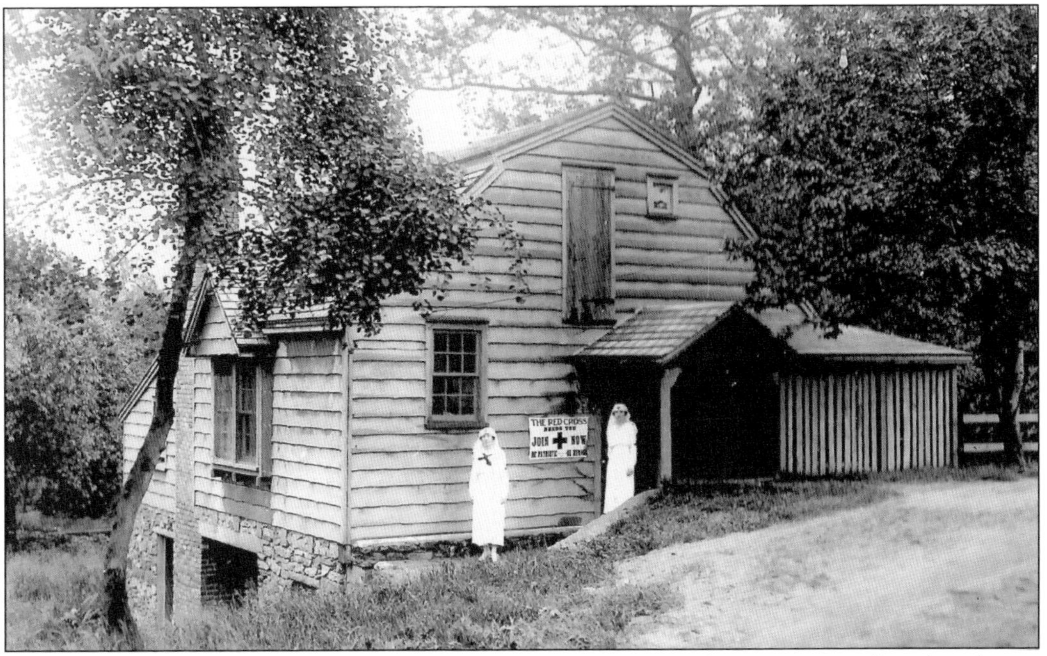

Red Cross nurses Helen Hennessy and Hazel McKay stand outside the paper mill replica during a 1918 blood drive. The one-story shed on the far side of the building covered the waterwheel, which then still made electricity. The paper mill replica stands today, although its electricity now comes from the grid, not from falling water. (Courtesy of RLS.)

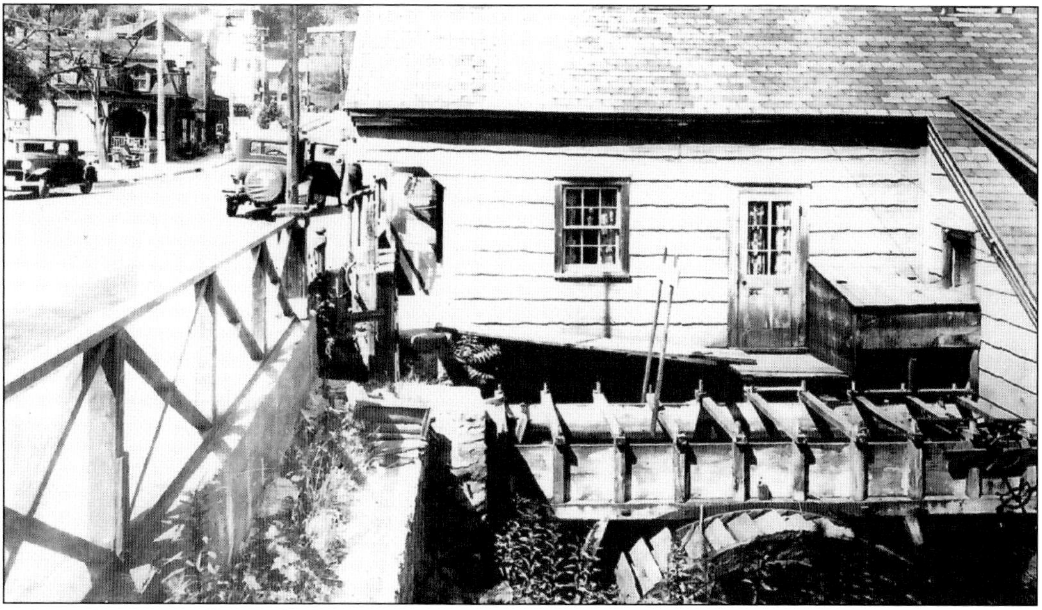

When the first mill was built, the head of the harbor was a spring-fed swamp. The dam (in front of the mill) created a pond from which water poured through a flume and over the wheel on the east side of the building. The revolving wheel engaged the gears, shafts, and belts to grind the grain and run other machines. Behind the mill to the right, Roslyn Creek runs out to Hempstead Harbor. (Courtesy of the Nassau County Department of Parks, Recreation and Museums, Cedarmere.)

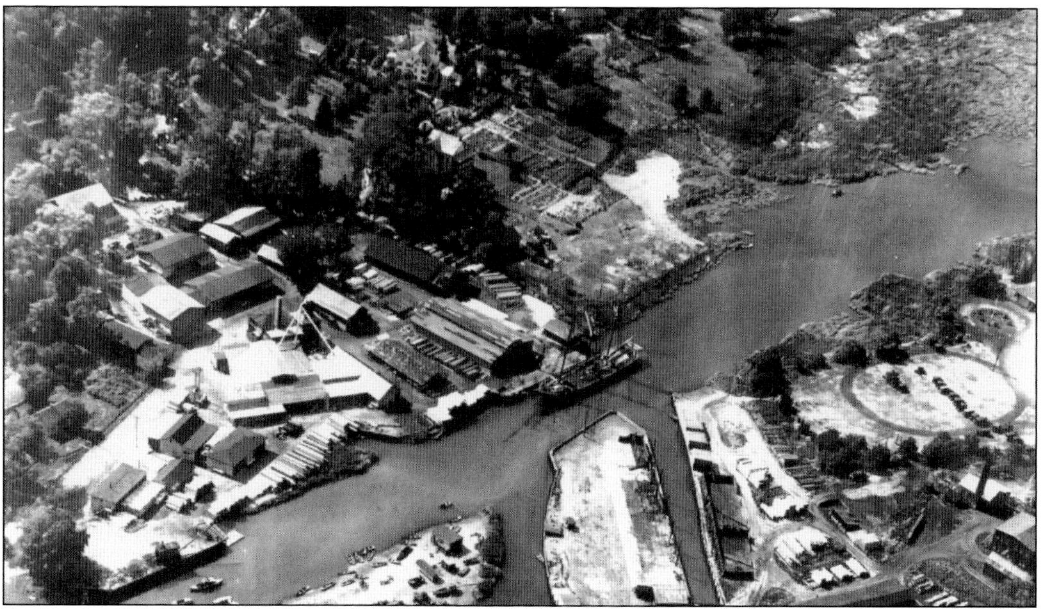

Quaker William Hicks started his lumberyard and sawmill near his Roslyn Harbor home in 1832. Further, he built a wharf and started a line of New York steamboats, kept a store, ran the post office, and was an overseer of highways. Before 1859, he moved his lumber operation down to Roslyn village, where it thrived and expanded to both sides of the creek. Here, in 1919, a lumber schooner lies at the lumberyard wharf. (Courtesy of RLS.)

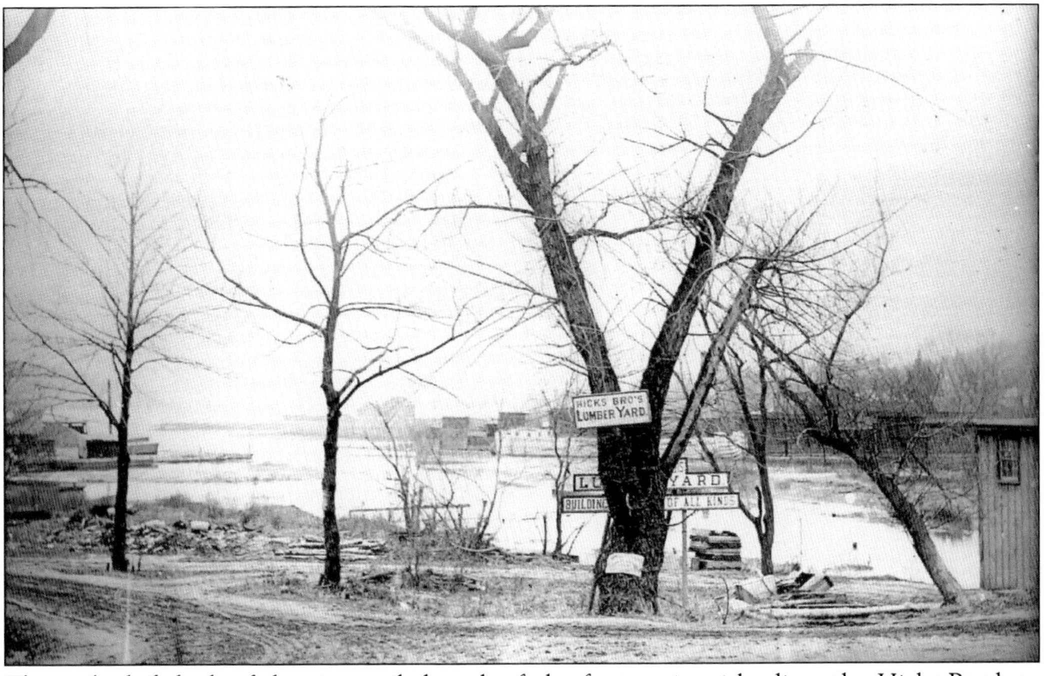

The makeshift look of the sign nailed to the fork of a tree is misleading; the Hicks Brothers Lumberyard and mills was the biggest industry Roslyn ever had. This view looks north from behind the Hendrick Onderdonk house. The building corner at the far right may have been part of the Roslyn Rescue Hook and Ladder engine house. (Courtesy of the Nassau County Museum Collection, Long Island Studies Institute.)

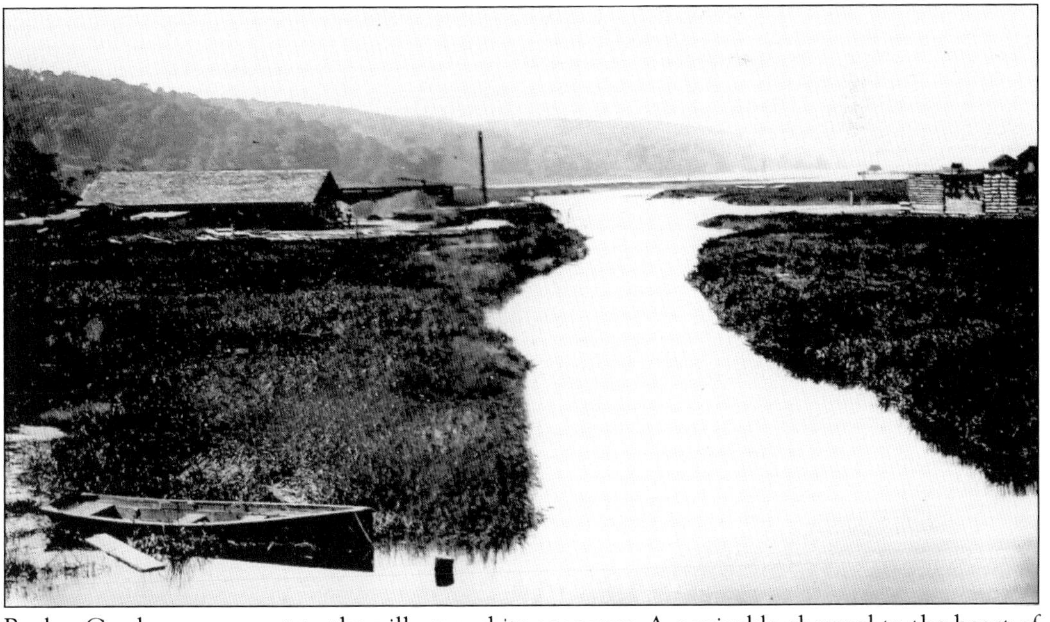

Roslyn Creek was an asset to the village and its economy. A navigable channel to the heart of the village, it was also a tailrace for the mills. The channel was most active at Hicks Brothers Lumberyard, where schooners brought timber, bricks, and coal and took away finished lumber and other Roslyn exports. (Courtesy of RLS.)

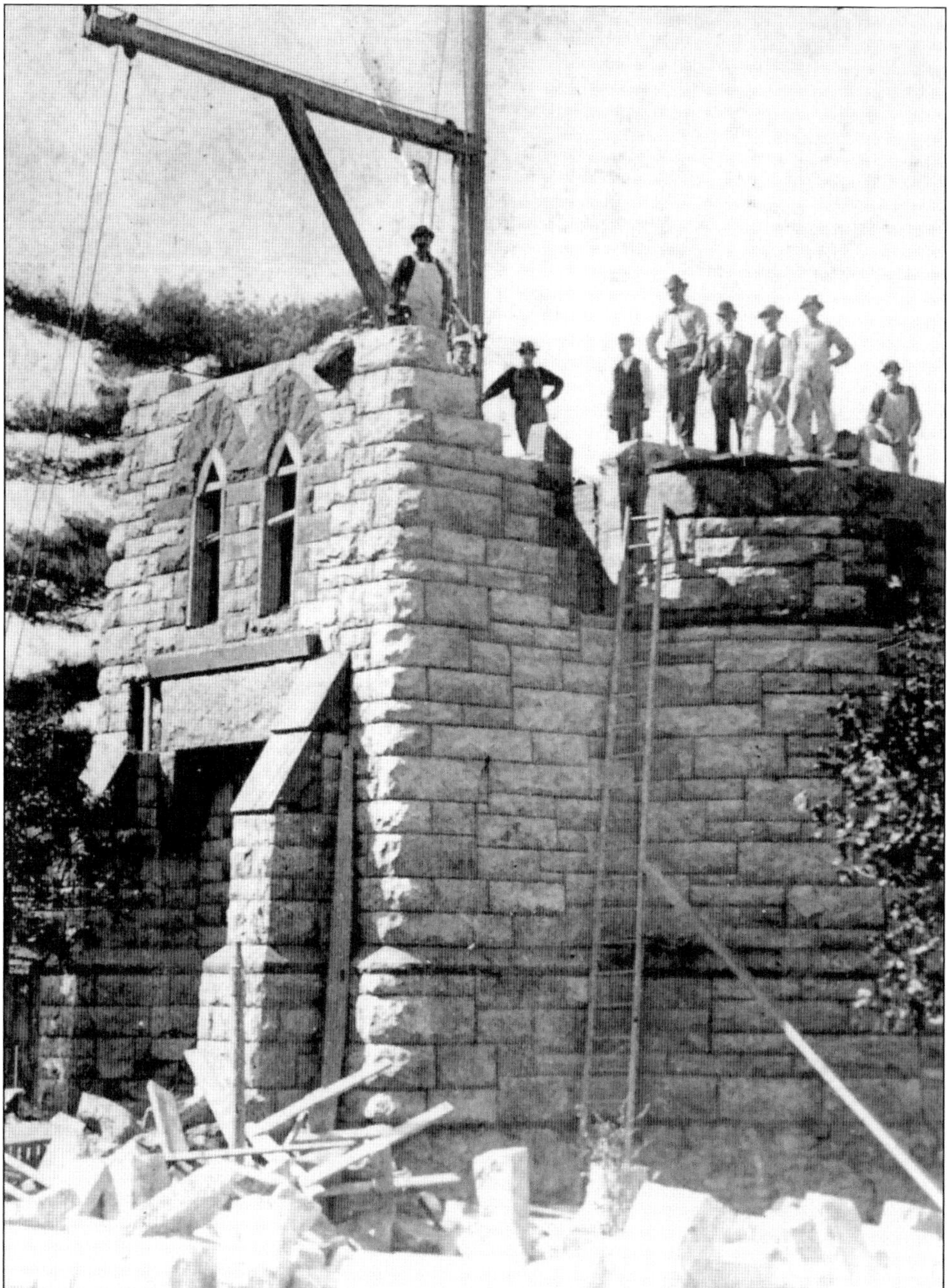

Hugo Lamb, the Roslyn clock tower's architect, also designed Theodore Roosevelt's Oyster Bay house, Sagamore Hill. The masonry foreman, Harry Skewes, moved to Roslyn to supervise the tower project. He and his wife bought a house on East Broadway; some of their descendants still live in the village today. Skewes may be among the masons shown atop the rising tower in the summer of 1895. They are about to build the clock-face level, into which would go the massive Seth Thomas works with its four six-foot-diameter marble-faced dials. The tower would be capped off by a belfry with a 2,500-pound bell to be used as a fire alarm. (Courtesy of the Bryant Library Local History Collection, Roslyn.)

Roslyn's clock tower, shown in 1910, is prominent on Tower Place. It was given in memory of Roslyn Harbor's Ellen Eliza Ward, a patron of Roslyn who died in 1893. The gift was announced in March 1895 with its architect to be Lamb and Rich of New York. The tower is Romanesque Revival, with rock-faced, coursed ashlar masonry, tightly massed forms, red granite colors, and round-arched openings. (Courtesy of John and Michelle Santos.)

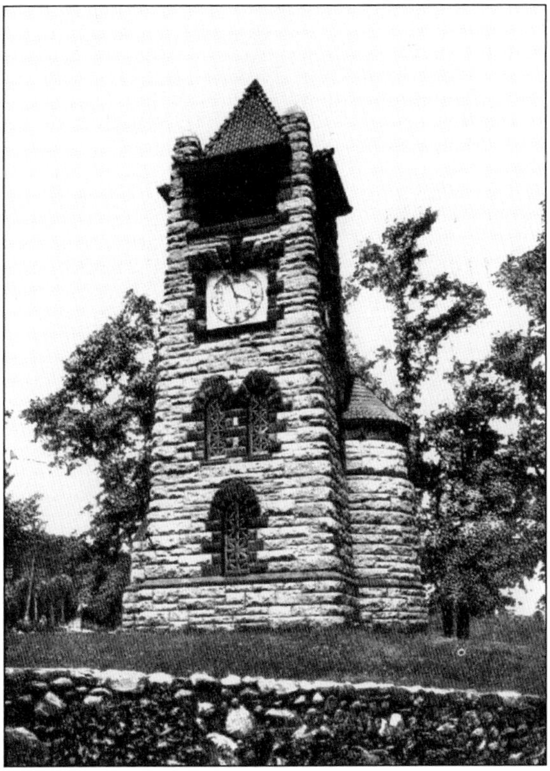

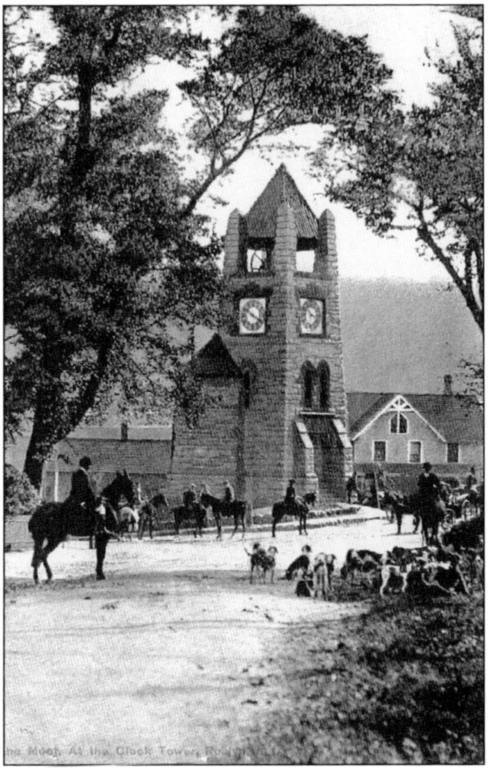

Long Island's North Shore was an equestrian paradise early in the 20th century, with a network of lanes linking estates and parks from the border of Queens to Cold Spring Harbor. Here the Meadowbrook Hunt, one of the nation's first organized hunt clubs, stands at the tower in 1904. (Courtesy of John and Michelle Santos.)

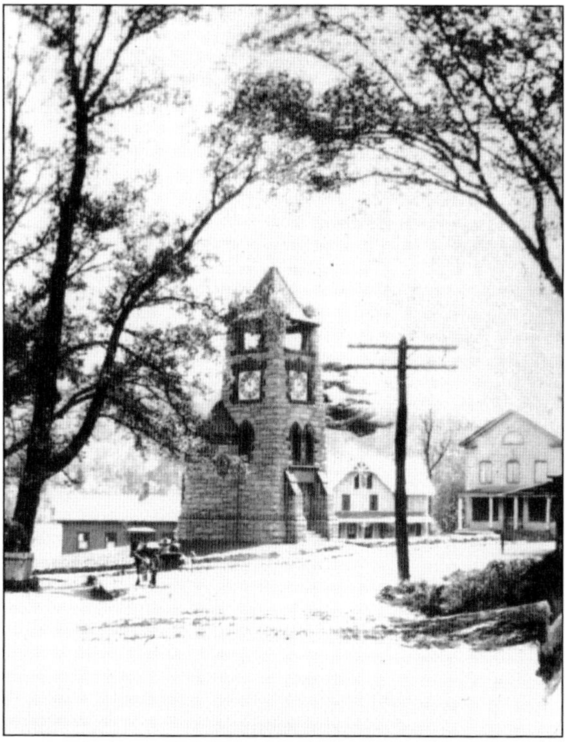

This pre-1917 view shows Roslyn's Negro school behind and left of the clock tower. Reportedly the last Negro school in the state of New York, it opened in 1864 with 15 students and closed in 1917 when its pupils were enrolled in the village school. The building to the right of the clock tower is a restaurant today. (Courtesy of the Queens Borough Public Library, Long Island Division, Illustrations Collection–Roslyn.)

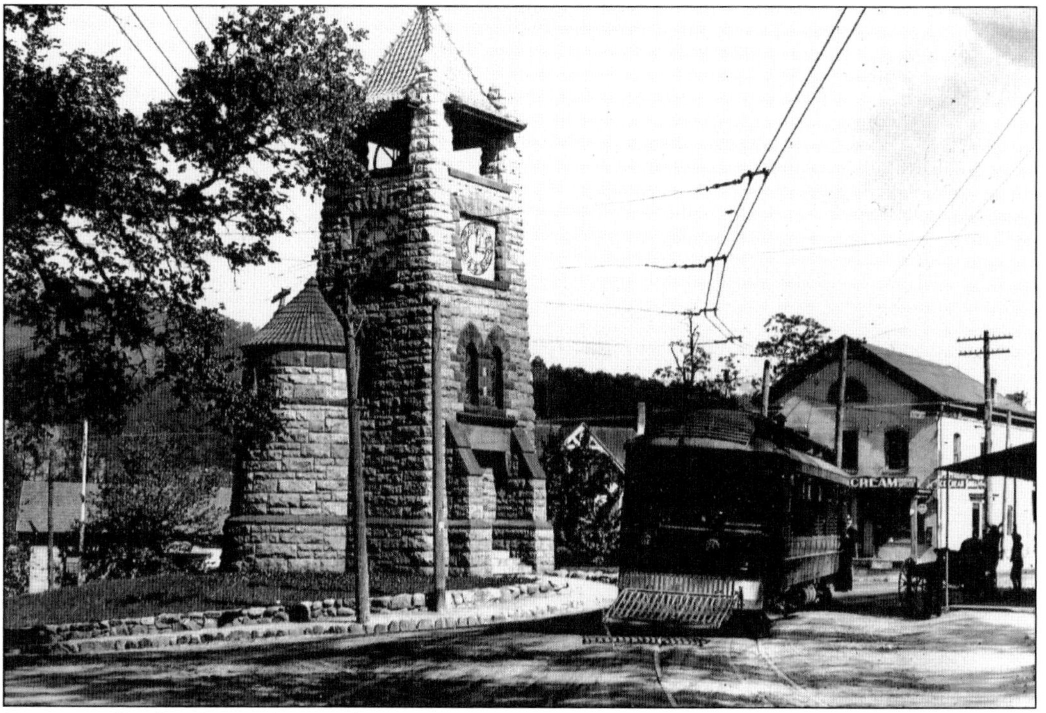

Here a trolley heads north out of Main Street en route to Port Washington. The New York and North Shore Traction Company brought the trolley to Roslyn in 1907. Behind the trolley car stands the 1862 William M. Valentine store on Main Street. (Courtesy of RLS.)

Three

Around the Town

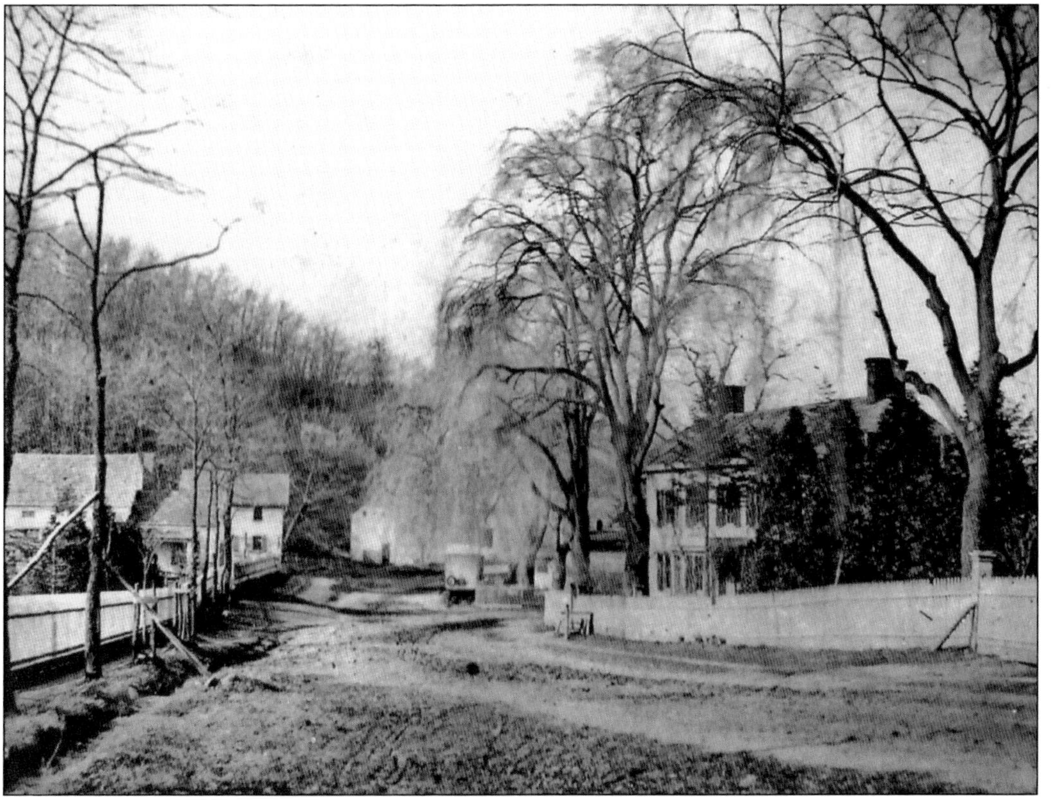

Roslyn's core is the inverted *A* formed by Main Street, East Broadway, and the milldam; the "point" of the *A* is Kirbys Corners, shown here around 1900. Today the elm-shaded Jacob Kirby mansion (right) has been replaced by brick apartments, and the 17th-century Dutch-type house across the street is a museum, one of more than 100 pre–Civil War buildings that survive in the core district. (Courtesy of RLS.)

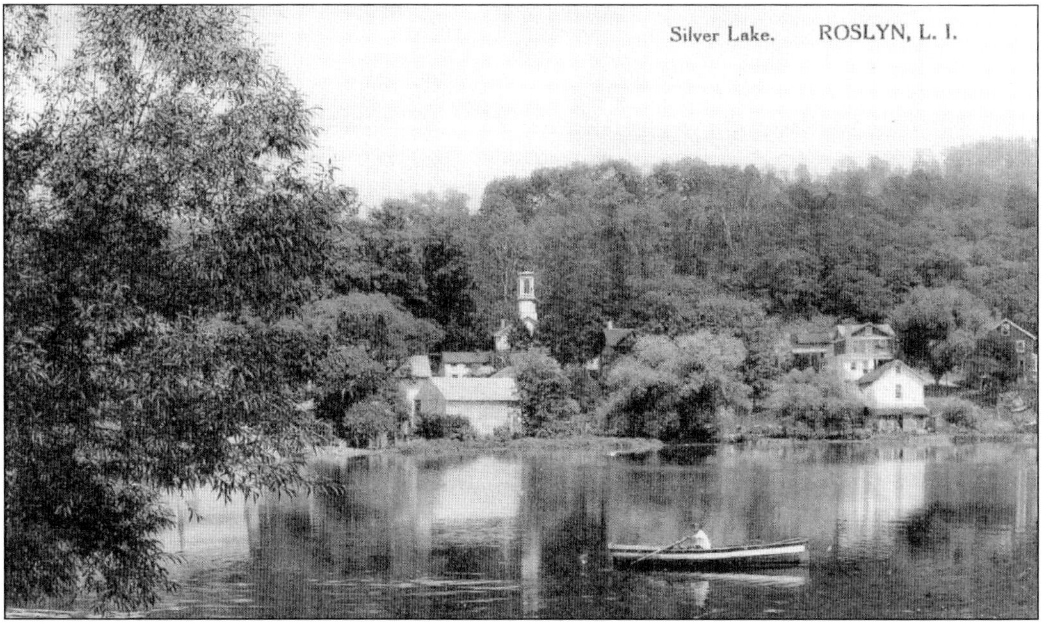

Around 1914, the Town of North Hempstead bought the village marsh. In the 1930s, Maj. George H. Robertson, a race car hero and local newspaper owner, discovered that a memorial had been funded, and he arranged for it to take the form of a park. By 1937, many thought the new park was "the most beautiful spot on all of Long Island." (Courtesy of John and Michelle Santos.)

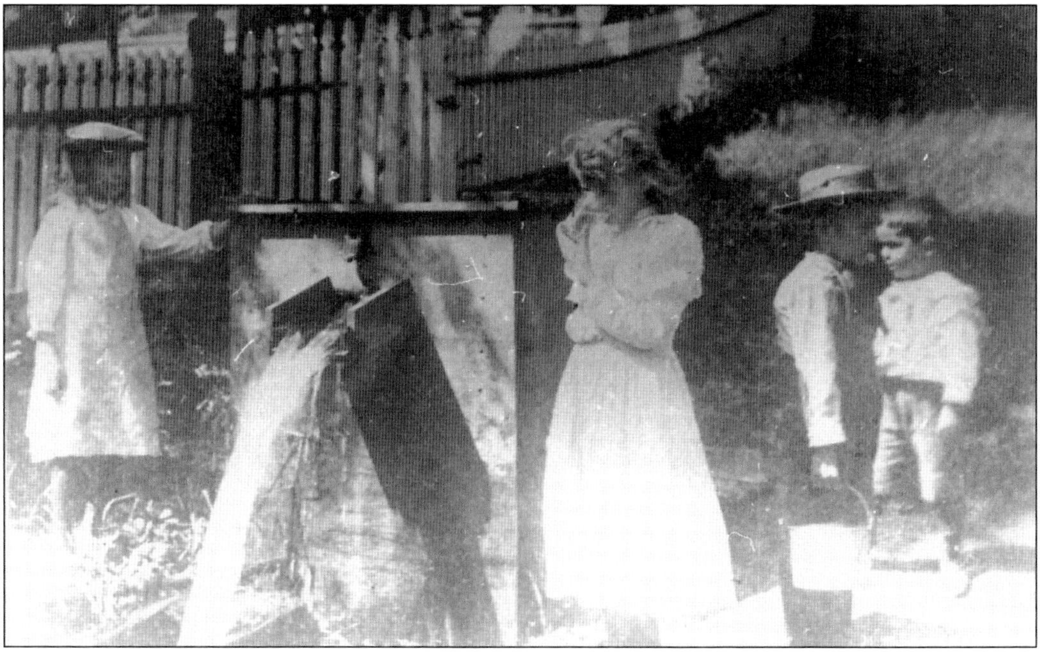

The millponds in Roslyn Park are fed by hillside springs. The Great Settling Spring rises in the side yard of the Smith house on Main Street, then, channeled under the street, once supplied this gushing fountain near Paper Mill Pond. Here, on a warm day in 1908, children have come to drink and fetch water. (Courtesy of the Nassau County Museum Collection, Long Island Studies Institute.)

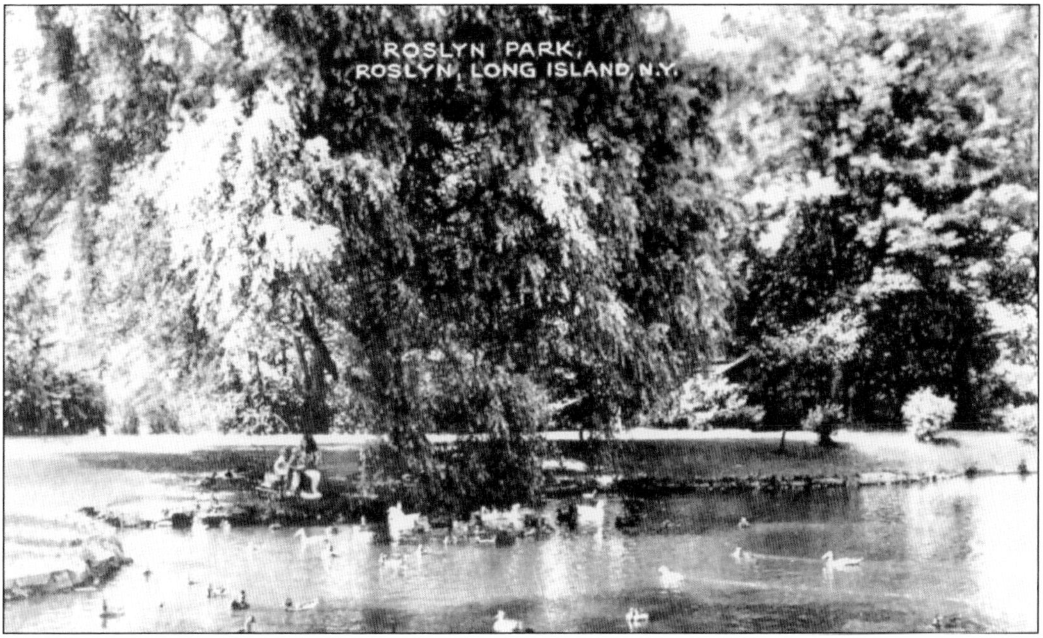

Roslyn Park's Paper Mill Pond has long been a haven for ducks (above), but the old millpond has not always been so calm. In the summer of 1955, Roslyn, like other Long Island towns, was slammed by Hurricane Hazel. The *Roslyn News* called this disaster "the end of the road." Below, a man examines what happened when the rampaging waters of Paper Mill Pond broke its dam. The damage shows how Paper Mill Road is simply a layer of pavement on top of a dam. (Above, courtesy of John and Michelle Santos; below, courtesy of the Queens Borough Public Library, Long Island Division, Illustrations Collection–Roslyn.)

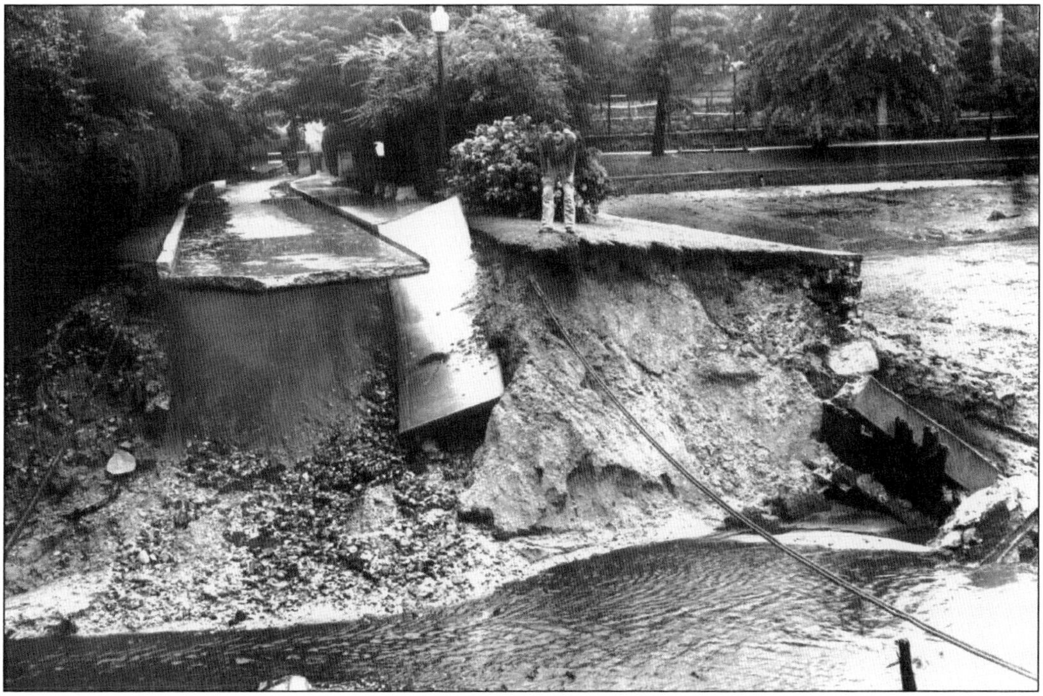

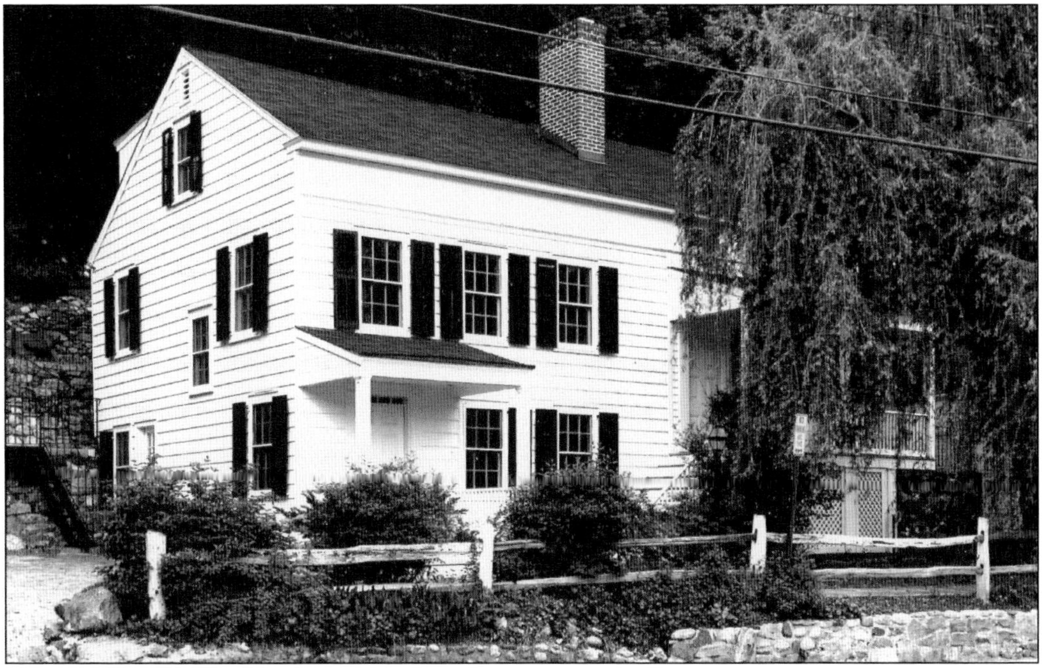

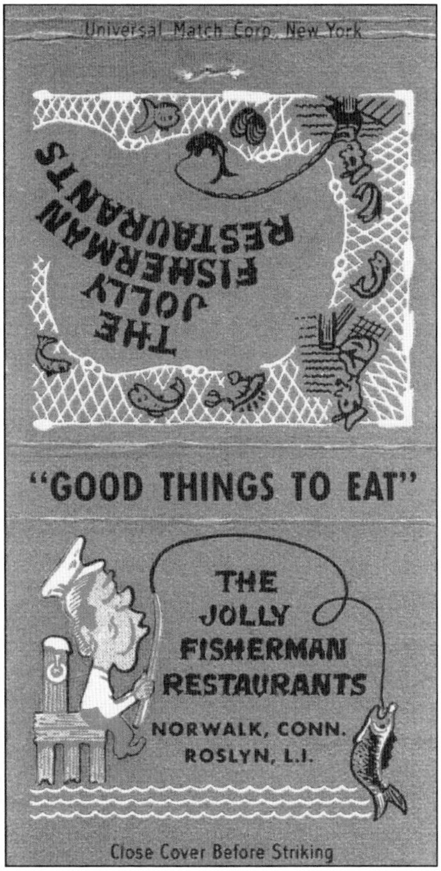

The oldest section of the house above was built around 1835 for George Allen, who lived next door. Listed as a "gentleman" in the 1850 census, Allen held several public offices, and he is said to have brought old New York cart horses to Roslyn to end their lives in comfort. After a fire in December 1974, Roger and Peggy Gerry bought and restored the George Allen tenant house. It is now the headquarters of the Roslyn Landmark Society. Across the street is the popular seafood restaurant the Jolly Fisherman, whose matchbook cover is shown at left. (Above, photograph by Ray Jacobs, courtesy of RLS; left, courtesy of Ian Zwerdling.)

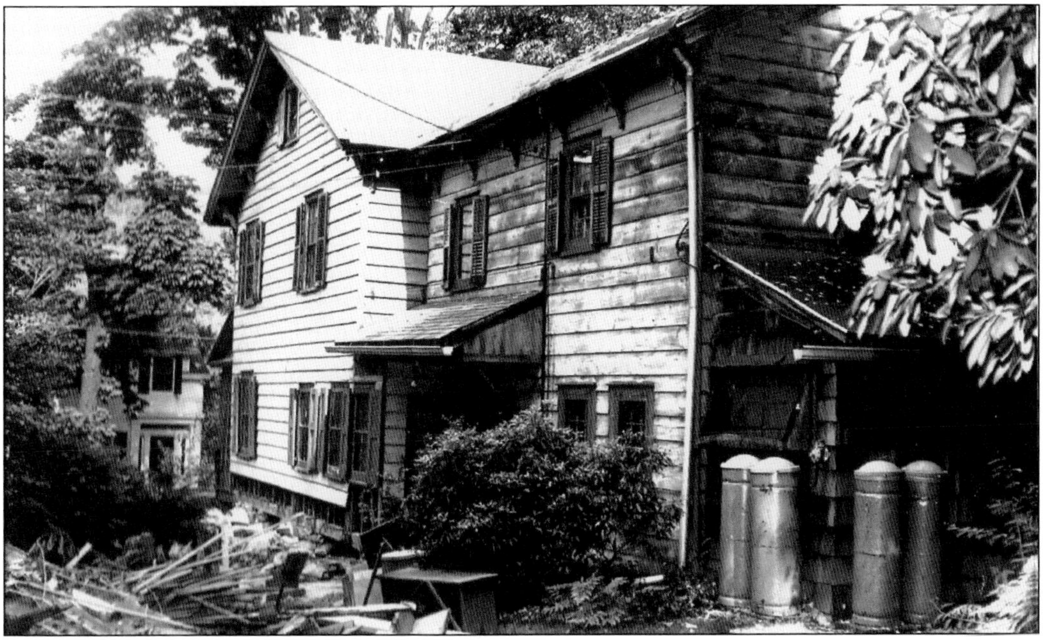

The top photograph shows the James and William Smith house at 106 Main Street under restoration in 1972. The original part of the house, at the front (left), was built in 1836 for Capt. James Smith, a merchant tailor. He was goaded by his young wife, Ann, into mortgaging his inheritance to build more house than he could afford. In 1840, Smith went bankrupt, but his father-in-law bought the house and Smith lived on here for another five years. The next two owners were blacksmiths, also named Smith. Their descendant Jessie Smith lived here until her death in 1970. By 1975, the house had become one of Roslyn's architectural stars. (Photographs by Ray Jacobs, courtesy of RLS.)

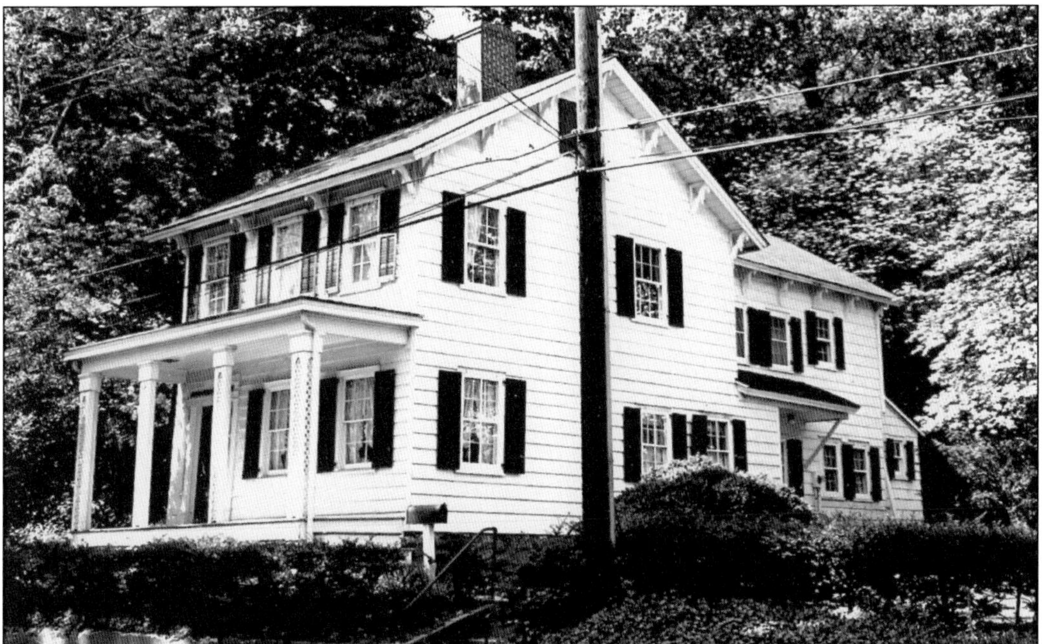

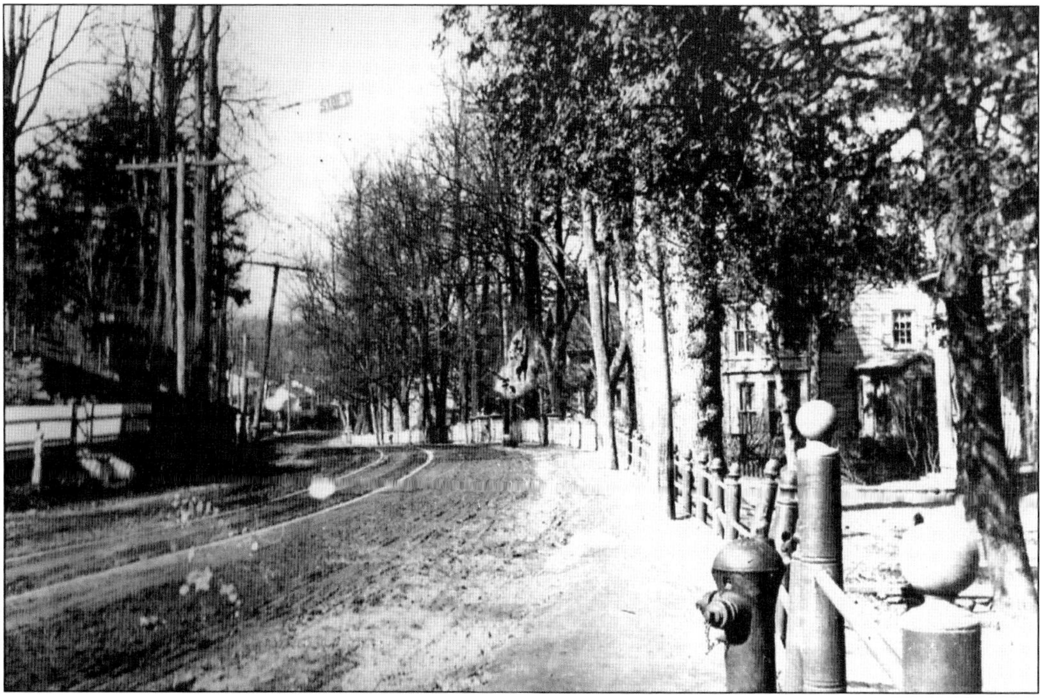

This view looking north on Main Street around 1910 shows the tracks of the Mineola, Roslyn, and Port Washington trolley and an early fire hydrant. A two-story bay window can be seen directly above the hydrant on the south side of the Henry Western Eastman house, and the George Allen tenant house is the last house visible up the street. (Courtesy of RLS.)

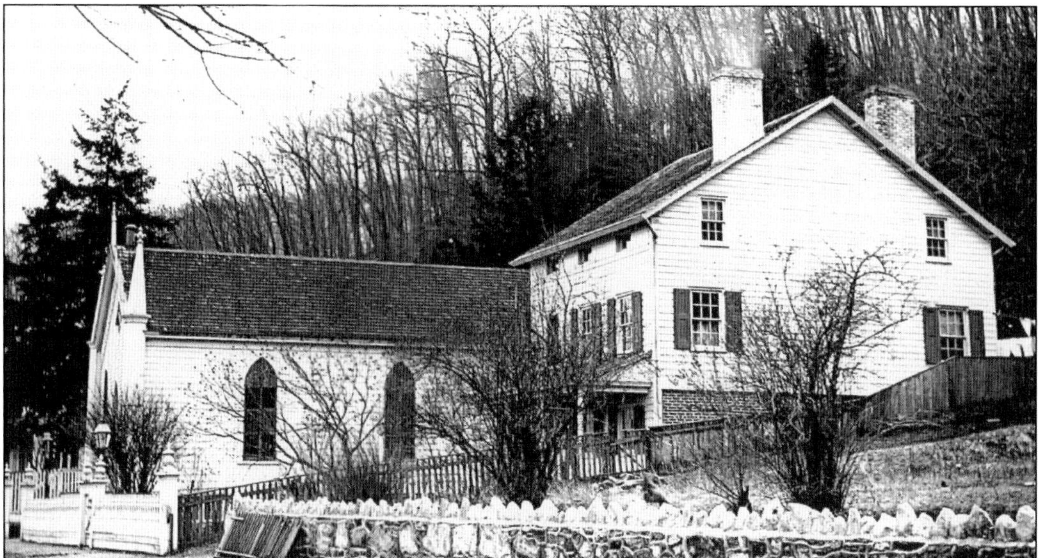

Hempstead Harbor's Methodists worshipped in the paper mill until this church was built on Main Street in 1814. It was described as "an uncomfortable and uncouth affair," but the only church in Roslyn for 30 years. The parsonage (right) was built in 1843, and the church was renovated in the Gothic Revival style in 1869. An early-20th-century fire destroyed the church and damaged the house, which now has a flat roof. (Courtesy of RLS.)

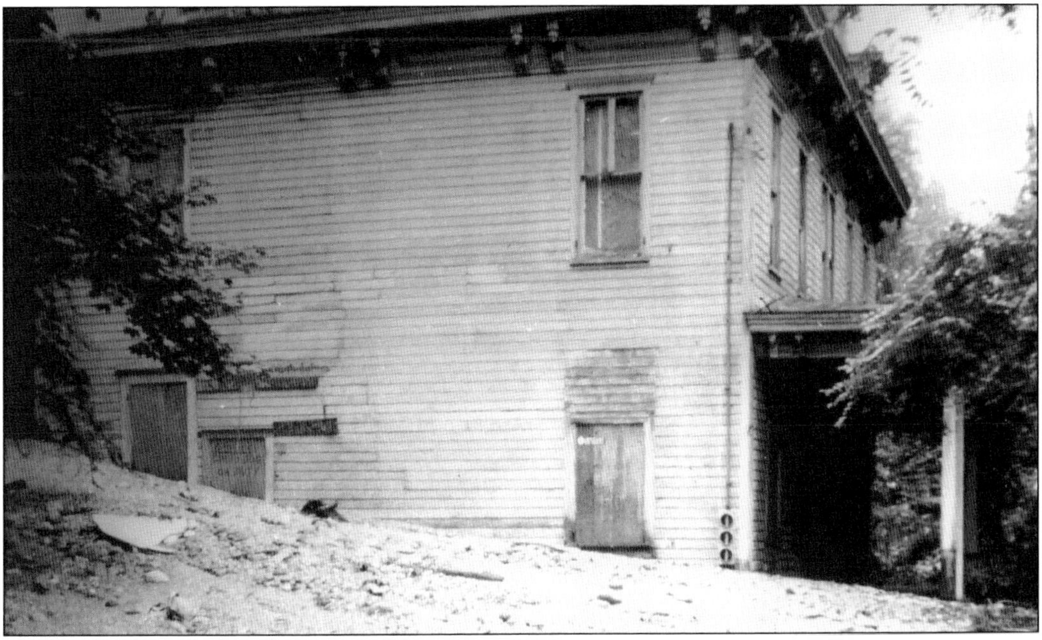

For nearly 50 years, the Warren Wilkey house on Main Street was a deteriorating eyesore. In 1969, as an apartment complex was being built on the hillside above, a landslide slammed into it, causing serious damage. Preservation leader Roger Gerry had the construction stopped and bought the house. The developer built retaining walls, and Gerry found that the Wilkey house was worthy of the authentic restoration he had in mind. (Photograph by Ray Jacobs, courtesy of RLS.)

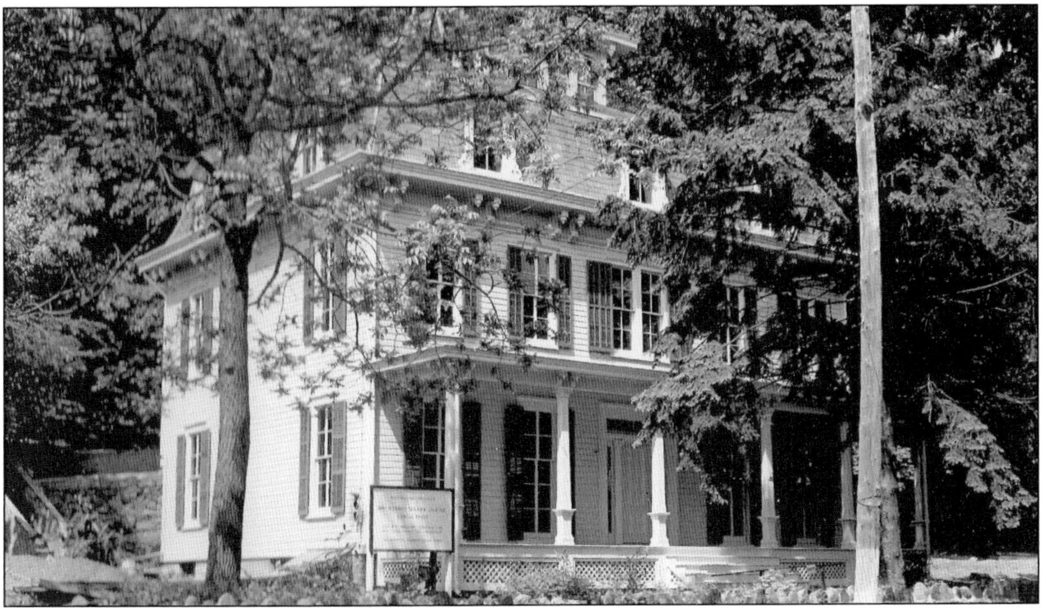

The Second Empire–style Warren Wilkey house, one of Roslyn's finest buildings, was built around 1865 by Wilkey's carpenter brother-in-law John S. Wood. Wilkey, a New York businessman, lived part-time in Roslyn. In 1925, this house was divided into small apartments, and the house slid deep into neglect. According to Roger Gerry, the restoration was "one of the major achievements of the Roslyn Preservation Corporation." (Photograph by Ray Jacobs, courtesy of RLS.)

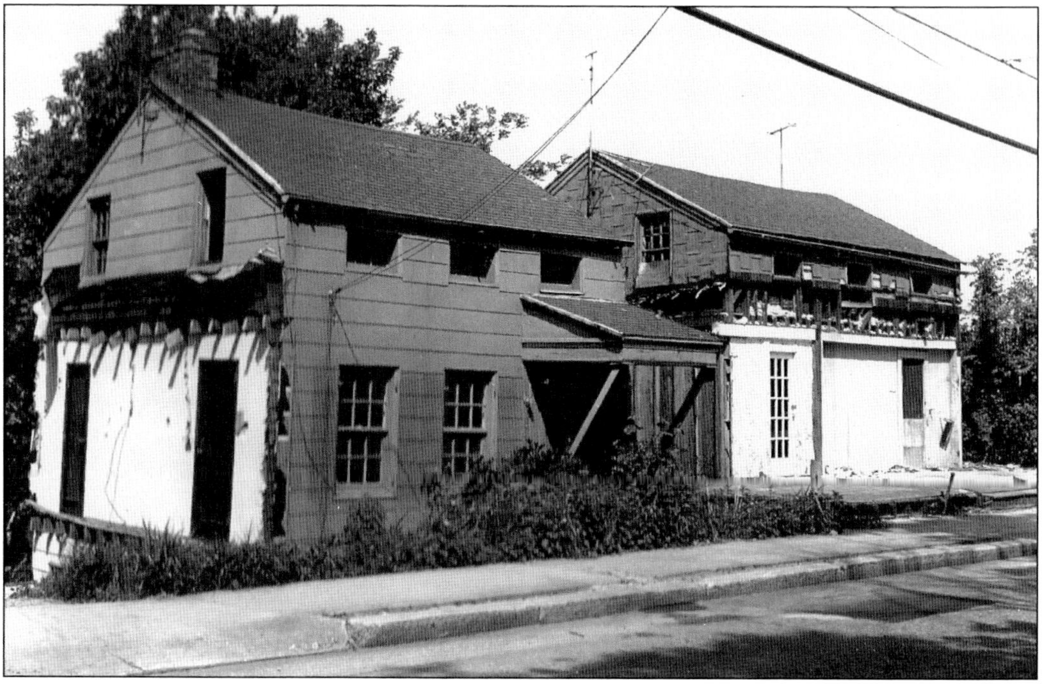

This little eyesore on East Broadway (above) stood in the way of a 1973 expansion of the Roslyn Savings Bank. Under the asbestos and asphalt siding lived two once-respectable Greek Revival cottages that had been cobbled together and used for years as a store and residence. One, the Smith-Hegeman cottage (below), was built for Capt. James Smith around 1845, after his bankruptcy and loss of the house at 106 Main Street. The bank donated them to the Roslyn Preservation Corporation, and Roger Gerry supervised a restoration that began with separating them and moving one to each side of the Wilkey house. By subdividing the large lot and putting the cottages on the new lots, Gerry preempted the threat of inappropriate future development. (Photographs by Ray Jacobs, courtesy of RLS.)

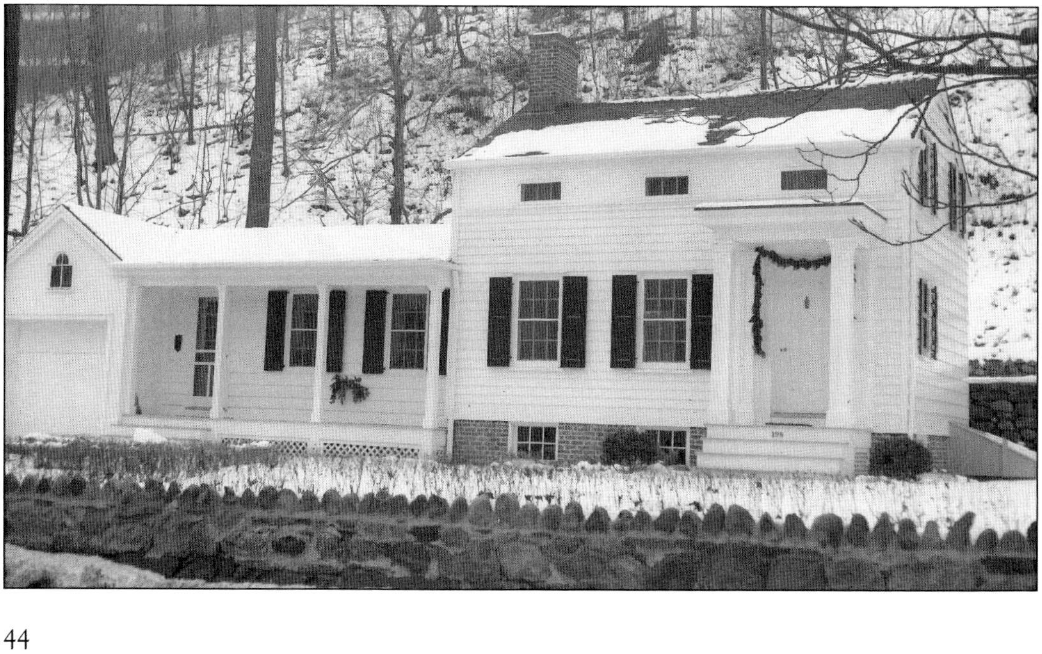

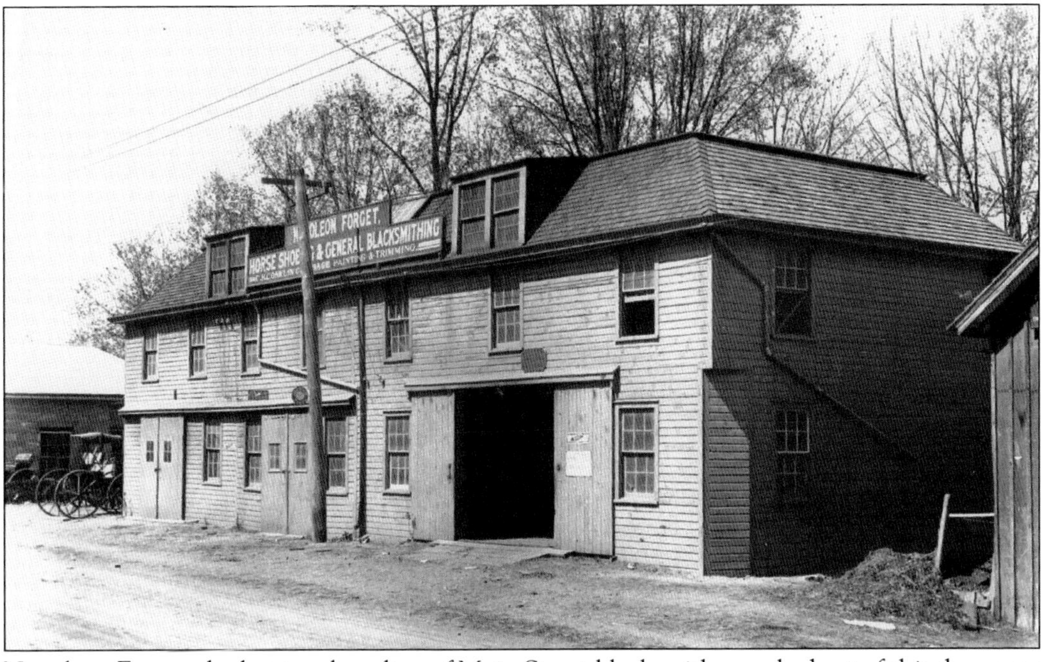

Napoleon Forget, the last in a long line of Main Street blacksmiths, worked out of this shop near the south end of the street. The blacksmith shop, shown here in 1909, replaced Thomas and John Wood's carpentry shop and was itself replaced by a garage that still stands on this site. (Courtesy of the Queens Borough Public Library, Long Island Division, Joseph Burt Photographs.)

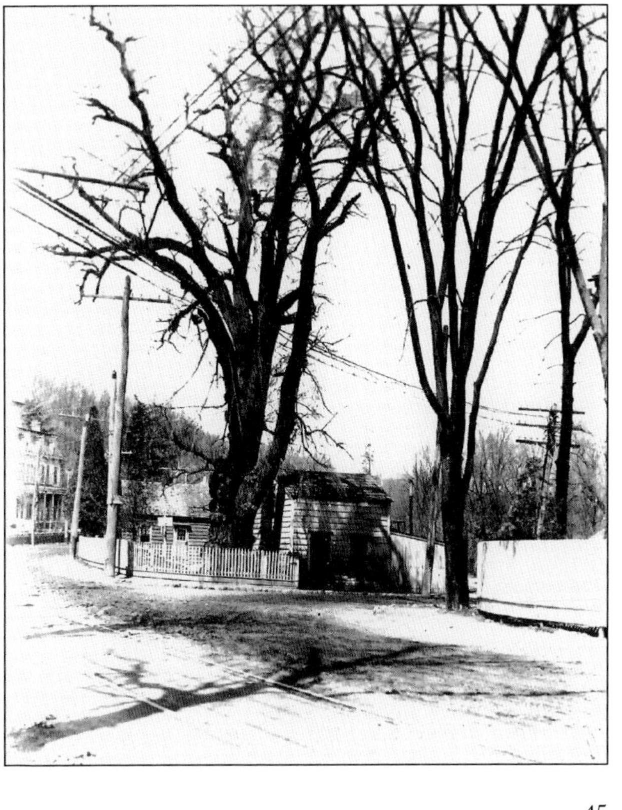

Kirbys Corners is shown around 1900, when a photographer's studio occupied the little house inside the corner (each windowpane holds a photograph). The sign on the tree advertises the "Roslyn Carriage Shop on the Mill Dam." In 1958, the little house was moved to become part of a larger dwelling then being built for Virginia Applegate Sammis, the last Kirby owner. (Courtesy of RLS.)

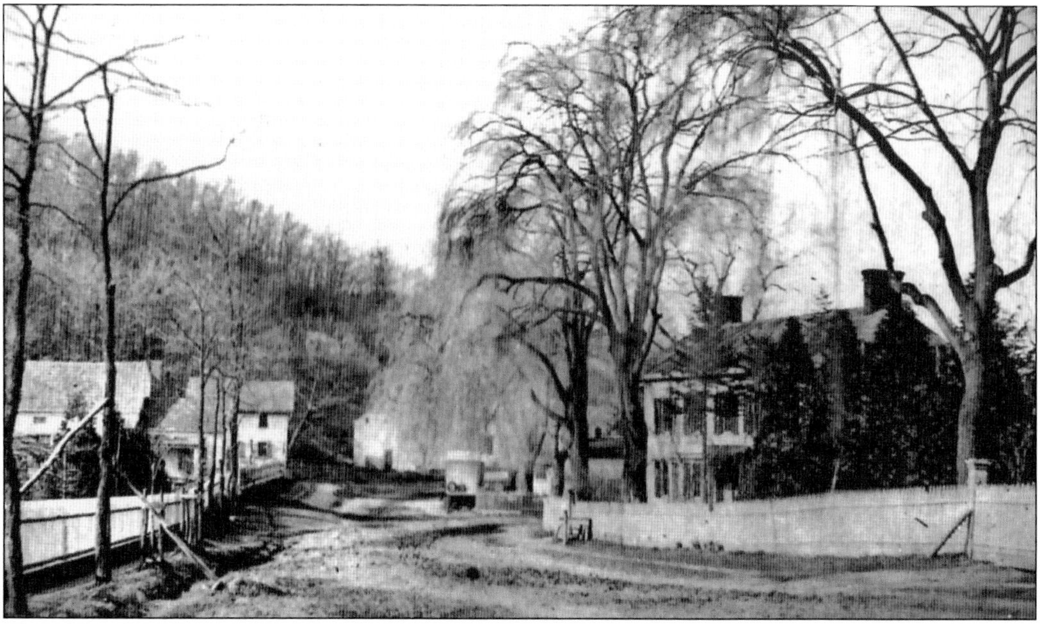

The oldest house in Roslyn, built Dutch-style around 1680, stands on the west side of Main Street at East Broadway (left). By around 1900, the Van Nostrand–Starkins house had been remodeled several times. The mounting block in front of the picket fence aided people in climbing into carriages. (Courtesy of RLS.)

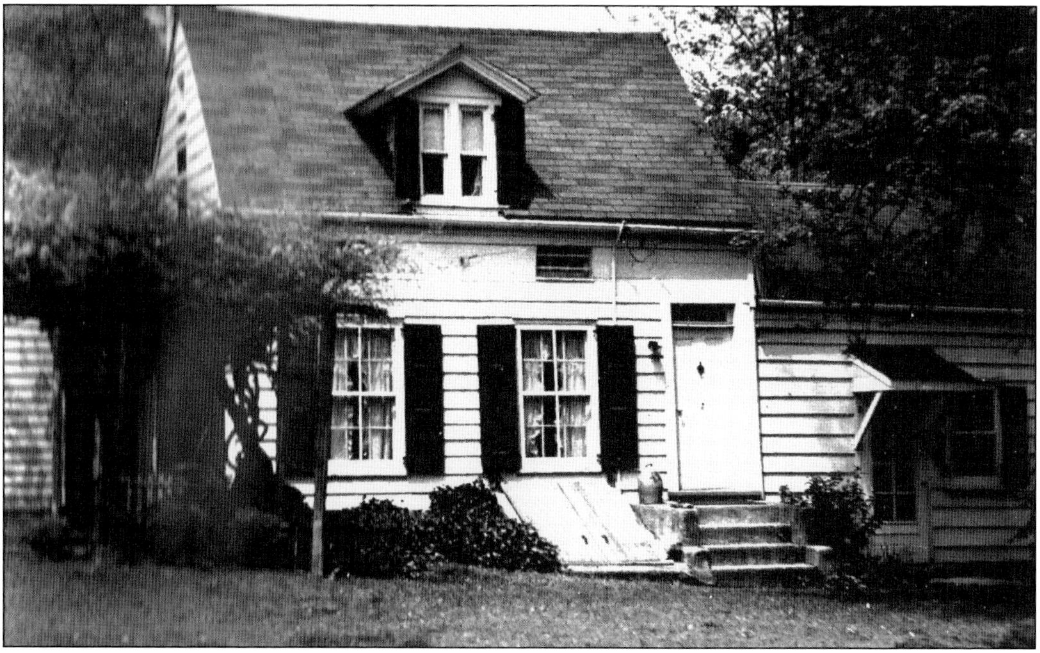

By 1970, the ancient Dutch house looked like a Greek Revival cottage with Victorian additions. If it had not been an important example of a rare architectural type, preservationists would have permitted it to remain in its evolved condition. But its significance as an early Long Island Dutch-type house required a restoration plan that sacrificed the charm it had acquired over centuries of change. (Photograph by Ray Jacobs, courtesy of RLS.)

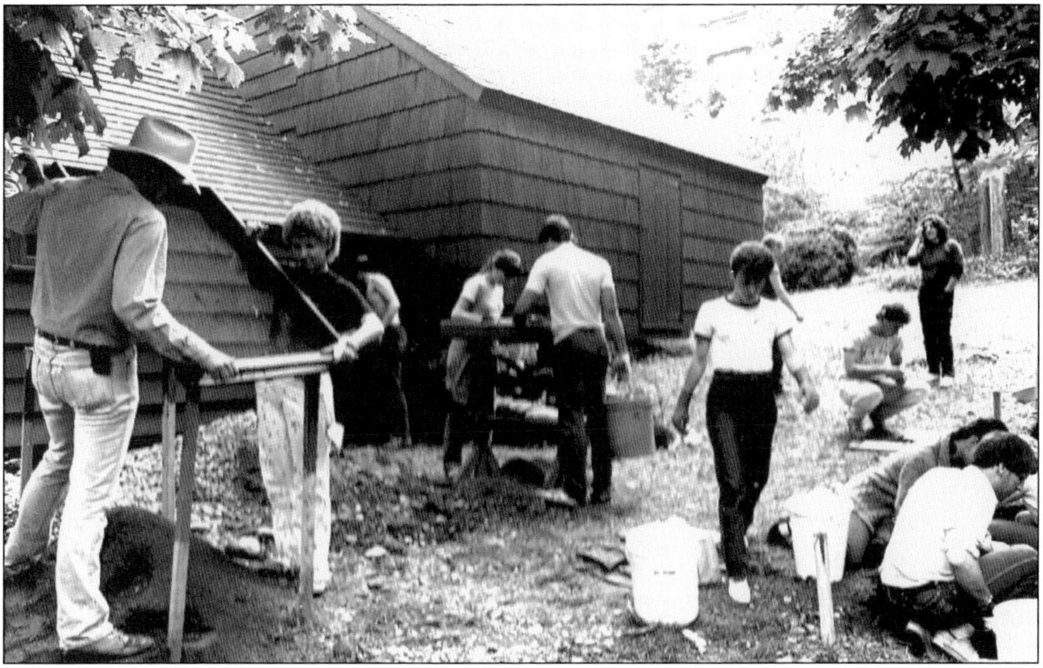

In 1982, archaeologists from New York University investigated the Van Nostrand–Starkins backyard for the fourth time. They hoped to learn about the domestic lives of the house's early residents. Artifacts discovered during the digs are displayed in the house along with items from other local buildings. (Courtesy of RLS.)

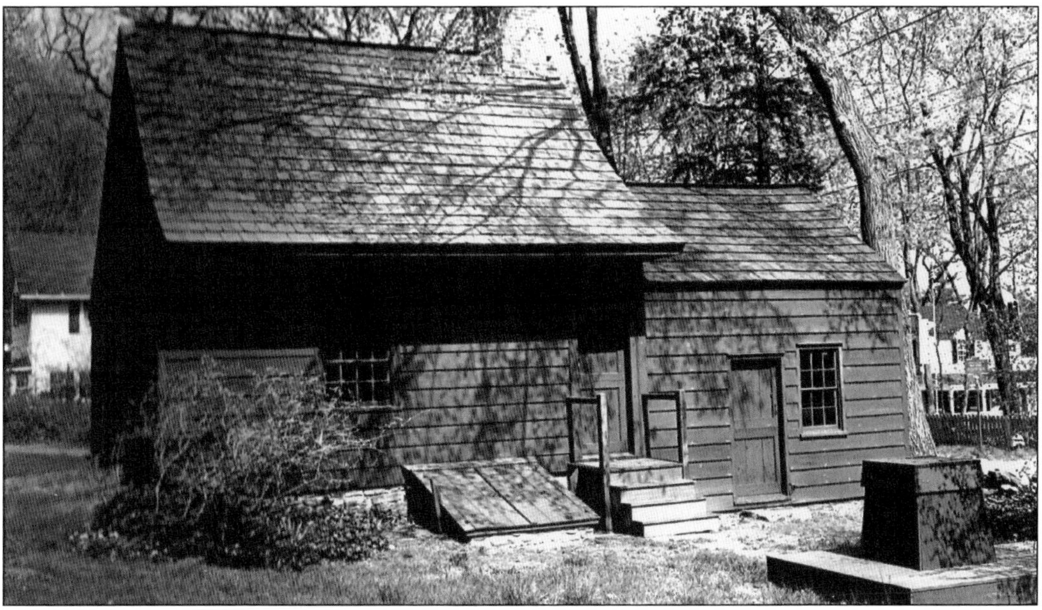

After study, the Roslyn Landmark Society chose to restore the Van Nostrand–Starkins house to the way it looked around 1830. At that date the house retained much of its original Dutch appearance, and a rear lean-to and a small west wing had been built. But the Greek Revival alterations that so changed its appearance had not yet been made (see page 46). (Photograph by Ray Jacobs, courtesy of RLS.)

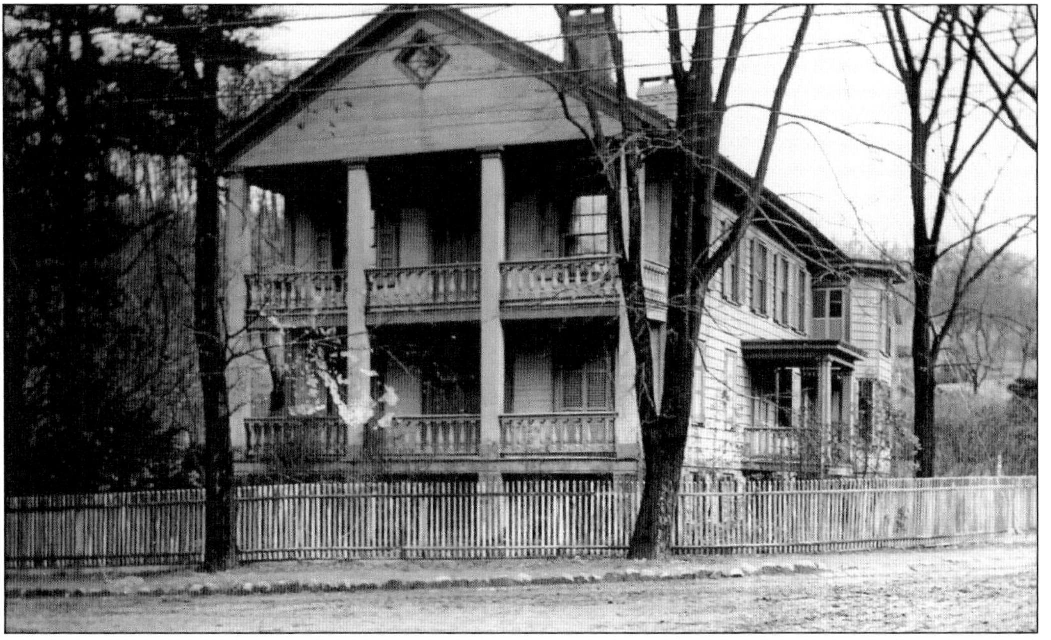

Around 1845, Jacob Kirby remodeled a house at Kirbys Corners as a Greek Revival residence. His widow, Elizabeth, continued living here with their son William Wallace, an attorney, minister, and justice of the peace. At the time of this *c.* 1900 picture, Wallace's widow, Susan Eliza, and son, Ralph, lived here. In 1941, the mansion was dismantled and the facade built into Cornelius Vanderbilt Whitney's Wheatley Hills house (now part of the Old Westbury Country Club clubhouse). (Courtesy of RLS.)

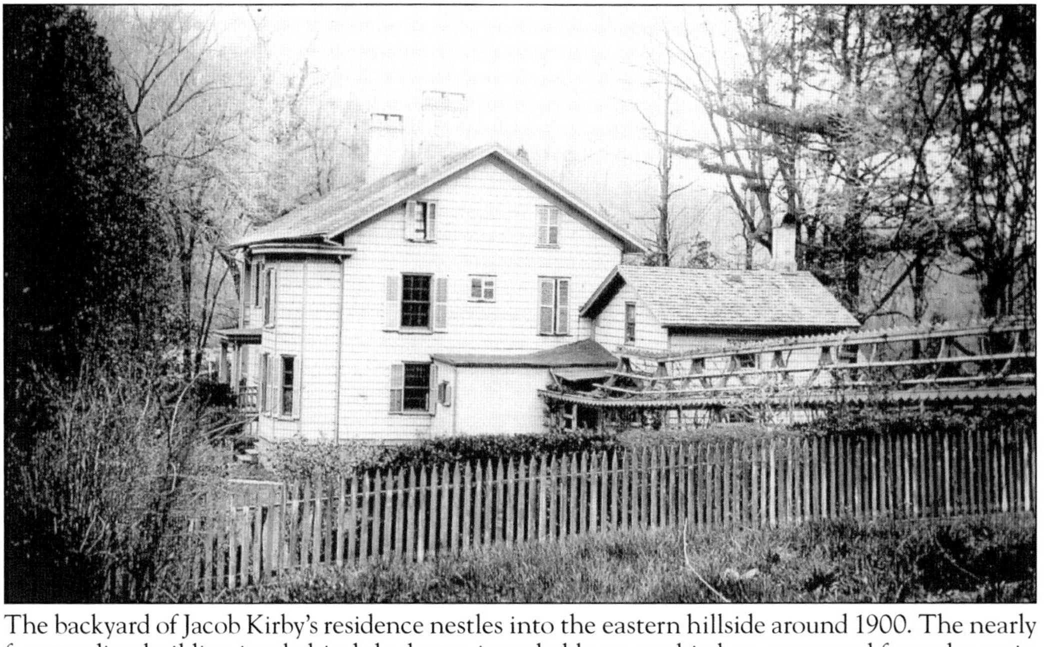

The backyard of Jacob Kirby's residence nestles into the eastern hillside around 1900. The nearly freestanding building just behind the house is probably an out-kitchen, separated from the main house to minimize the chance of fire. The long garden structure with the sawtooth crest running toward the back of the yard appears to be a grape arbor. (Courtesy of RLS.)

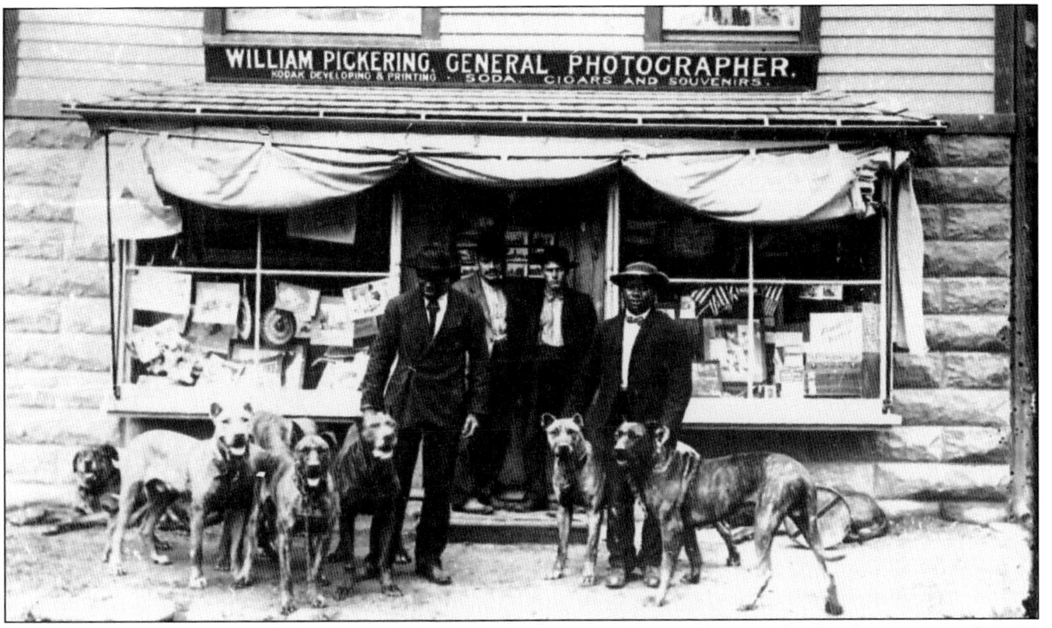

William H. Pickering was a well-known Roslyn photographer and news dealer from around 1900 through the 1920s. An English immigrant, Pickering worked on nearby estates until 1901, when he and his wife Emma moved into this house and shop on East Broadway. Pickering, a self-taught photographer, also sold newspapers, books, candy, and stationery. His photographs and postcards are the best visual record of Roslyn life in the early 20th century. Some of the postcards feature the Pickering children, all nine of whom were cute and photogenic. In the image above, men outside Pickering's shop hold fighting dogs, probably Italian mastiffs. In the lower view, a boy and a cat stand before windows displaying framed photographs. (Above, courtesy of the Nassau County Museum Collection, Long Island Studies Institute; below, courtesy of the Queens Borough Public Library, Long Island Division, Joseph Burt Photographs.)

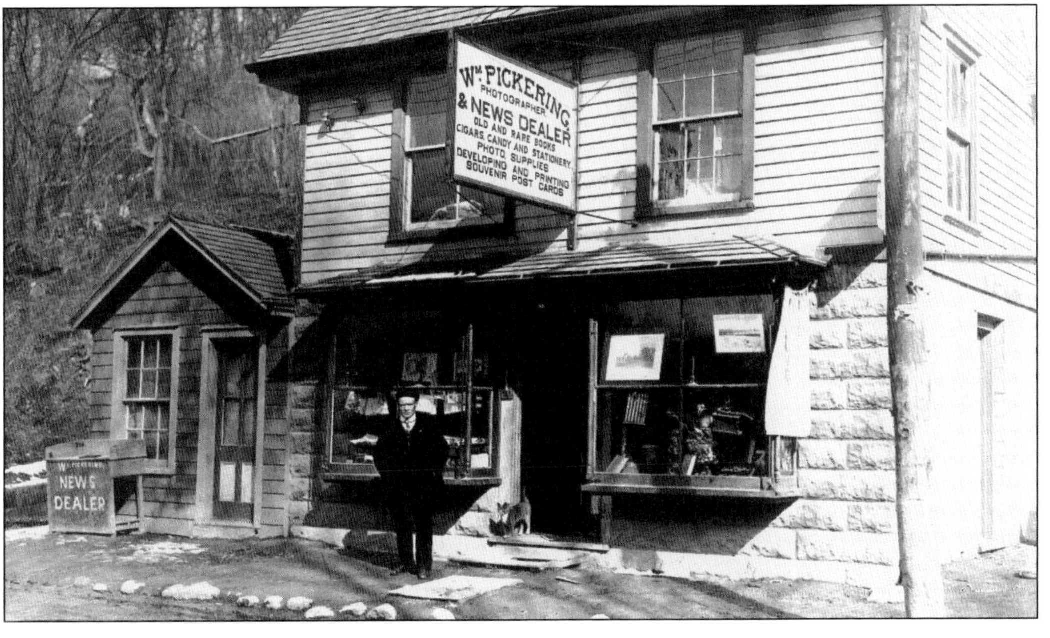

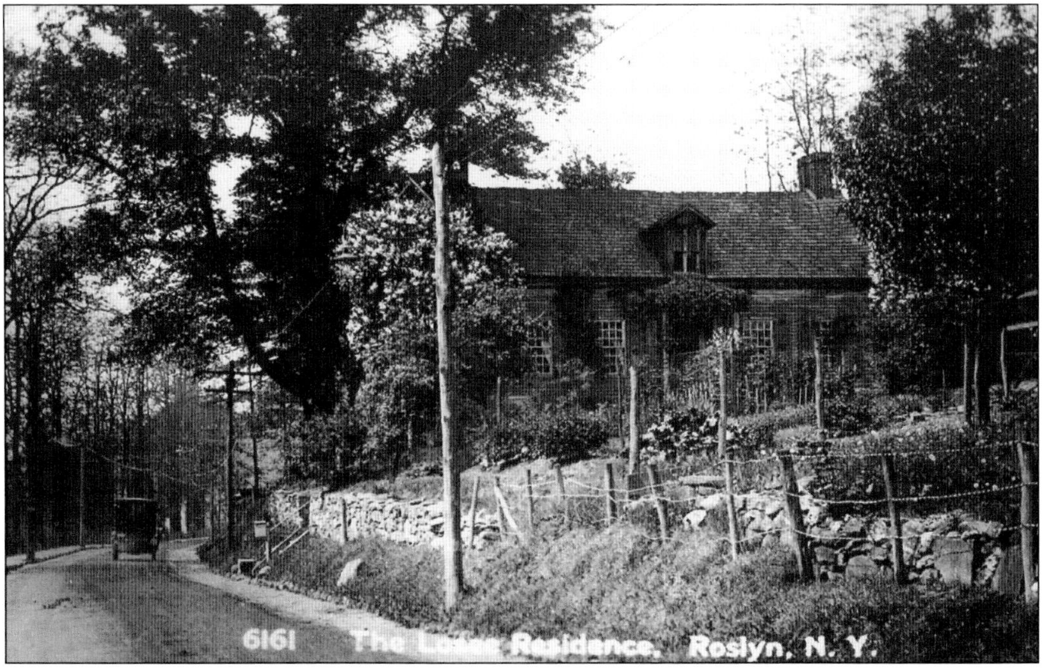

Both photographs show the south front of the Valentine-Losee house on East Broadway. Built around 1743 by John Valentine, it is the third-oldest building in Roslyn, following the Van Nostrand–Starkins house and the Roslyn gristmill. Like these, it is Dutch built. One of William Pickering's most popular postcards features the quaint old house and its riotous garden. The very old automobile heading north on East Broadway dates the postcard to 1920 or earlier. The lower view shows the house after its 1996 restoration by Peggy Gerry with John Stevens and Guy Ladd Frost. (Above, courtesy of RLS; below, photograph by Ray Jacobs, courtesy of RLS.)

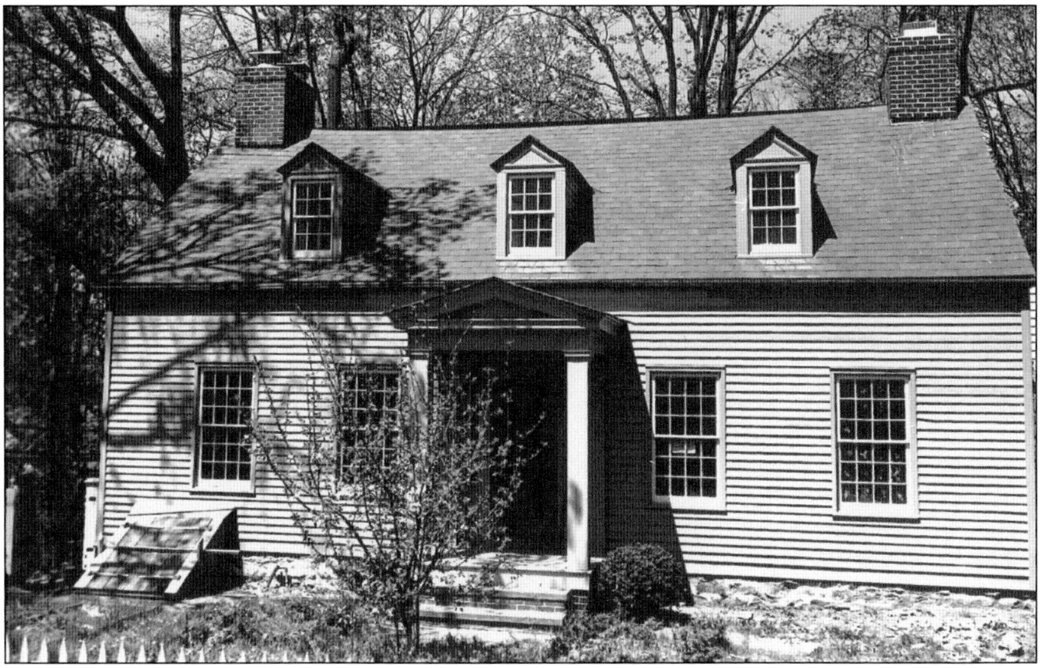

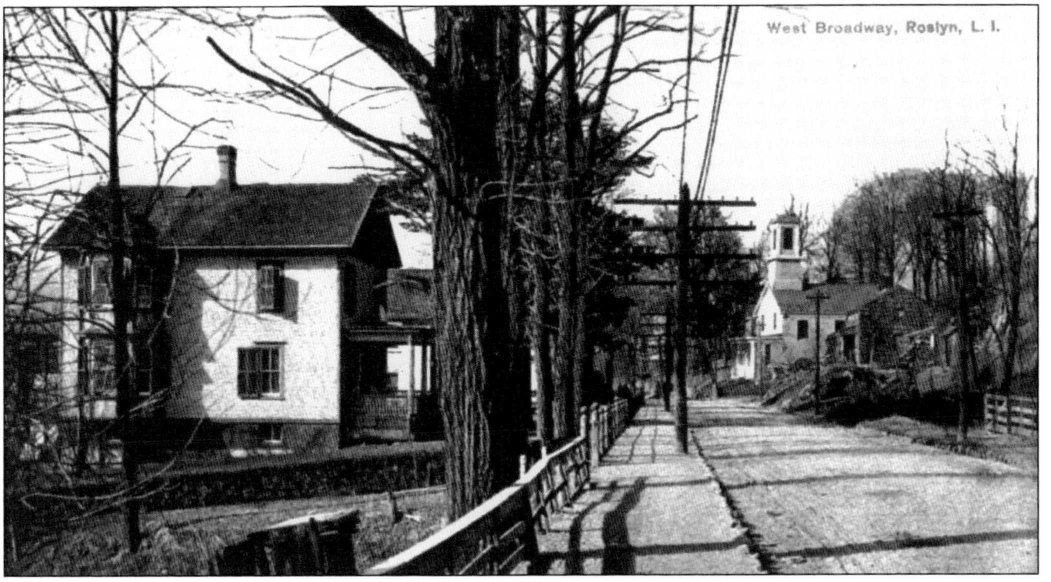

This East Broadway house, left, belonged to Herbert Conklin around 1910. Queen Anne in style, it was built in 1889 by Conklin's brother Eugene. Both were partners in the firm of Conklin, Tubby and Conklin, which bought the John D. Hicks Lumber Company, the great Roslyn lumber business that occupied acres at the head of the harbor. Conklin descendants lived here until 1986. (Courtesy of John and Michelle Santos.)

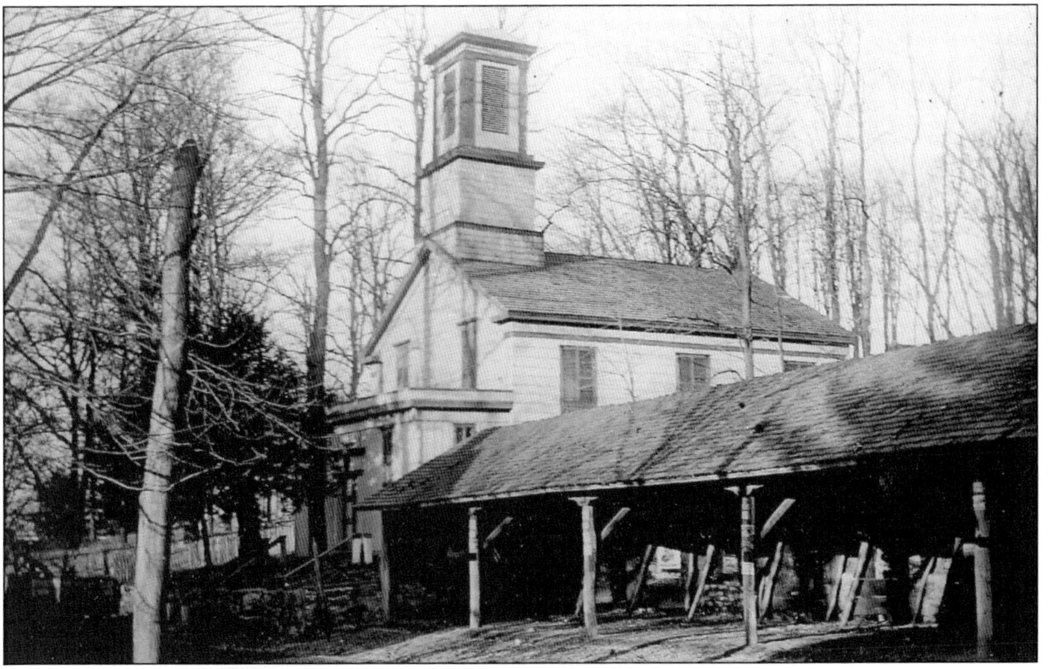

Seen here around 1910, Roslyn's Presbyterians built this church on East Broadway in 1851. The second pastor was the distinguished Dr. Samuel Rose Ely of Main Street. Ely baptized William Cullen Bryant's wife Fanny here in 1858, and Bryant himself worshipped here "because Dr. Ely invited all . . . to join in the communion service." After 1928, the church was deconsecrated, it lost its steeple, became a gallery, and finally a residence. (Courtesy of RLS.)

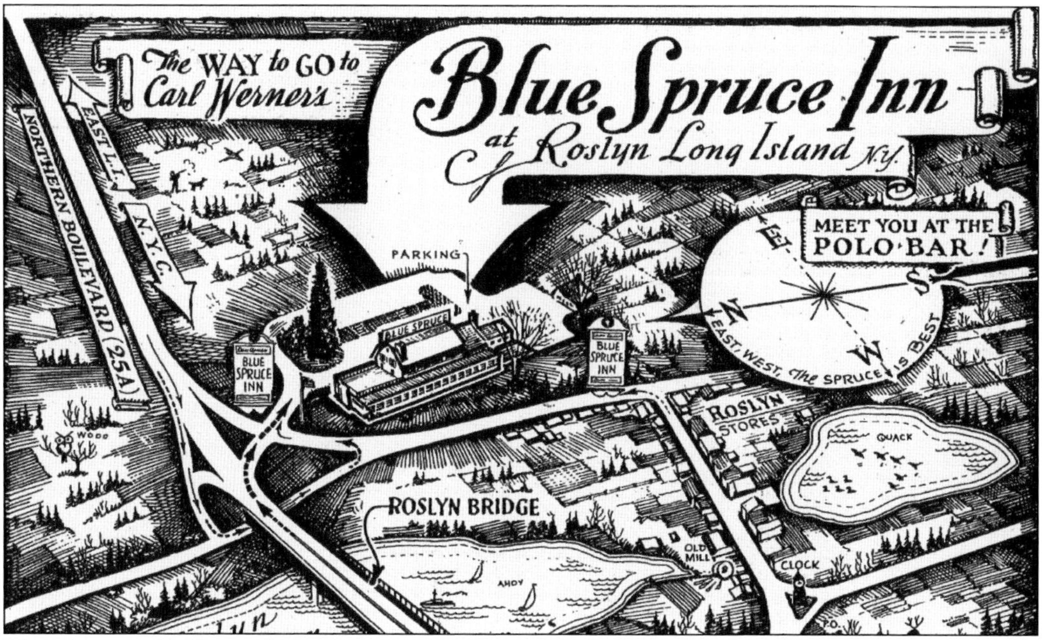

The Francis Skillman house was part of a farm Skillman inherited from his grandfather Onderdonk. It became the Blue Spruce Inn after Skillman's daughter Elizabeth Andrews died in 1922. The inn was favored by the North Shore equestrian set. The inn burned twice and was finally destroyed by fire in 1981. In its place now is the Harbour View Shopping Center. (Courtesy of Ian Zwerdling.)

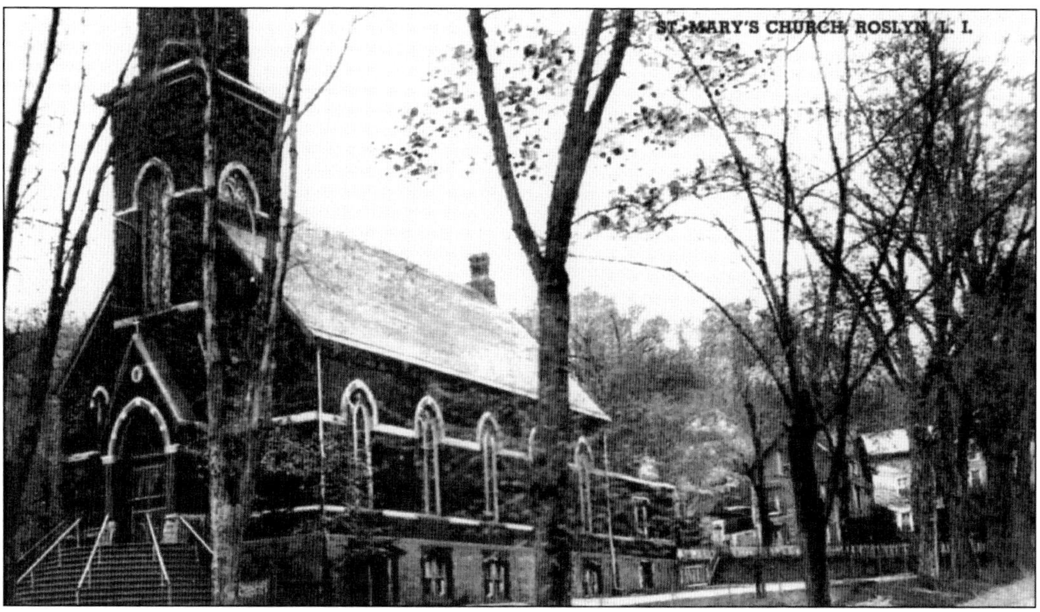

St. Mary's Roman Catholic Church was built on Bryant Avenue from 1871 through 1878. Until after the Civil War, Roslyn Catholics had worshipped in Manhasset. In 1865, a petition to celebrate mass locally was signed by all the local Catholics, as well as their non-Catholic landlords and employers. A chapel was built in 1867 and later replaced by this handsome brick church. (Courtesy of John and Michelle Santos.)

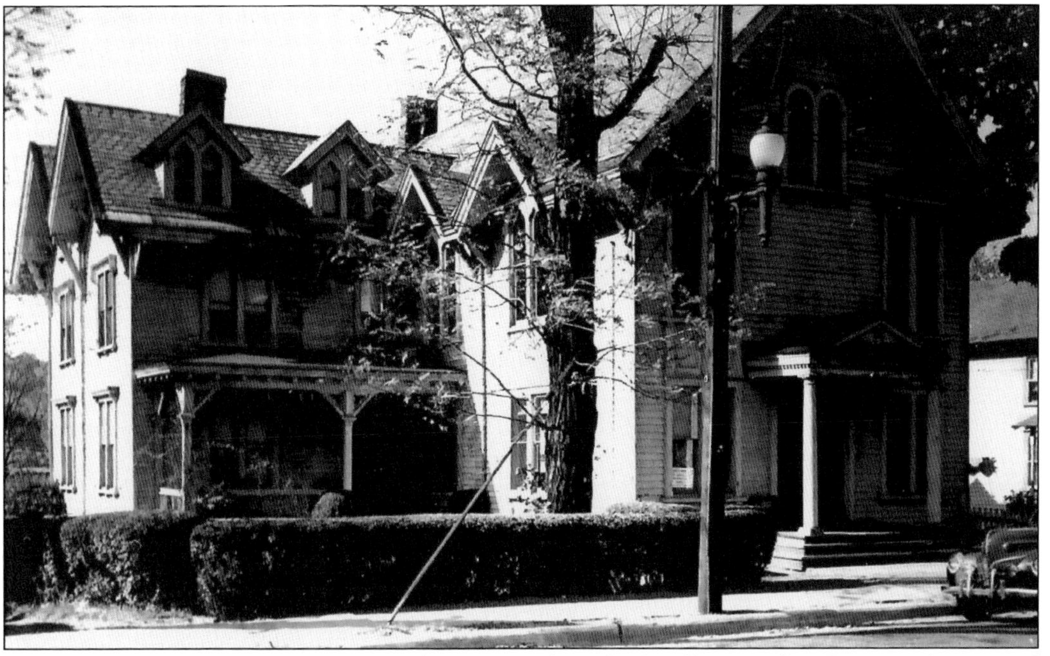

This building (above), seen here around 1900, was the gift of William Cullen Bryant, who wanted Roslyn to have a meeting place for social and intellectual activities. In 1873, he bought land south of Cedar Mere to build "the Hall," which was completed by Independence Day, 1876. A few months after the poet's death, the Bryant Circulating Library was organized, and, according to his wish, Bryant's daughter Julia deeded the building to the association. Still operating today, this is the oldest library in Nassau County. The reading room (below), seen here in the 1940s, resembled Bryant's own library in most ways. In 1946, when the Northern Boulevard viaduct was planned, the library moved to temporary quarters and this Victorian Gothic hall was demolished. (Above, courtesy of the Nassau County Department of Parks, Recreation and Museums, Cedarmere; below, courtesy of RLS.)

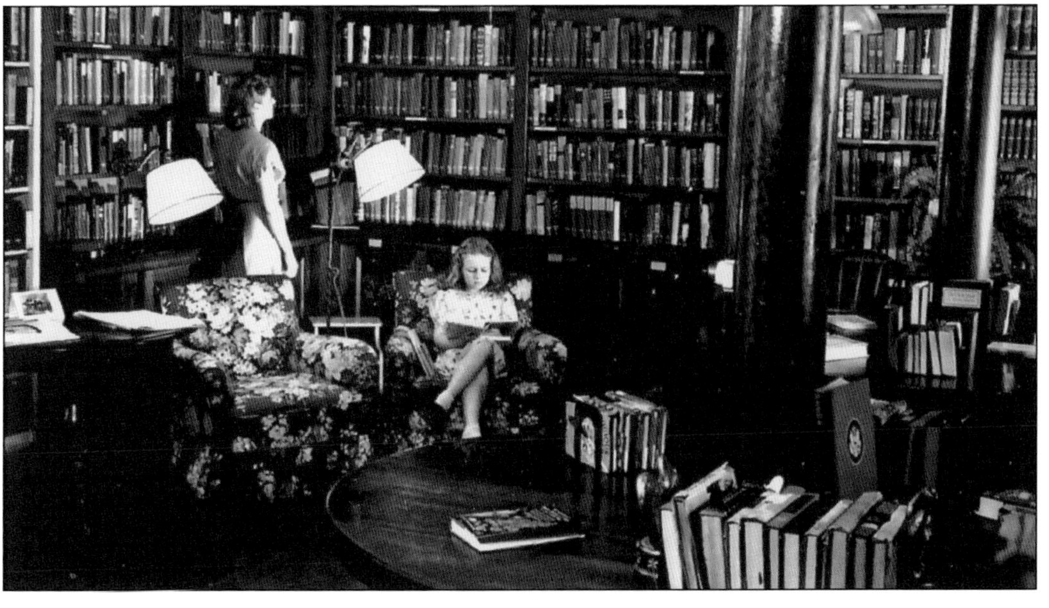

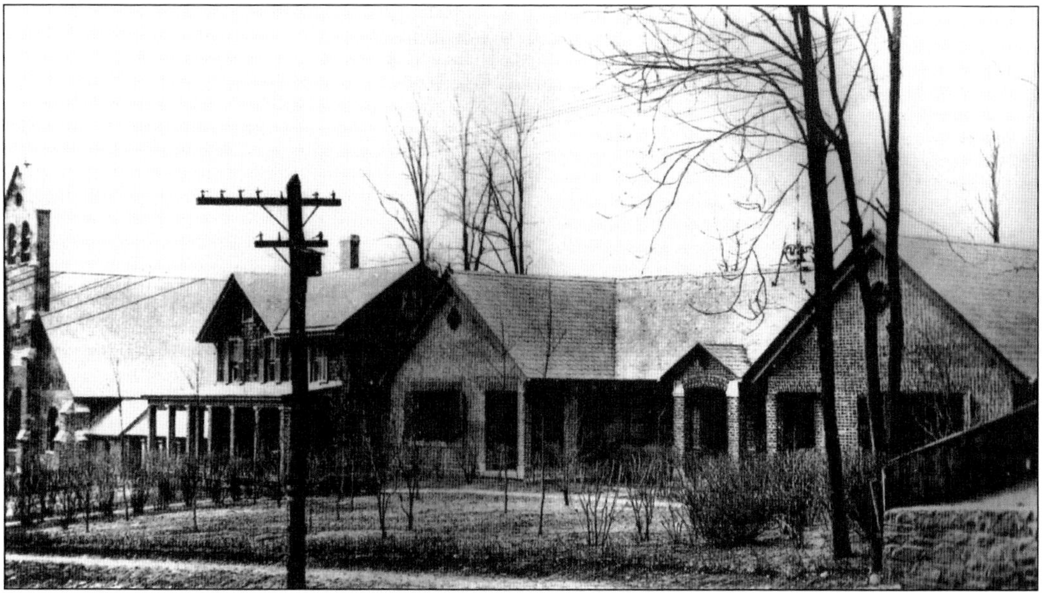

Hempstead Harbor's first Episcopal services were held in the 1780s, and in 1862 Christ Church Chapel was built on this Northern Boulevard site. An 1873 rectory is shown far left. In 1908, Katherine Duer Mackay of Harbor Hill donated money to build and furnish a parish house, shown here around 1906. She also engaged Stanford White to design a new Trinity Church, completed in 1907, in memory of her mother. (Courtesy of RLS.)

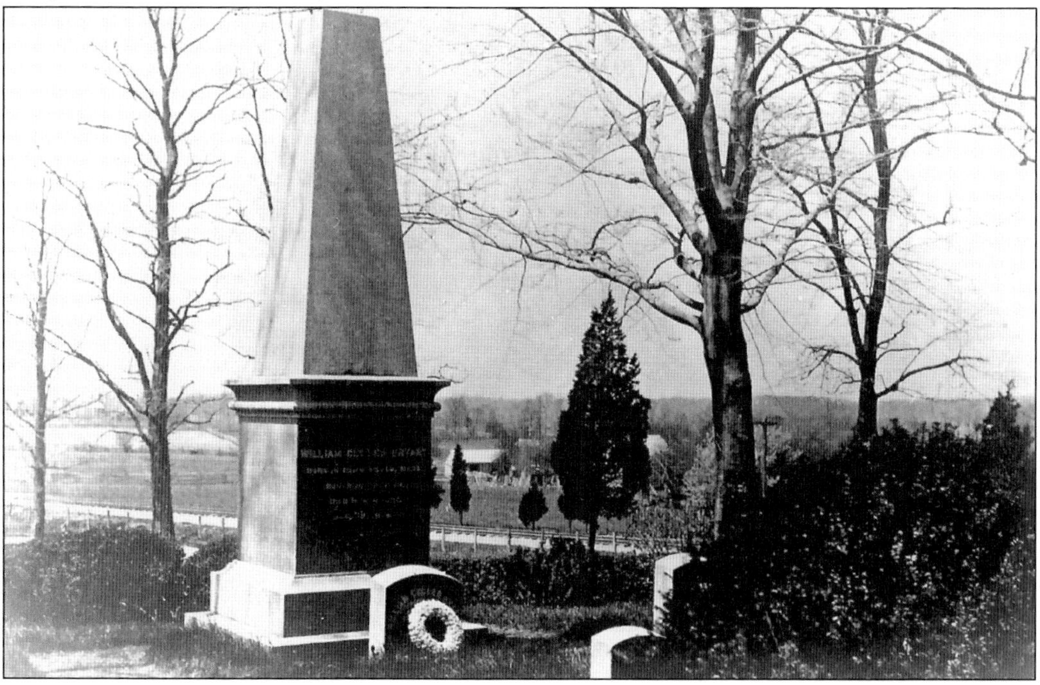

William Cullen Bryant died in New York City on June 12, 1878. He was buried under an obelisk in the Roslyn Cemetery. The most prominent monument in the 1861 cemetery is the Civil War memorial topped by the bronze figure of a Union soldier. Near Bryant's grave is buried Frances Hodgson Burnett, the author of *Little Lord Fauntleroy.* (Courtesy of RLS.)

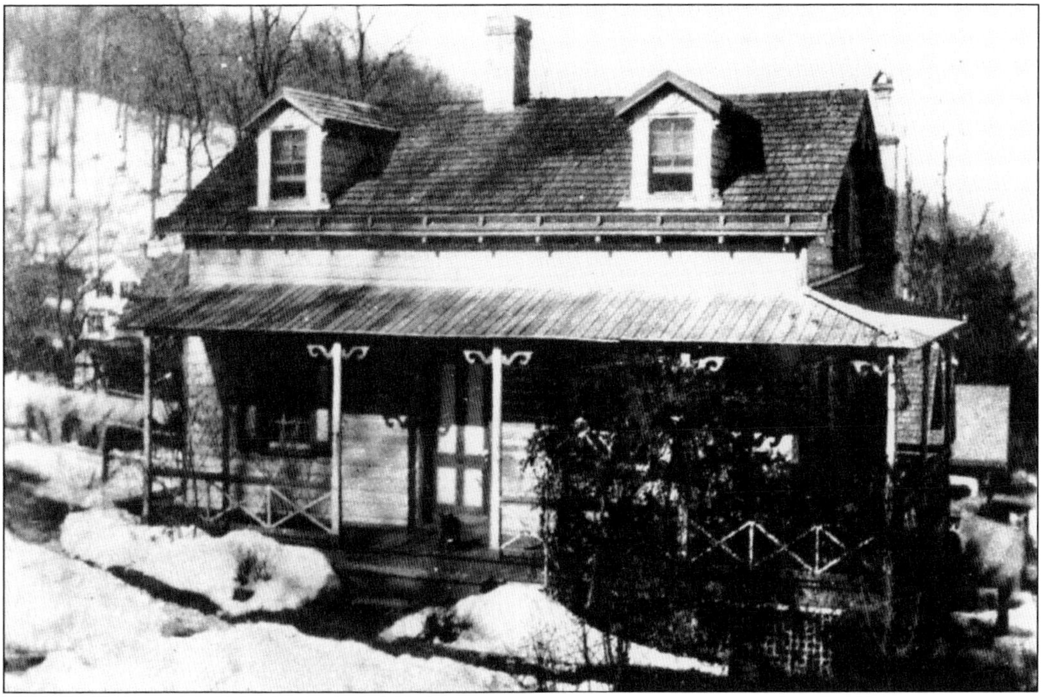

During the late 19th century, the Flushing–North Hempstead Turnpike (Northern Boulevard) was organized as a toll road. Roslyn had two tollgate houses, the one shown here around 1900 near West Shore Road and another in the cemetery. This one was owned by local carpenter Stephen Speedling. At the tollgate house, the toll collector raised the pole barrier after collecting the toll. (Courtesy of the Nassau County Museum Collection, Long Island Studies Institute.)

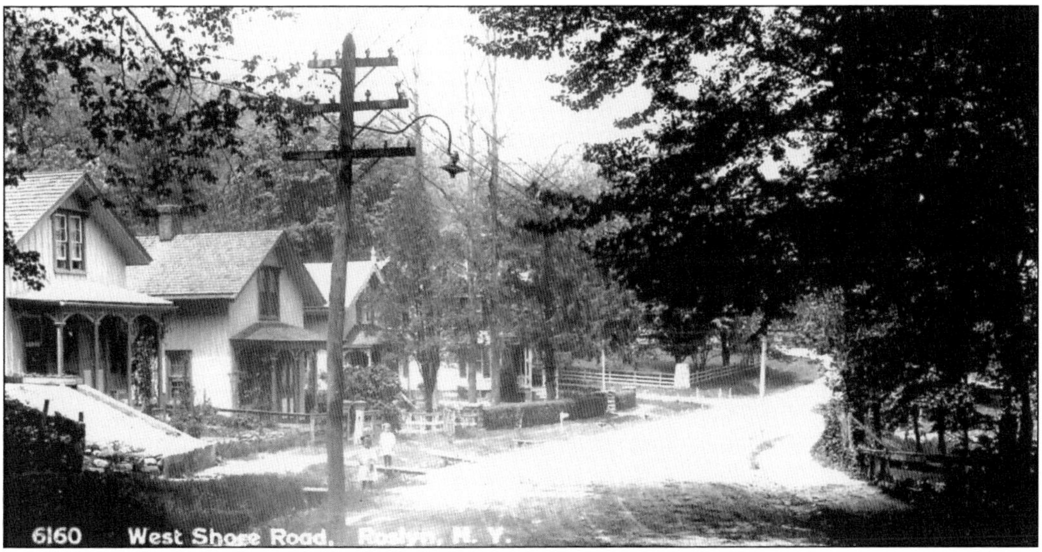

This *c.* 1900 postcard shows the West Turnpike hill descending into Roslyn's valley, where an artisan's neighborhood developed after Frederick M. Eastman and Benjamin D. Hicks subdivided farmland into small house lots. These houses were built in the 1880s, many for investors. Houses here were restored starting in the 1980s and 1990s, and it has become a desirable and affordable place to live. (Courtesy of John and Michelle Santos.)

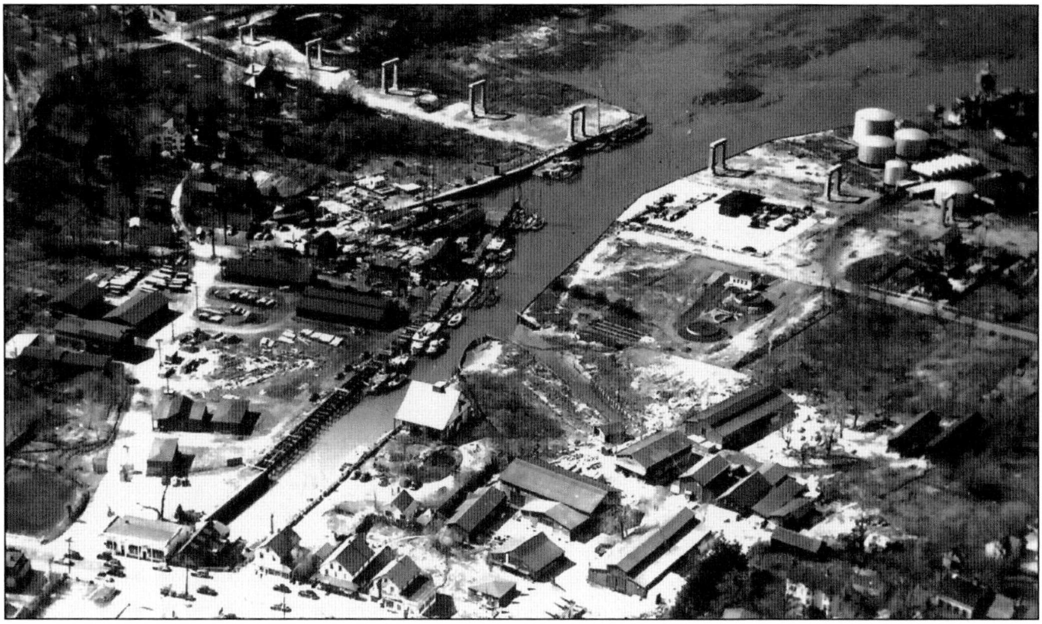

Novelist Christopher Morley (considered eccentric) suspected that the U.S. Department of War planned to eliminate Roslyn as an obstacle to civilians fleeing from a disaster in the city. The answer was the great white viaduct on Northern Boulevard, which would sweep traffic past the village. Here, in 1949, the viaduct's pylons stand ready to carry the four-lane highway over the harbor. (Courtesy of RLS.)

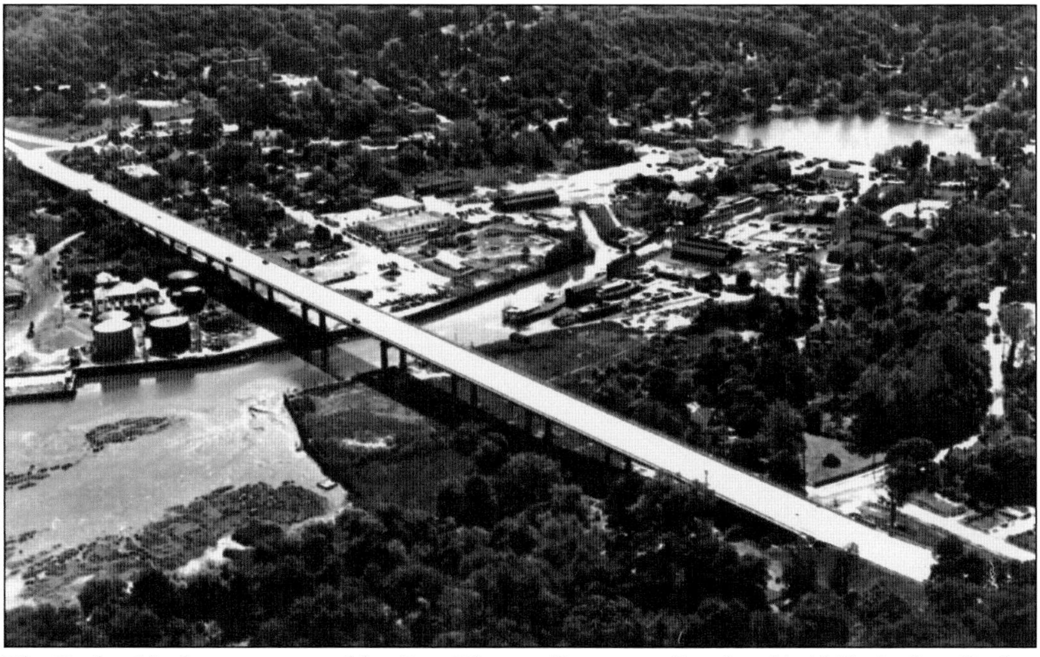

The Roslyn Viaduct was opened by Gov. Thomas Dewey on October 21, 1949. At first, Roslyn merchants complained that the diversion deprived them of business, but by 1960, when this photograph was taken, traffic had increased so much that the milldam was crowded again. (Courtesy of the Nassau County Museum Collection, Long Island Studies Institute.)

Four

LEADERS AND LUMINARIES

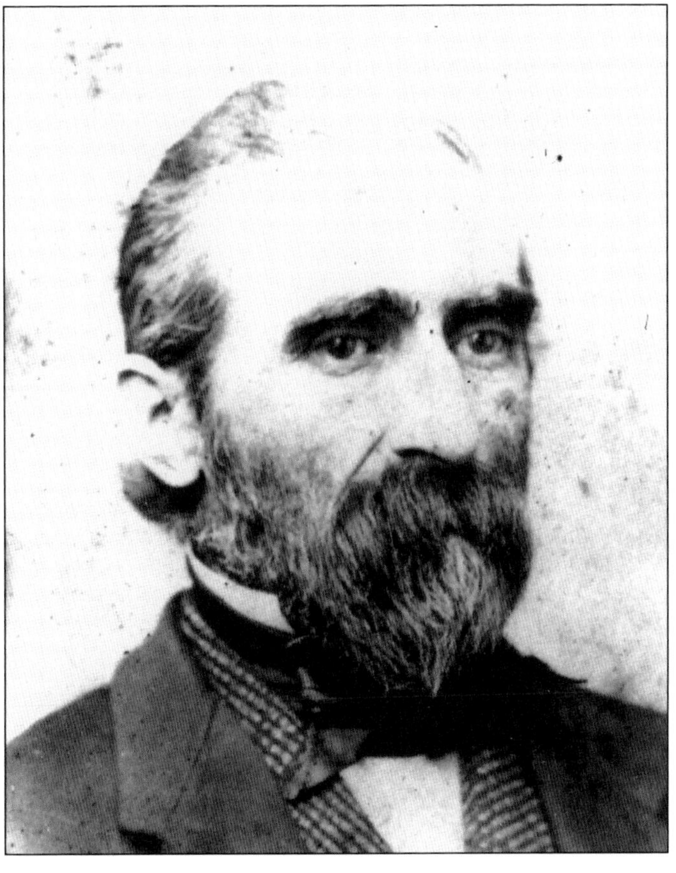

In every era, key people have altered Roslyn and left it more prosperous, comfortable, or beautiful. Squire Francis Skillman (1817–1898) was such a leader, seen here around 1868. He was state assemblyman in the 1860s, and Roslyn's justice of the peace from 1851 through 1875. Skillman held court in a building behind his house. Historians prize his 1895 letter describing mid-19th-century people, places, and events. (Courtesy of the Bryant Library Local History Collection, Roslyn.)

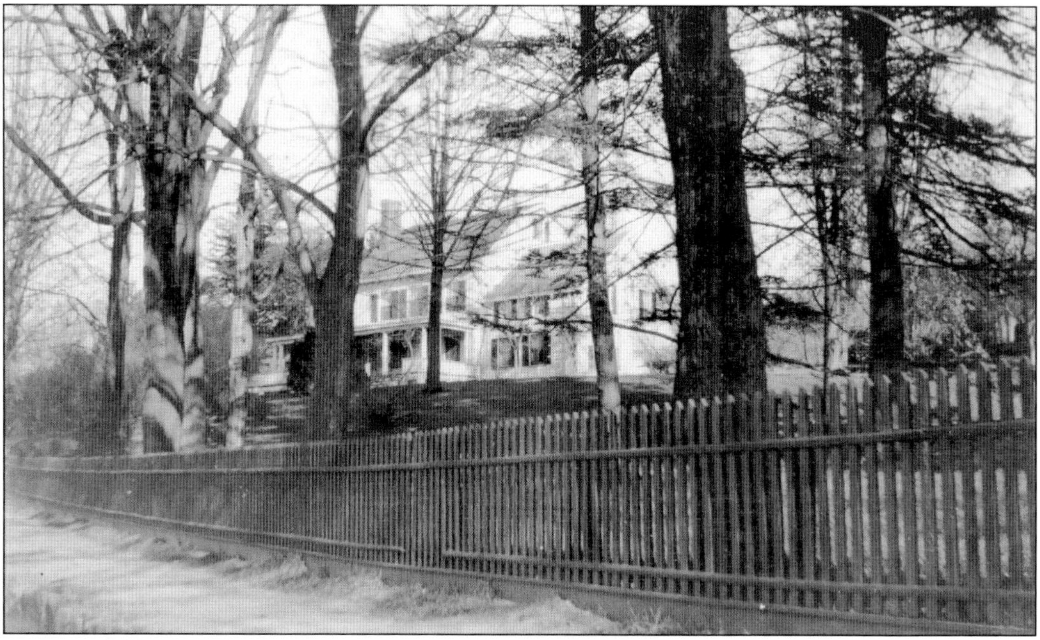

Francis Skillman's house came with a history. It was said to have been owned by Richard Valentine, a Revolutionary War patriot who transferred ownership to a Tory relative to avoid its confiscation during the British occupation. After the peace he was unable to get it back, which, with other troubles, broke his heart, and ruined, he died, drunk in a ditch. Later the house was owned by the paper mill Onderdonks; after Skillman's time it was a popular restaurant, the Blue Spruce Inn. (Above, courtesy of the Queens Borough Public Library, Long Island Division, Eugene L. Armbruster Collection; below, courtesy of John and Michelle Santos.)

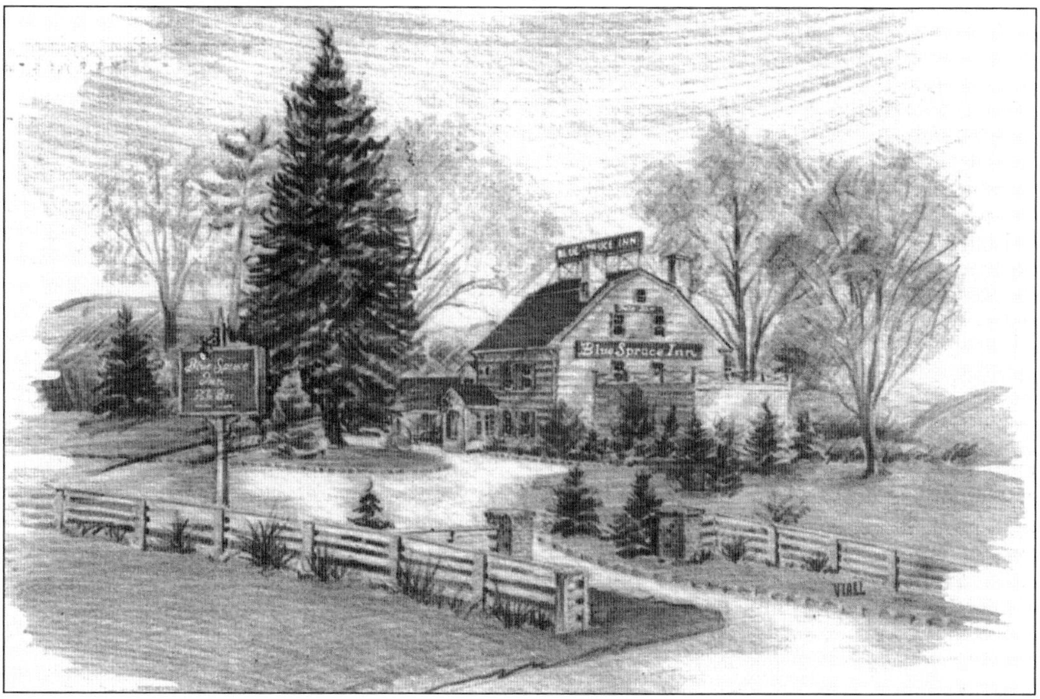

Born in New York in 1724, Dutch-speaker Hendrick Onderdonk settled in Hempstead Harbor in 1752. He bought a house and land, a store, and the gristmill. In 1773, Onderdonk built the first paper mill in New York State, astute because paper was a high-value item, and the suppression of its manufacture in the colonies was ending. Onderdonk may have spied for Gen. George Washington. After 1783, he went to the state assembly, was a supervisor of the town of North Hempstead, and overseer of highways. One April morning in 1790, the new president paid Onderdonk a visit en route to New York. Afterward, Washington wrote that he had been "kindly received and well entertained." The portrait at right shows prosperous Hendrick Onderdonk, who died in 1809; below is his house around 1895. (Right, courtesy of Ian Zwerdling; below, courtesy of RLS.)

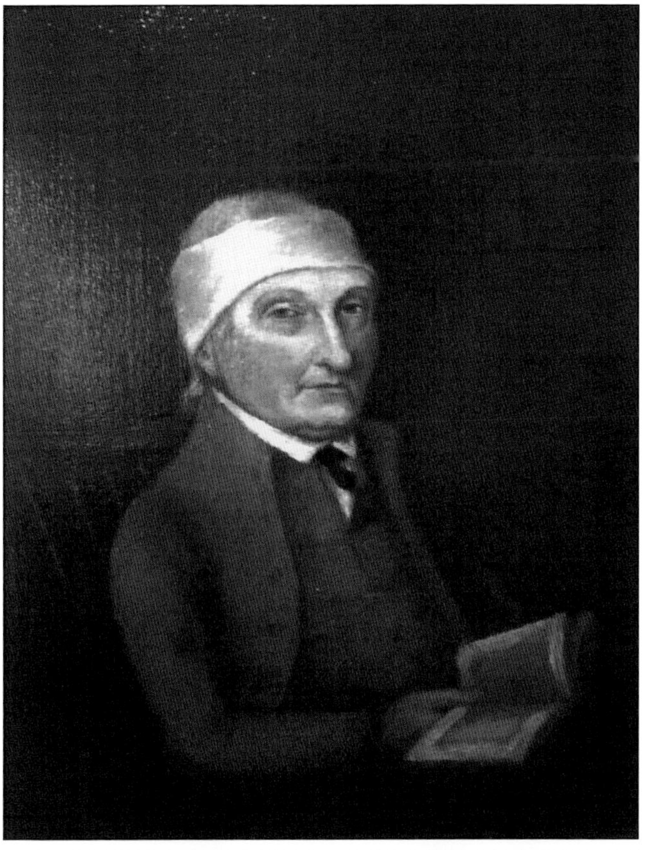

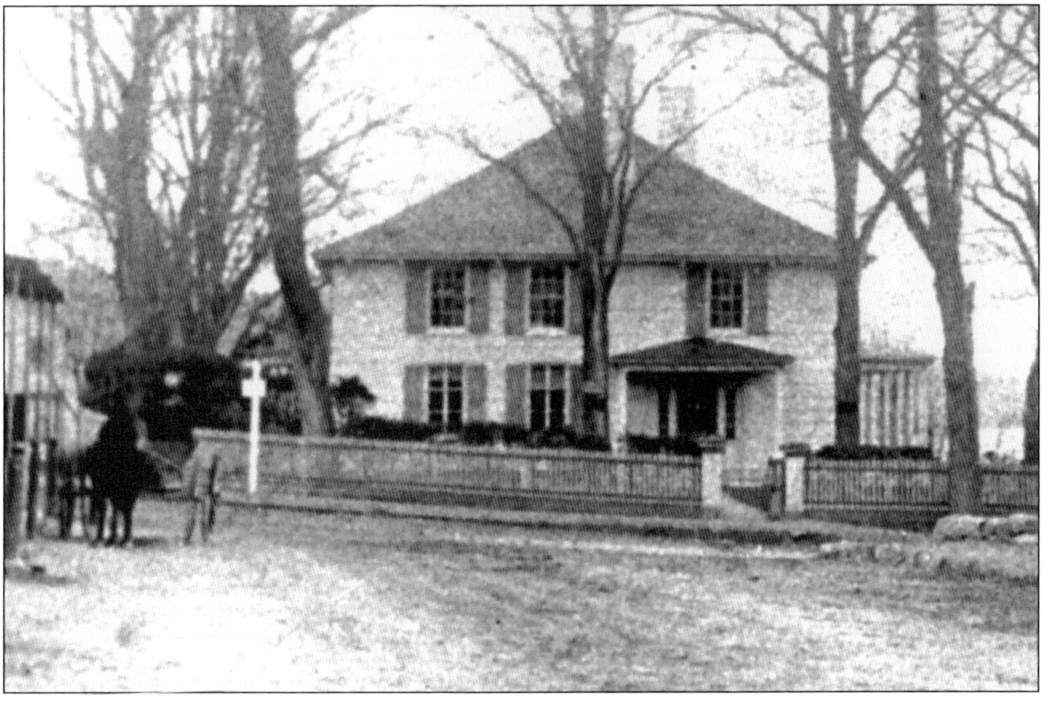

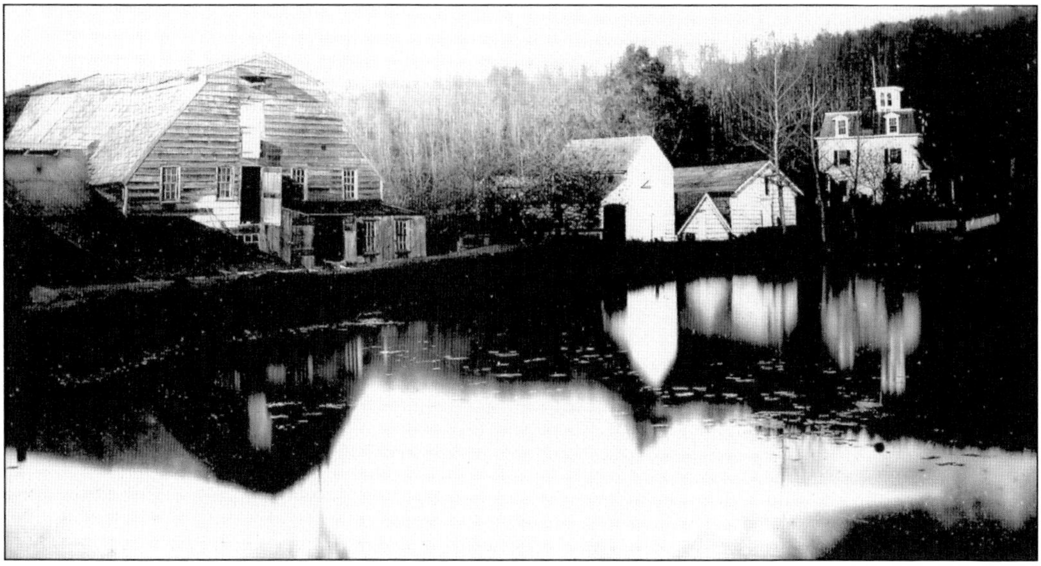

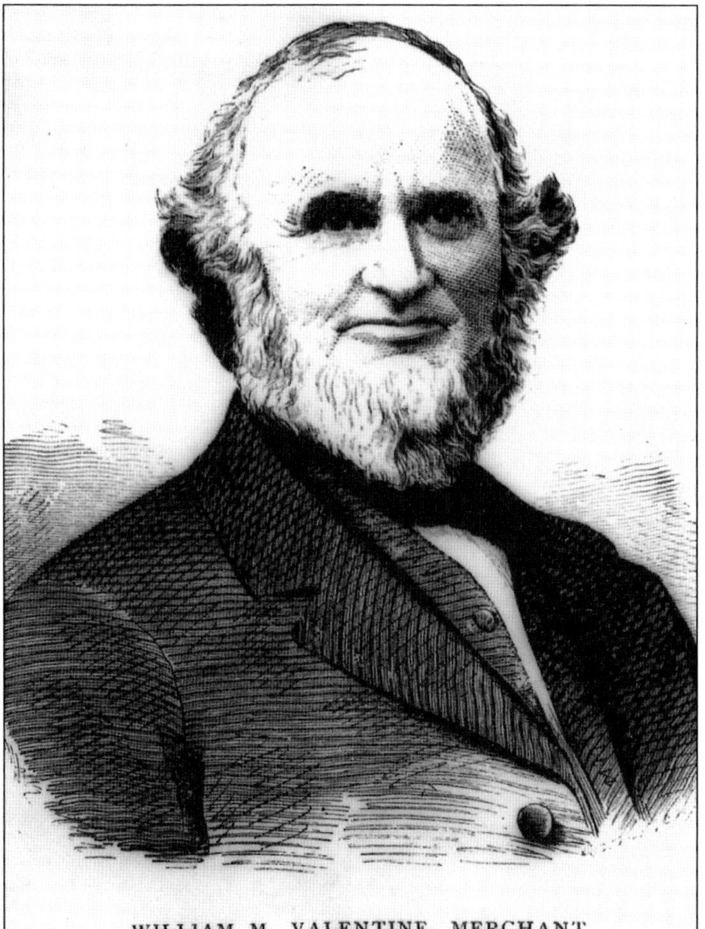

WILLIAM M. VALENTINE, MERCHANT.

The Valentine family, English-speaking Quakers, was prominent in early Roslyn. In 1801, William M. Valentine's father bought the paper mill from Hendrick Onderdonk. The family built houses and operated the paper mill until 1891. William M. Valentine was born in Roslyn in 1809. The house (above, on the right) was his home. Regarded as "a trifle eccentric," Valentine was widely admired. He ran the paper mill until 1837, then became a merchant. In 1862, he built a large brick store that stood until recently on Main Street at Tower Place. One night in 1882, Valentine left his store to row home across the millpond. Nearly there, he was assaulted by thugs, and although he lived two more years, he never recovered. (Above, courtesy of Ian Zwerdling; left, courtesy of the Bryant Library Local History Collection, Roslyn.)

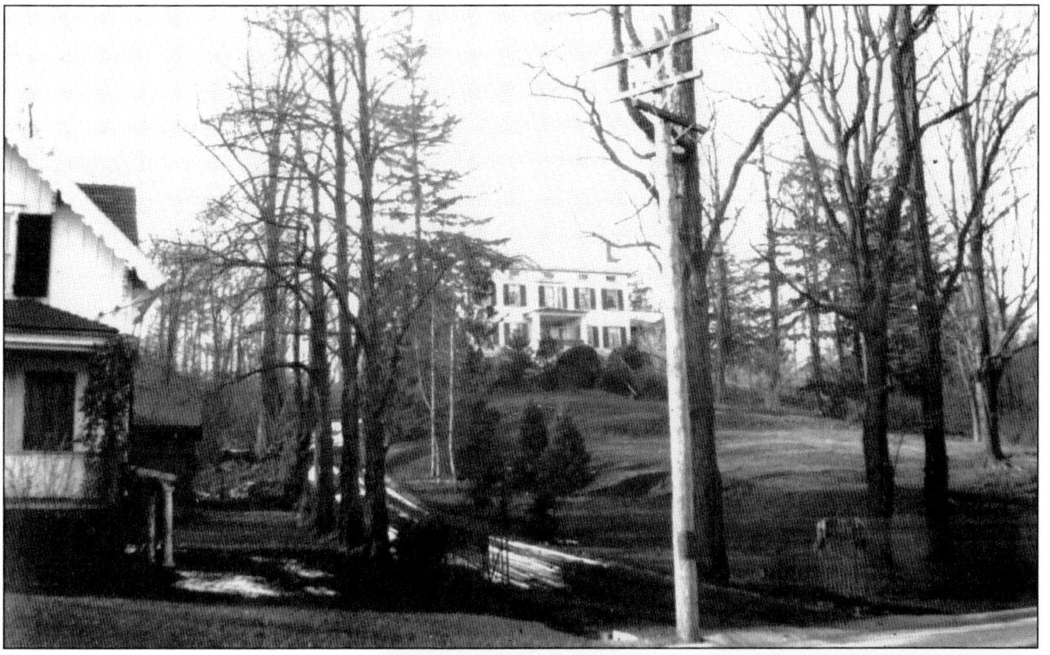

Samuel Rose Ely, born in 1803 in Massachusetts, was a distinguished cleric long before Roslyn. Educated at Williams College and Princeton, he had preached in East Hampton and Brooklyn before 1853 when he came seeking "repose and the quiet of country life." Soon he was pastor of the Presbyterian church, and opened the Locust Hill Academy on his Main Street property. Henry Western Eastman taught there and became a partner. In 1861, Ely helped to establish the Roslyn Cemetery. He retired from the ministry in 1871, and died two years later. Afterward, his widow, Mary Van Gilder, and son Samuel Rose Ely Jr. continued to live in the house until 1911. (Above, courtesy of the Queens Borough Public Library, Long Island Division, Eugene L. Armbruster Collection; right, courtesy of the Nassau County Department of Parks, Recreation and Muscums, Cedarmere.)

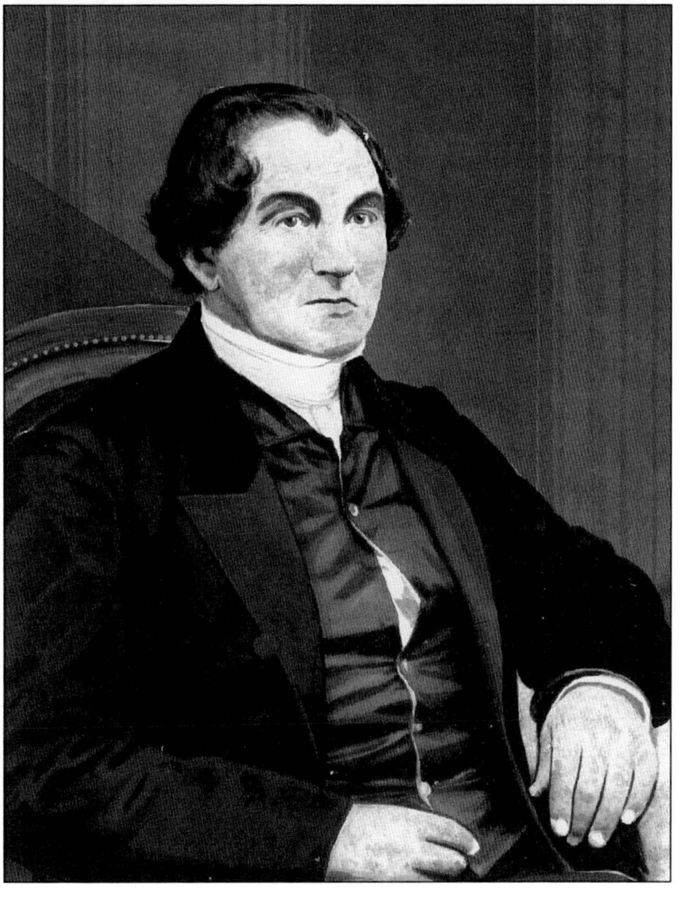

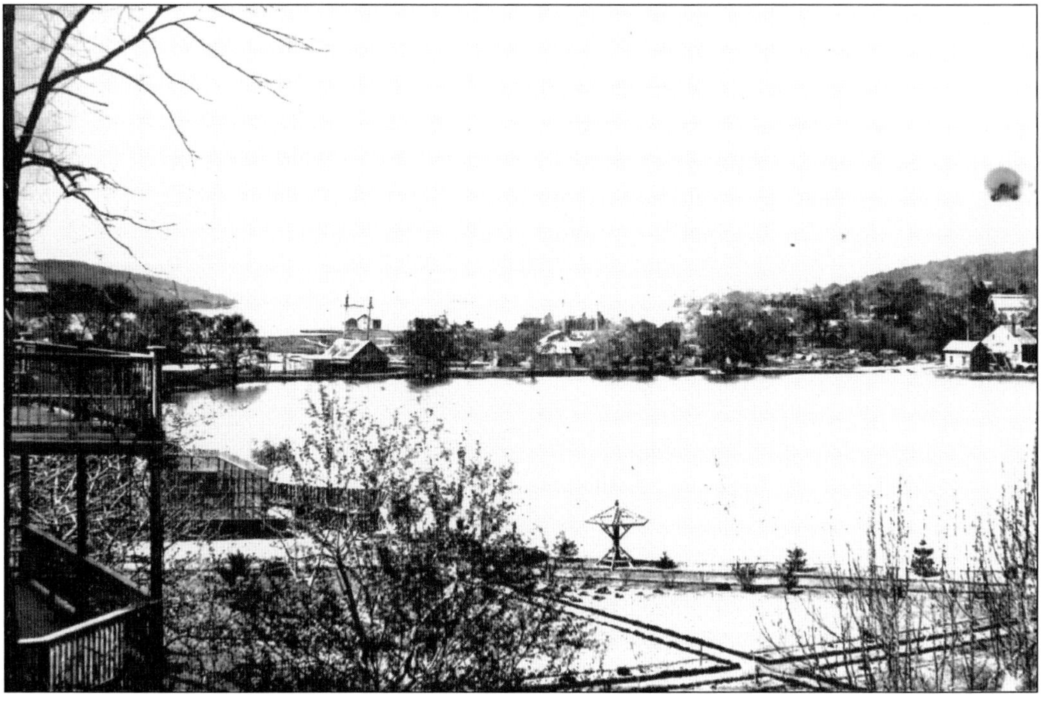

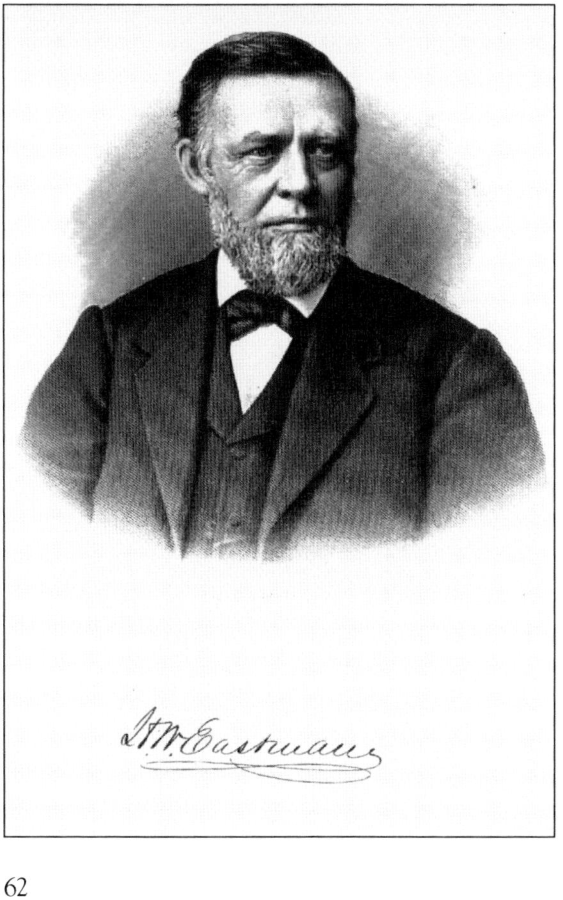

Henry Western Eastman, seen here in this 1882 portrait, was Roslyn's most influential late-19th-century business and professional man. Born here in 1826, Eastman studied law, and in 1847 practiced from Bryant Hall. When the law failed to support him, he taught at the Locust Hill Academy. He helped found the Bryant Circulating Library in 1878 and the *Plaindealer*, Roslyn's first newspaper. The Roslyn Savings Bank, constructed in 1876, was largely his own creation. Eastman's main contribution was in community development. Specializing in real estate law, he developed neighborhoods in key places. He subdivided and promoted the area around the railroad station that started Roslyn Heights. The artisan neighborhood on the western hillside was also his project. Eastman bought his Main Street house (above) in 1854. His garden, shown around 1880, was landscaped down to Silver Lake. Eastman died in 1882 at the age of 55. (Above, courtesy of RLS; left, courtesy of Sargent and Ellen Russell.)

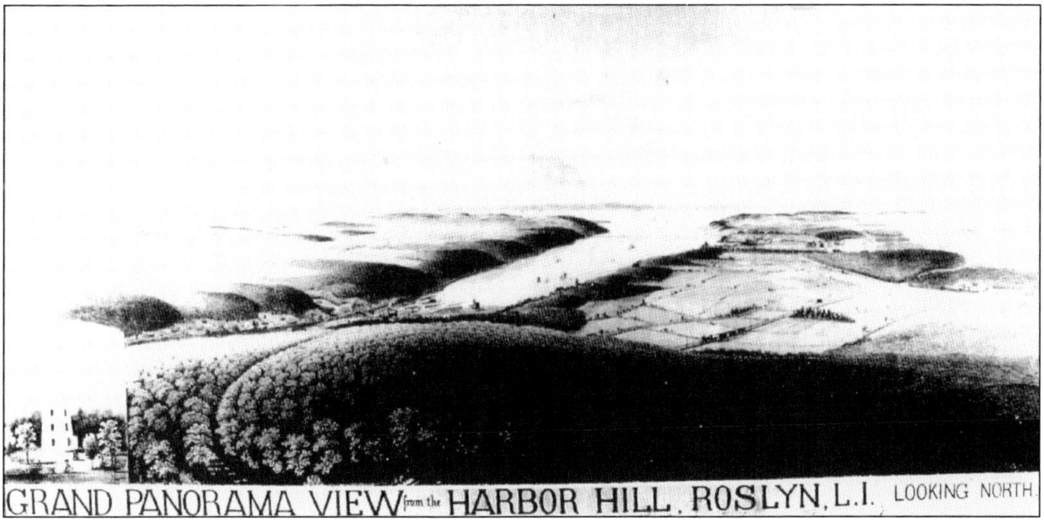

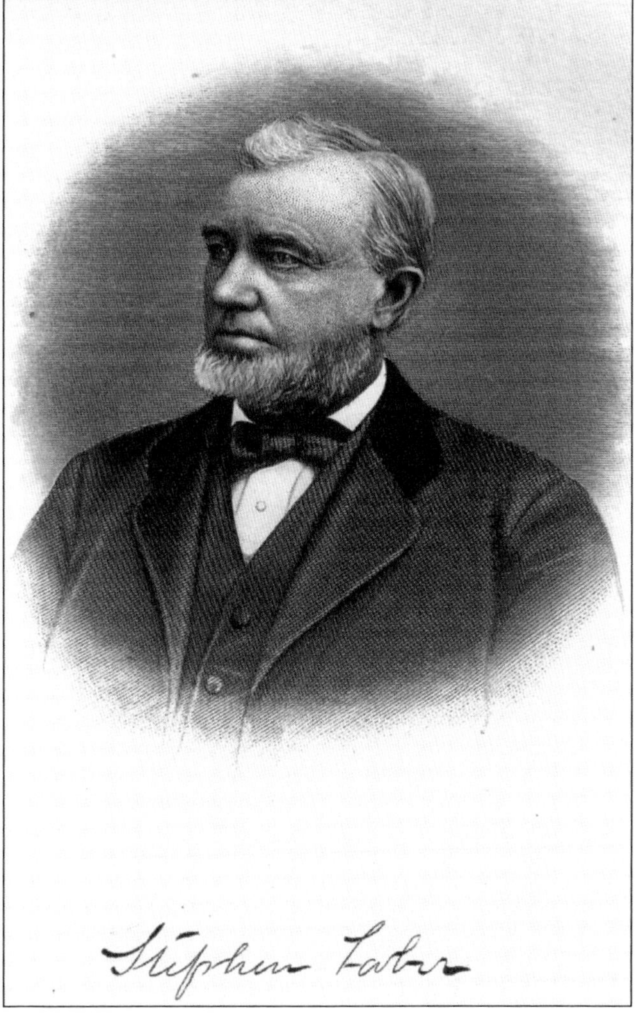

In 1856, Stephen Taber inherited part of a large Roslyn farm. It included Harbor Hill, which Taber, an engineer, measured and concluded to be Long Island's highest point (it was later demoted to second place). Taber's efforts made Roslyn more accessible to New York and the rest of the world. He was a director of the Long Island Rail Road when the Roslyn station was built and established a steamboat line to New York City. As these improvements increased Roslyn's resort trade, Taber built an 84-foot-tall observation tower and a popular picnic park atop Harbor Hill. Stephen Taber was elected to the state legislature several times in the 1860s, and in 1876 he became the first president of the Roslyn Savings Bank. (Above, courtesy of the Society for the Preservation of Long Island Antiquities; right, courtesy of Sargent and Ellen Russell.)

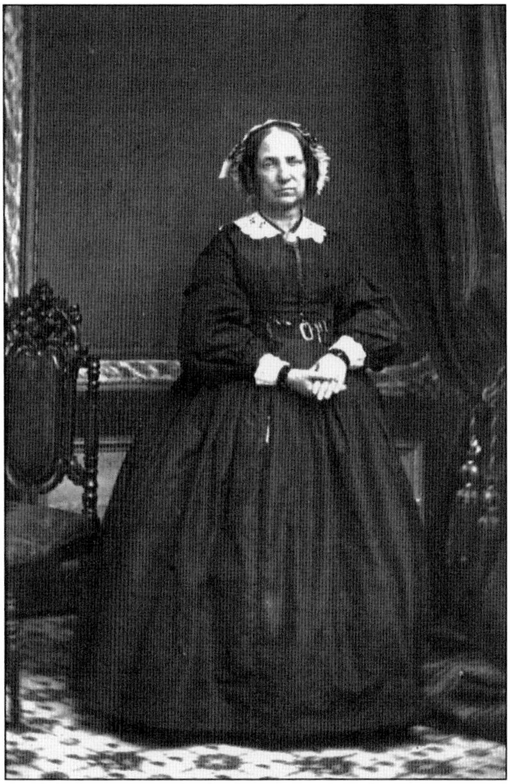

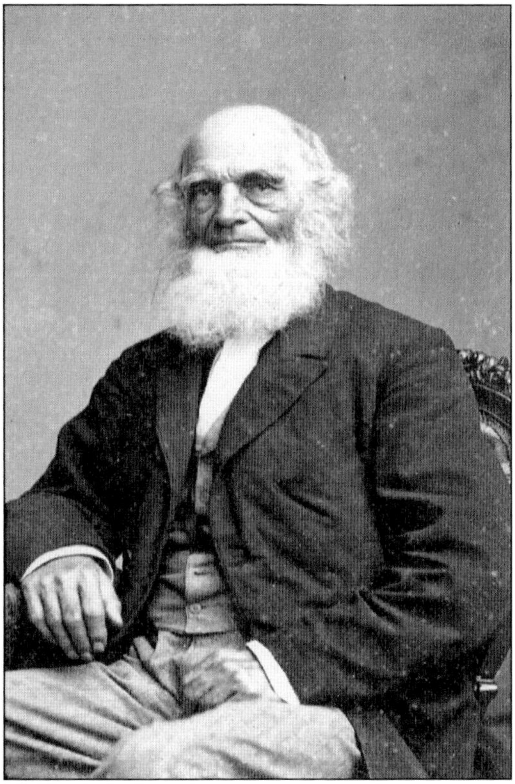

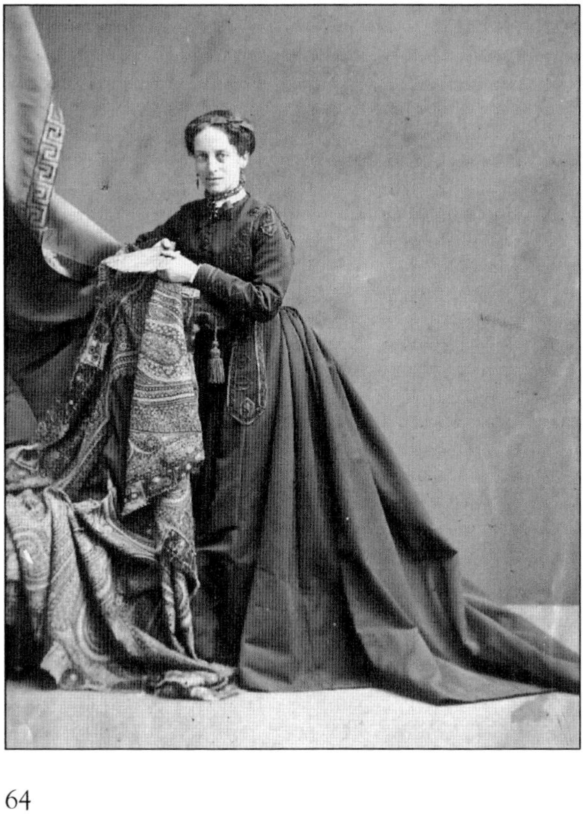

Poet and editor William Cullen Bryant moved to Roslyn in 1844, and his family cared for its people. In August, when his pears were ripe, he invited children to a fruit feast. At Thanksgiving he gave out chickens. In 1875, to give the people a meeting place, Bryant built a reading and lecture hall. He thought his wife's goodness exceeded his own. "The last time she went out," Bryant wrote after her death, it "was for the purpose of providing a poor worthy man in the village with a garden near his house." The Bryants worked to establish the Roslyn Cemetery, where Frances was buried in 1866 and Bryant himself in 1878. Both of these images are from around 1862. Frances Fairchild and William Cullen Bryant are seen above. At left is their daughter Julia Sands Bryant. (Courtesy of the Nassau County Department of Parks, Recreation and Museums, Cedarmere.)

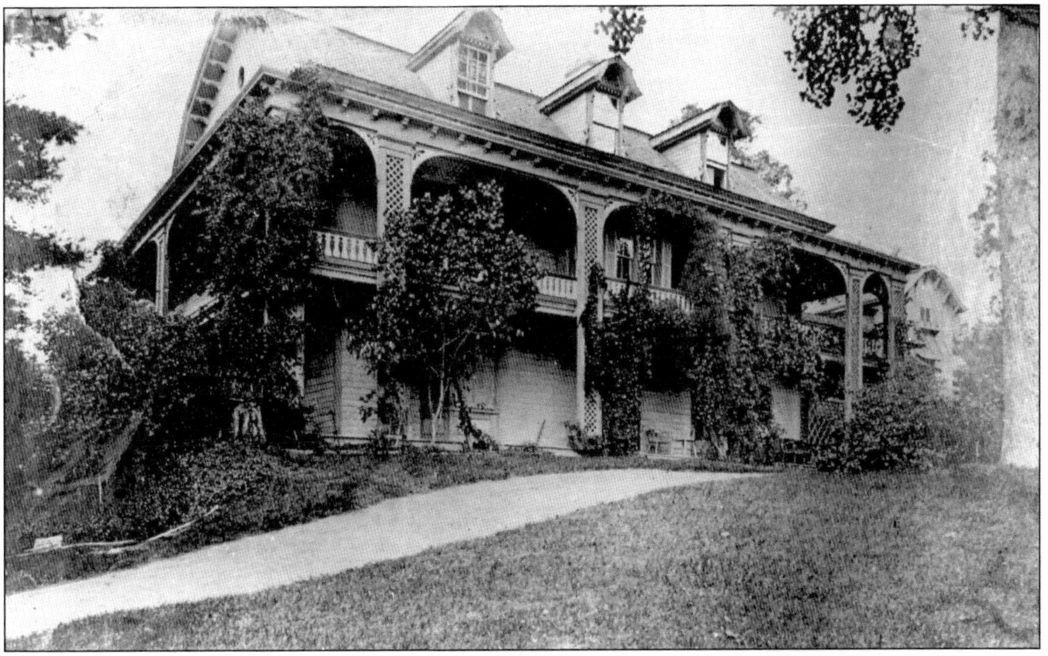

William Cullen Bryant became America's first internationally recognized poet with "Thanatopsis" in 1817, yet he earned his living through journalism. In 1825, he came to New York City to edit the *New-York Evening Post*. For nearly 20 years, the Bryants lived in a Manhattan apartment; finally, in 1843, they were able to buy this old Roslyn Harbor house. Bryant named it Cedar Mere for the trees that ringed the pond (grandson Harold Godwin renamed it Cedarmere). Bryant lavished attention on his home, enlarging the house and beautifying the grounds. He built several handsome guesthouses, designed by talented architects. By the time he died, Bryant owned nearly 200 acres that stretched from the harbor shore to an inland farm. Bryant is seen in the *c.* 1862 photograph at right in a Turkish costume, and Cedar Mere appears above around 1874. (Courtesy of the Nassau County Department of Parks, Recreation and Museums, Cedarmere.)

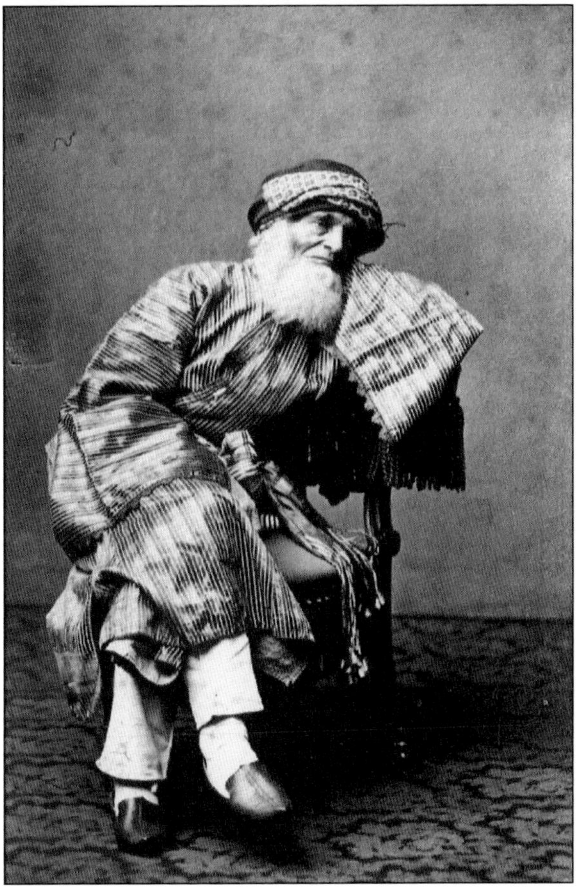

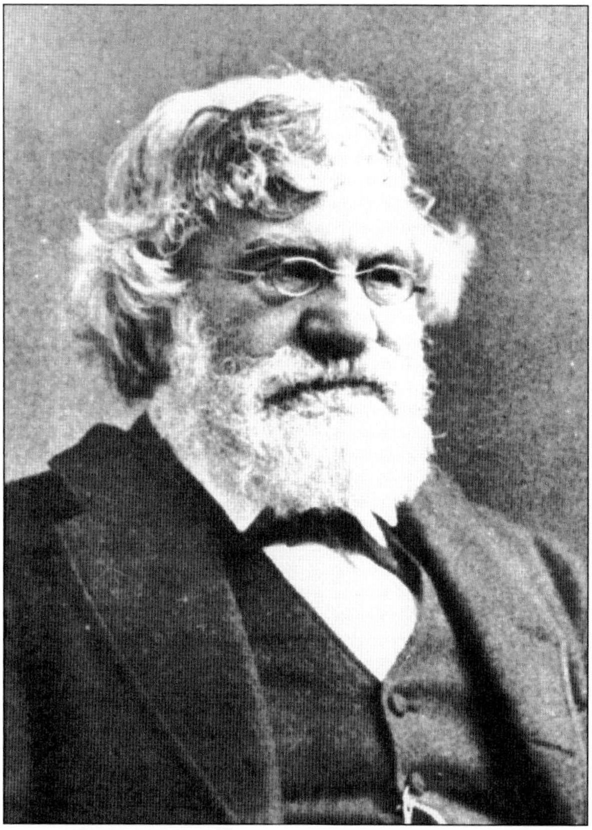

Parke Godwin (left) was a young lawyer when William Cullen Bryant hired him for a temporary job at the *New-York Evening Post*. The job lasted 45 years, and Godwin married Bryant's oldest daughter, Frances. They later lived in Montrose, the William Hicks house, which they had remodeled by Central Park architect Calvert Vaux. Harold Godwin, born in 1857 (below) was Parke Godwin's seventh child. An artist and art editor for the *New-York Evening Post* and other journals, Harold was a Roslyn benefactor. He restored the gristmill and revitalized the Bryant Library. After Cedarmere burned down in 1902, he rebuilt it. Godwin's wife Elizabeth Love Marquand founded the Roslyn District Nursing Association, and husband and wife were ceaselessly active on civic and humanitarian projects. (Left, courtesy of the Nassau County Museum Collection, Long Island Studies Institute; below, courtesy of the Nassau County Department of Parks, Recreation and Museums, Cedarmere.)

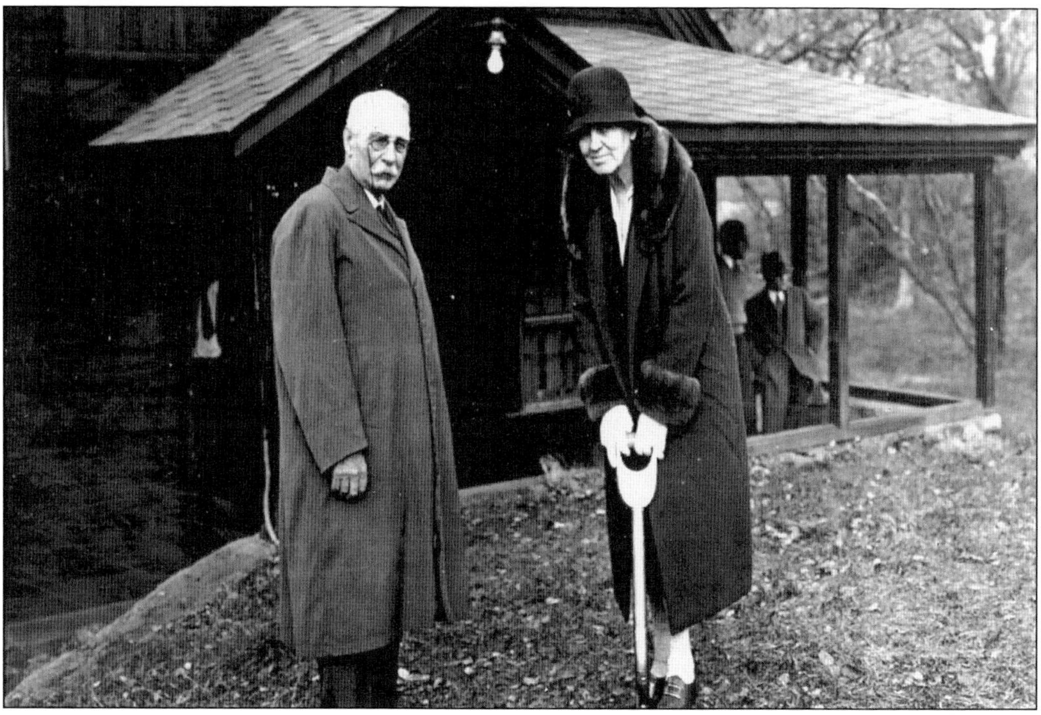

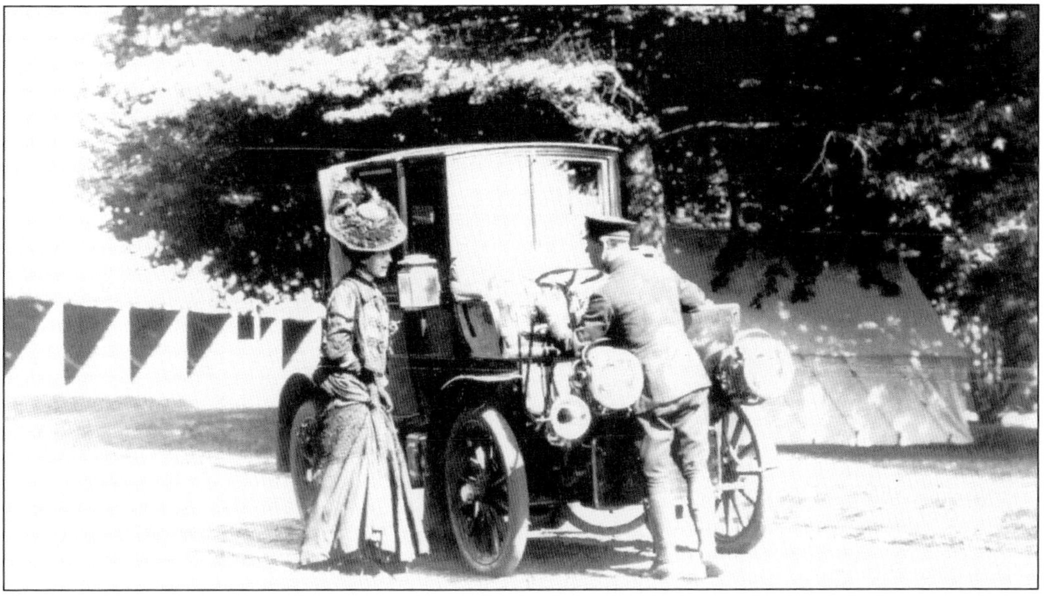

Katherine Duer Mackay, from an old New York family, was an imperious beauty. Her husband Clarence was the son of John Mackay, a miner who struck it rich in the Comstock Lode in Virginia City, then in the telegraph cable business. For the young couple's 1898 wedding, his parents gave them Roslyn's Harbor Hill property. Katherine engaged Stanford White to design the house; by 1903, the Mackays were seasonal residents. They employed more than 100 people, some of whose descendants still live in town. Katherine donated three Stanford White buildings and sat on the school board. After initial coolness, Roslynians warmed to the Mackays and enjoyed their hospitality. The *c.* 1902 image above shows Katherine with chauffeur Jim Havigan. The photograph below shows children playing in front of the mansion around 1907. (Courtesy of the Bryant Library Local History Collection, Roslyn.)

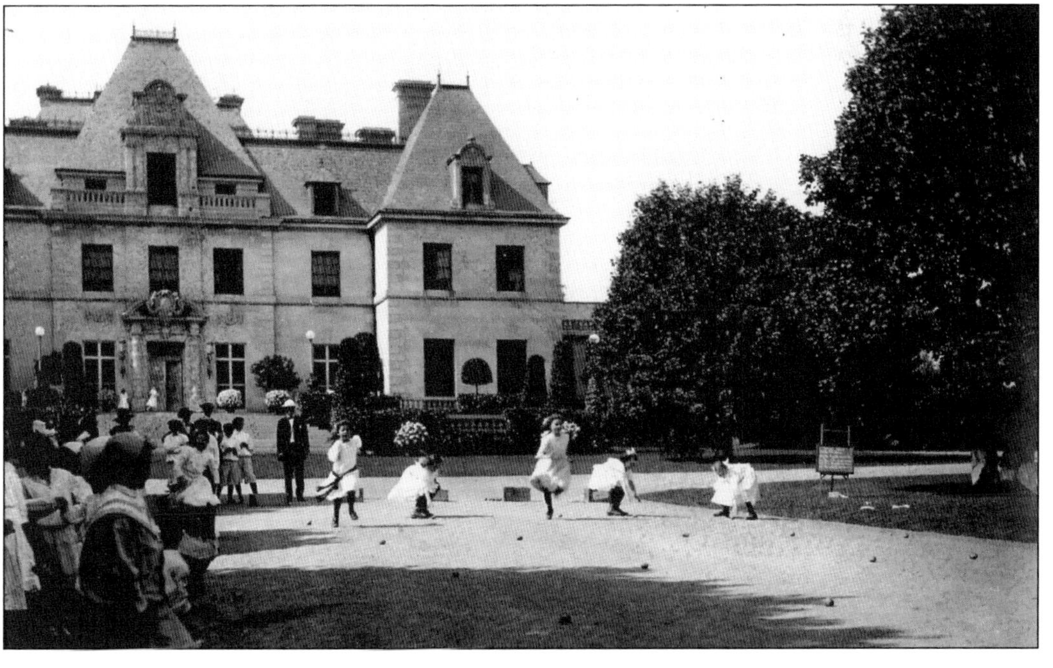

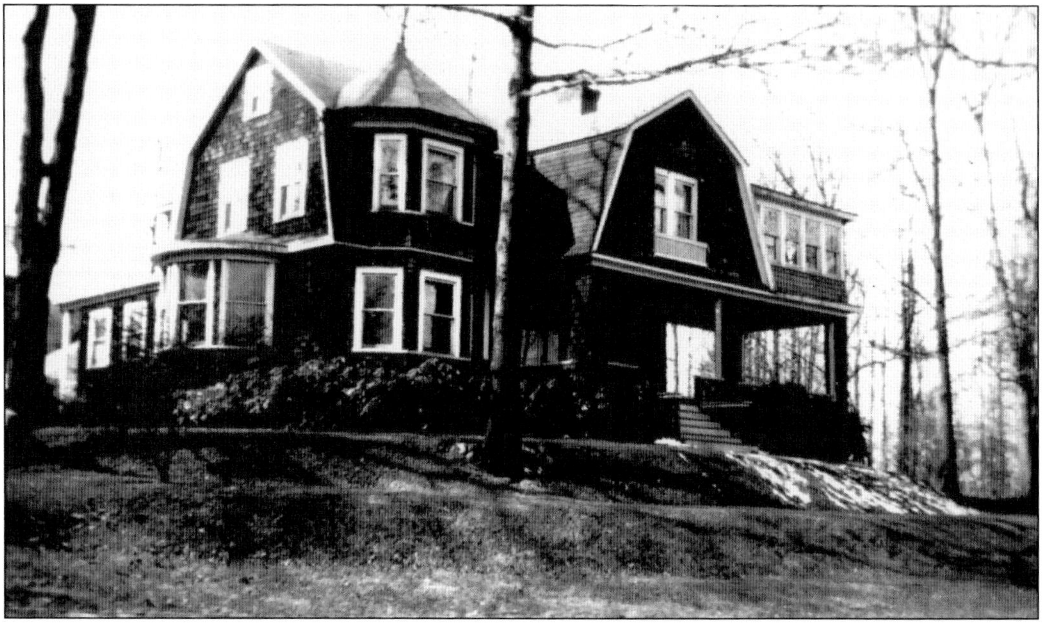

Born in Haverford, Pennsylvania, in 1891, Christopher Morley was a well-known writer from the 1920s until his death in 1957. After moving to Roslyn Estates in 1920, Morley disguised Roslyn in his writing under the name "Salamis." Morley's neighbors found him eccentric. He tended his wartime victory garden wearing a male Mother Hubbard, one recalled, and called himself the commissar of beets. Morley's home on the Birches is seen above, and he is seen below (on right) with Nigel Bruce. (Above, courtesy of the Bryant Library Local History Collection, Roslyn; below, courtesy of the Nassau County Museum Collection, Long Island Studies Institute.)

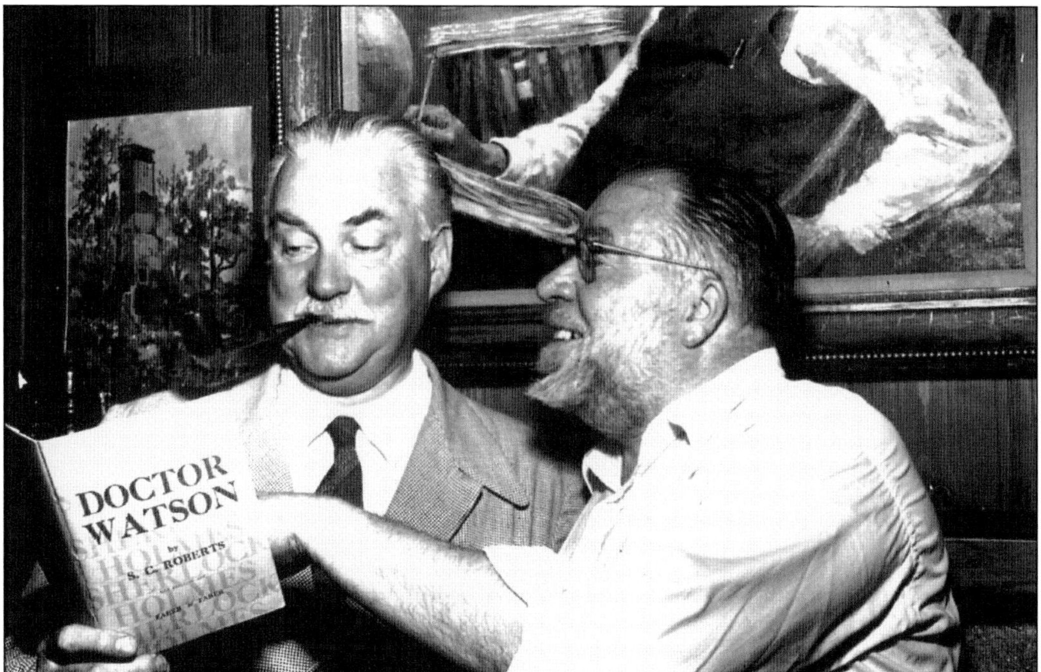

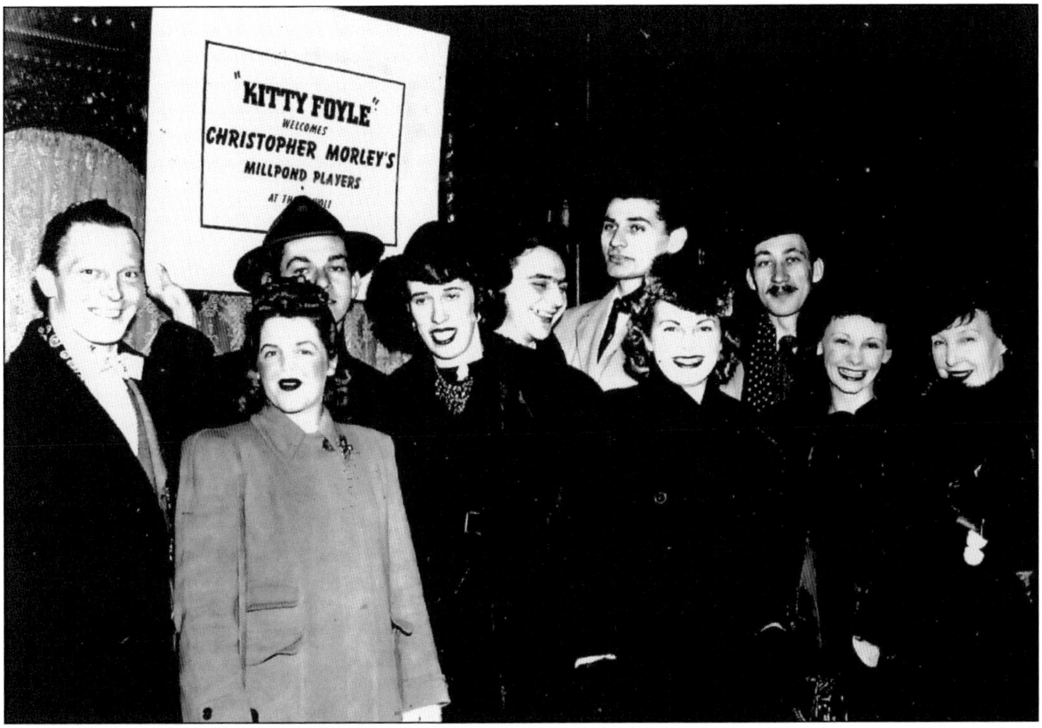

In the 1920s and 1930s, Morley staged his plays at the theater operating in the Roslyn War Memorial. The troupe of young actors (above) appeared in his popular work *Kitty Foyle* at the Millpond Playhouse. After several years commuting to Manhattan, enjoying his "Three Hours for Lunch Club," in 1935 Morley built himself a rustic studio in his front yard. The Knothole had many wonderful features, including a "dymaxion" bathroom designed by the radical architect Buckminster Fuller. In 1966, a friends group moved the Knothole to a nearby park, which was later named for the writer. (Above, courtesy of RLS; below, courtesy of the Nassau County Museum Collection, Long Island Studies Institute.)

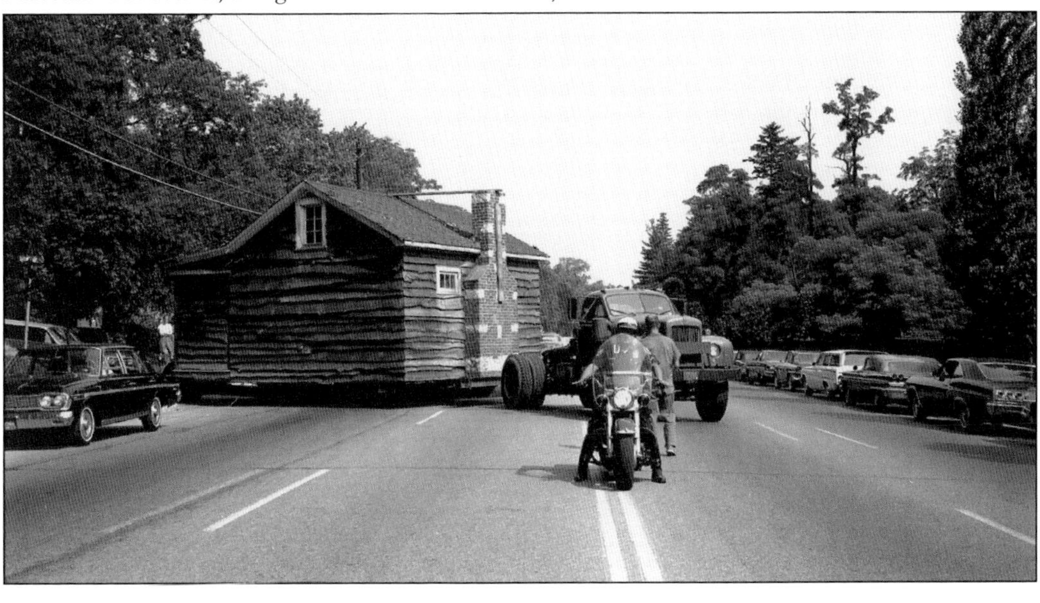

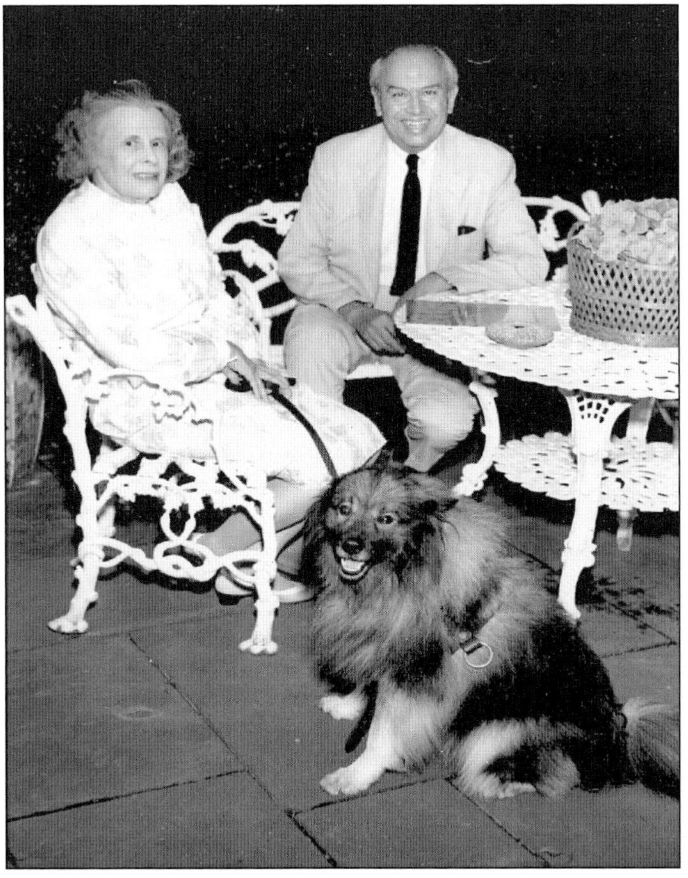

When Roger and Peggy Gerry arrived in 1951, the postwar world surged over most of Long Island. In Roslyn they found a quiet harbor town, threatened by progress and in danger of losing all that made it special. For nearly 50 years, these two talented and committed people used their skills and resources to protect Roslyn's character and its heritage. They worked in local government; formed organizations; bought, restored, and sold buildings; and attracted like-minded others to join them in the effort. The result is a village that has not been overwhelmed by suburban sprawl, one that looks a lot like it has for centuries. The Gerrys are shown with Bogey at their home in the late 1980s at left. The photograph below shows 105 Main Street. (Photographs by Ray Jacobs, courtesy of RLS.)

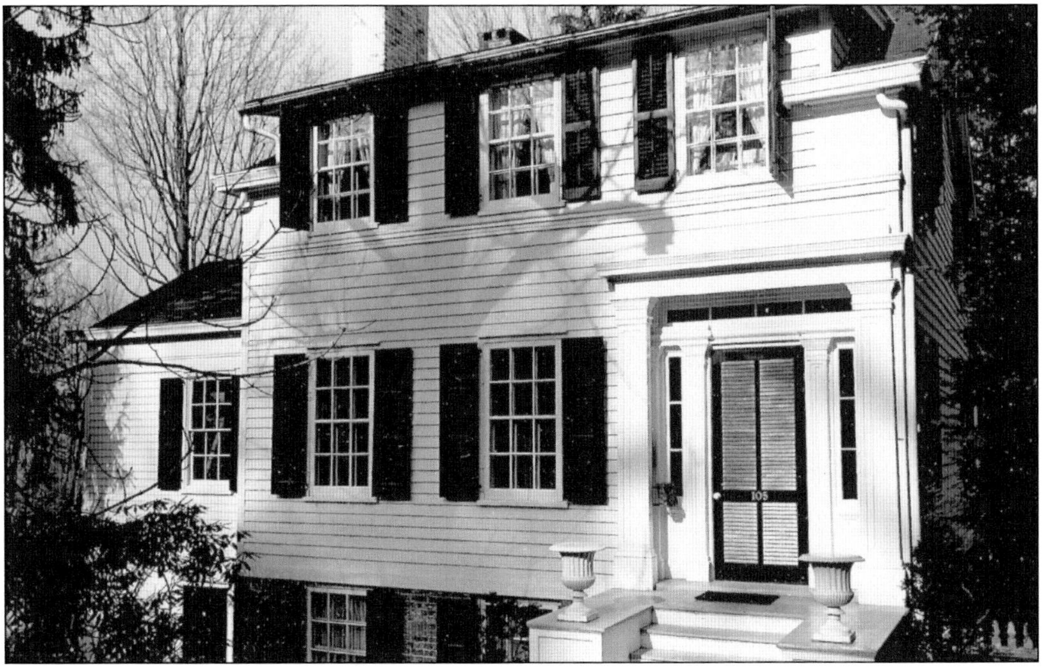

Five

ROSLYNIANS

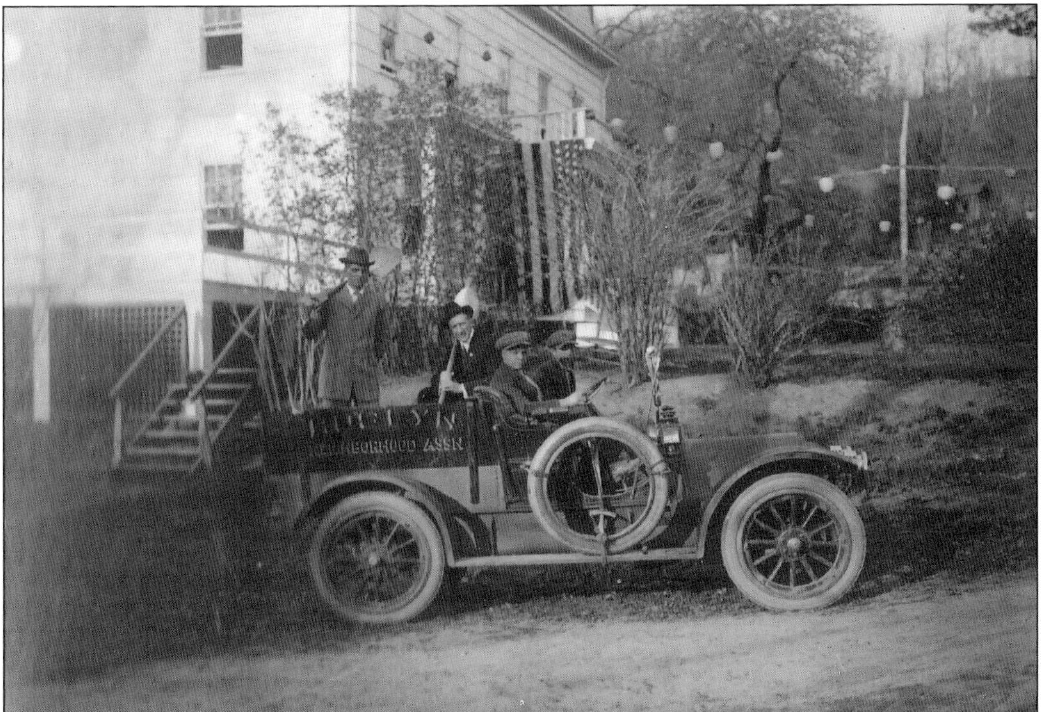

The Roslyn Neighborhood Association was formed in 1915 to "promote the recreational, industrial, intellectual and moral welfare of Roslyn." It acquired the William M. Valentine house for a community center and to house services and clubs. The association sponsored such activities as citizenship classes, a canning kitchen, a library, and community sings. In the *c.* 1920 photograph above, members are ready for work, perhaps on building Roslyn Park. (Courtesy of RLS.)

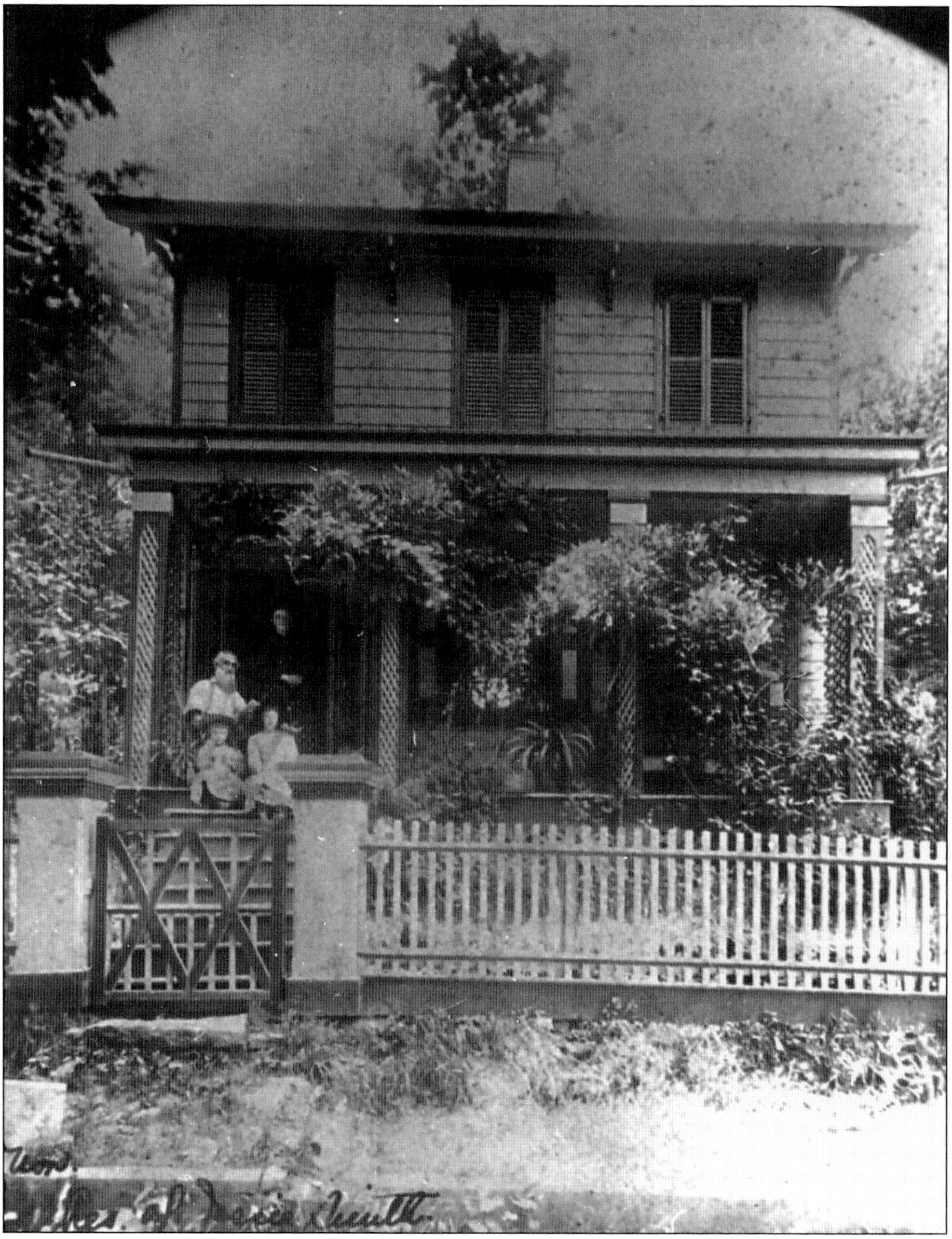

In 1856, this house was purchased by blacksmith William H. Smith, who also bought the previous owner's blacksmith shop. Smith updated the house with Gothic Revival bracketed eaves and a porch with lattice piers. After his death in 1896, his son William C. Smith, also a blacksmith, bought the house and lived there with his family. This *c.* 1900 photograph shows William C. Smith on the front steps with his wife Martha, daughter Jessie, and young son. Years later, when Jessie had grown old and the traffic on Main Street became heavy, she was known to brandish her umbrella to halt traffic so she could cross. Jessie worked as a bank teller in Mineola and lived in her family house until her death in 1970. (Courtesy of the Nassau County Museum Collection, Long Island Studies Institute.)

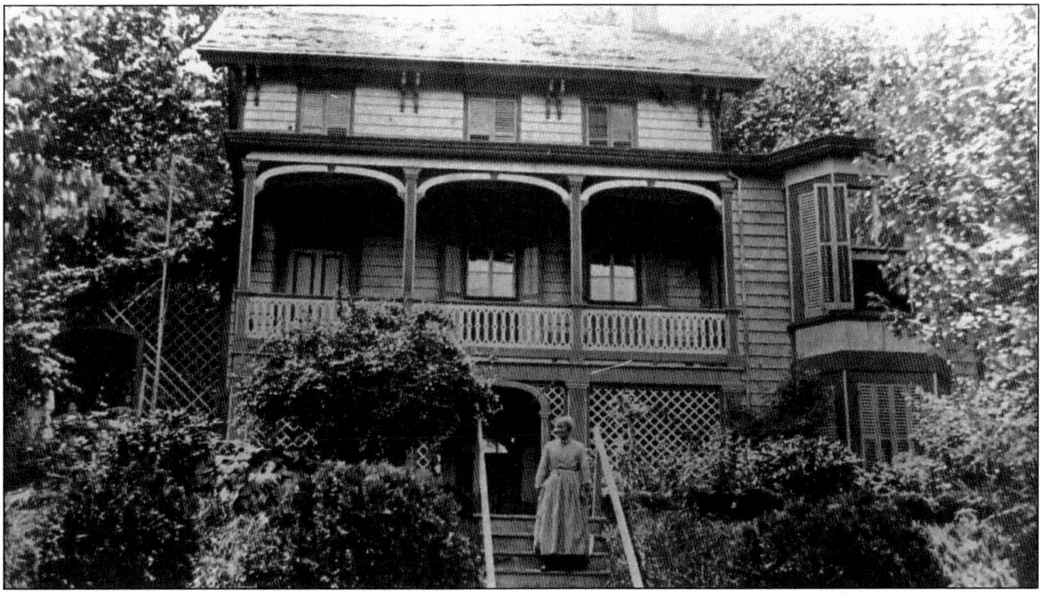

Belfast stonemason Samuel Dugan immigrated to Roslyn around 1853 with his Scottish wife Anngine, two young sons, and his brother John. He built his Main Street house (above) in the Italianate style around 1855. A few years later, Samuel was the master mason for the Long Island Rail Road overpass at Roslyn Road. The charming bungalow, seen below around 1897, was built by local businessman John F. Remsen when he married Norah Hicks Smith in 1885. At first it stood on Remsen Hill near Remsen's School Street harness shop. Remsen descendants lived here until 1951. Later a developer acquired the property and the house was doomed—until the Roslyn Preservation Corporation stepped in. Disassembled, the house was moved across town to another hillside site overlooking the clock tower. (Above, courtesy of RLS; below, courtesy of the Nassau County Museum Collection, Long Island Studies Institute.)

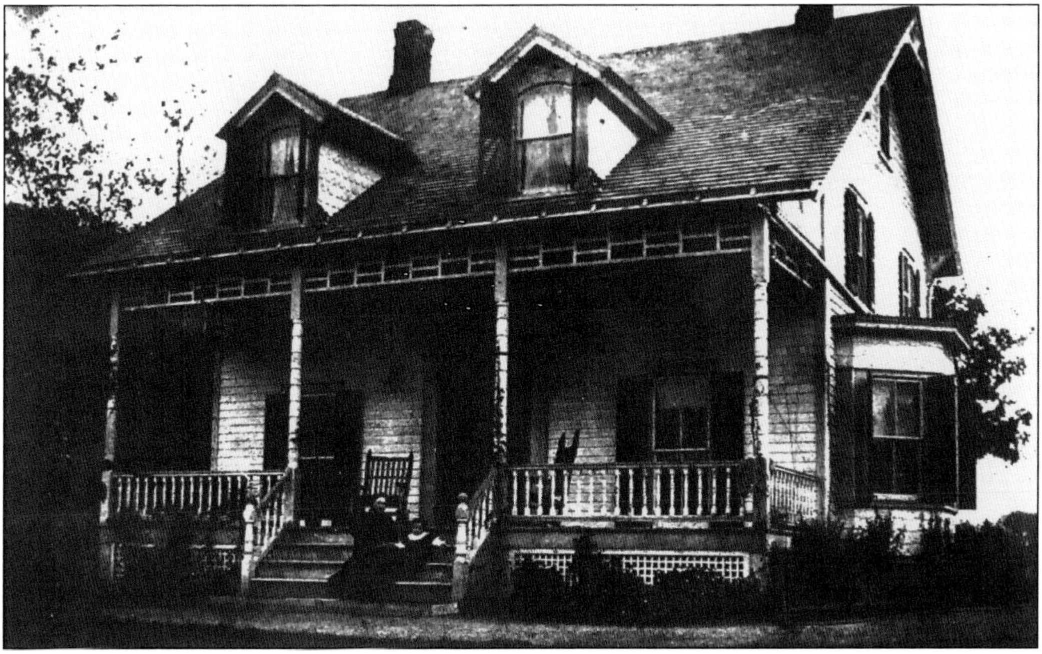

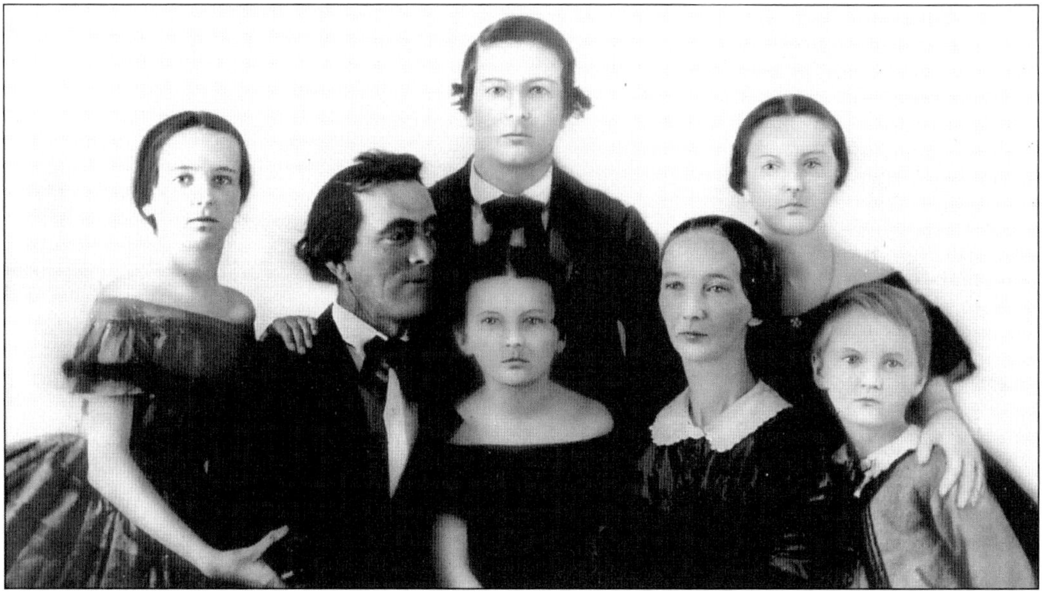

Myers Valentine and family wear their best around 1860. Born in 1818, Myers, a son of William Valentine, married Caroline Searing in 1840. He learned paper-making in nearby Motts Cove. After Washington Valentine's death in 1854, Myers was the last operator of the paper mill, which was abandoned after his death in 1891. Pictured with their parents are, from left to right, Ann Augusta, Theodore Searing, Mary Amelia, Phoebe Louise, and Eugene. (Courtesy of RLS.)

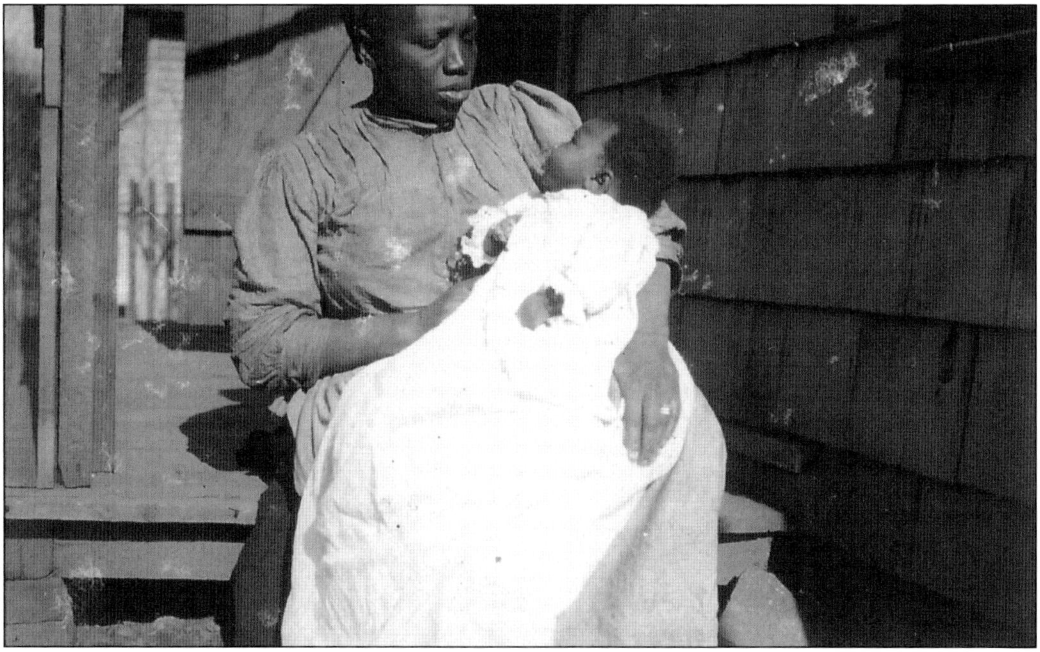

Annie Eato, who had worked for Parke Godwin, holds her baby on the porch in 1908. The photograph was taken at Mudge Cottage, one of several guesthouses on William Cullen Bryant's property. Bryant built it in 1868 for Amy and Elizabeth Mudge, who moved from their ancient farmhouse when it was bought for Parke and Fanny Godwin. (Courtesy of the Nassau County Department of Parks, Recreation and Museums, Cedarmere.)

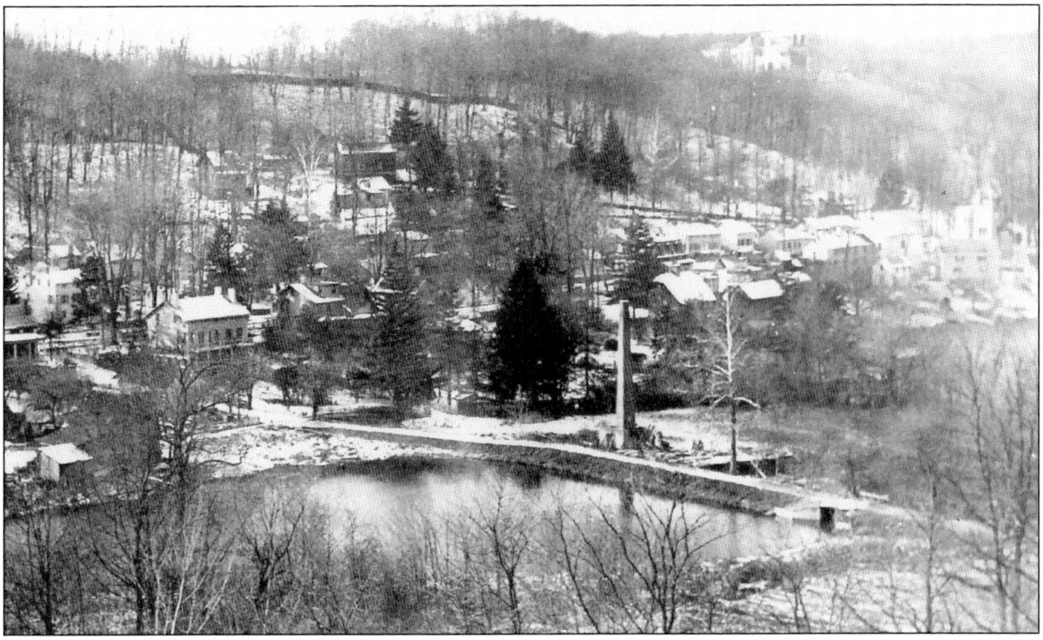

O. W. Pollitz immigrated from Belfast in Northern Ireland in the 1840s, shortly before his friends the Dugans. Pollitz built two houses on Glen Avenue (above, right), his own around 1850 and another, probably a rental, a few years later. Pollitz centers the family group (below). The young man standing is John Codman Pollitz. Johnny died in the Civil War, having saved his soldier's pay to buy the bell for Trinity Episcopal Church (built in 1862). (Above, courtesy of RLS; below, courtesy of the Nassau County Department of Parks, Recreation and Museums, Cedarmere.)

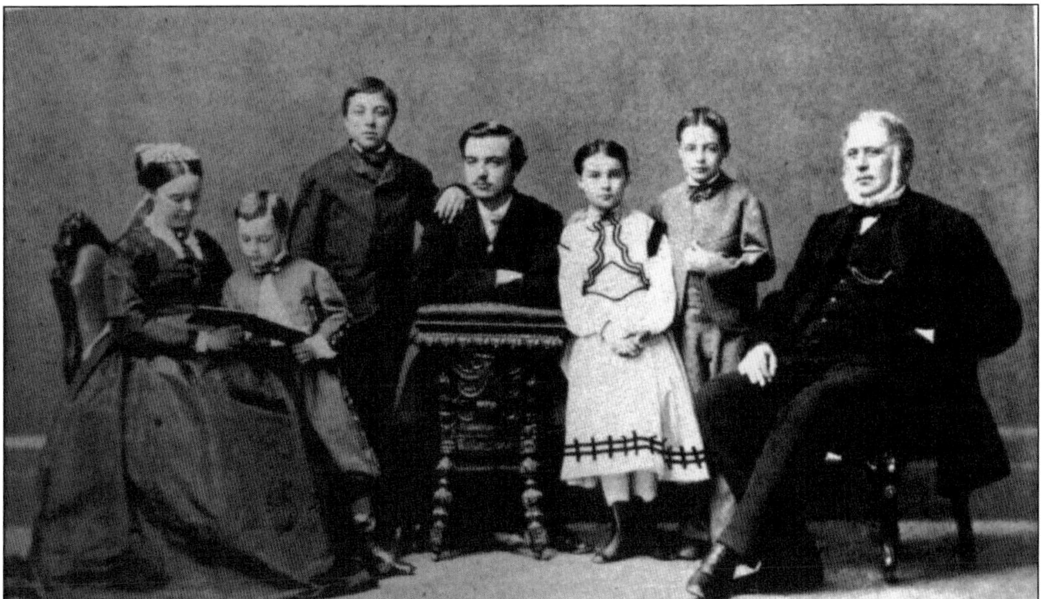

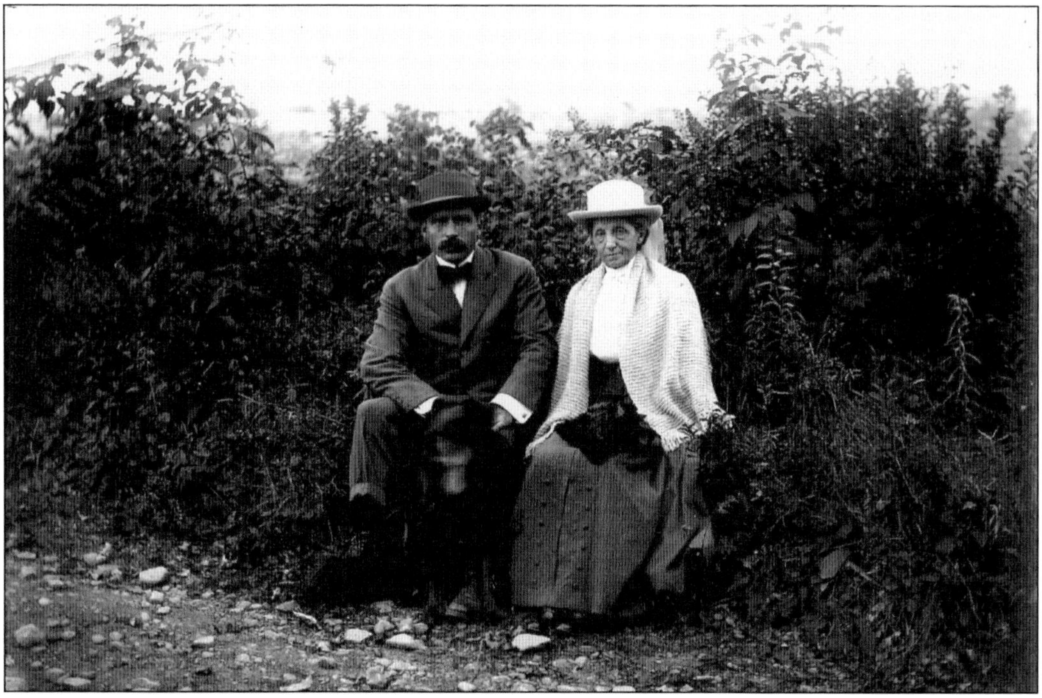

Shown in the *c.* 1915 photograph above are Jacob M. Kirby's daughter-in-law Susan Eliza and her younger son, successful civil engineer Isaac Henry Kirby. The captain's descendants lived at Kirbys Corners until 1971. During the early 20th century, two young Kirby women had a photography studio there. Ralph Kirby, Susan Eliza's elder son, was a lawyer and also a photographer. Susan Eliza's husband was Roslyn's late-19th-century Presbyterian minister William Wallace Kirby. The couple on the right, below, may be Isaac Henry Kirby and his wife. (Courtesy of RLS.)

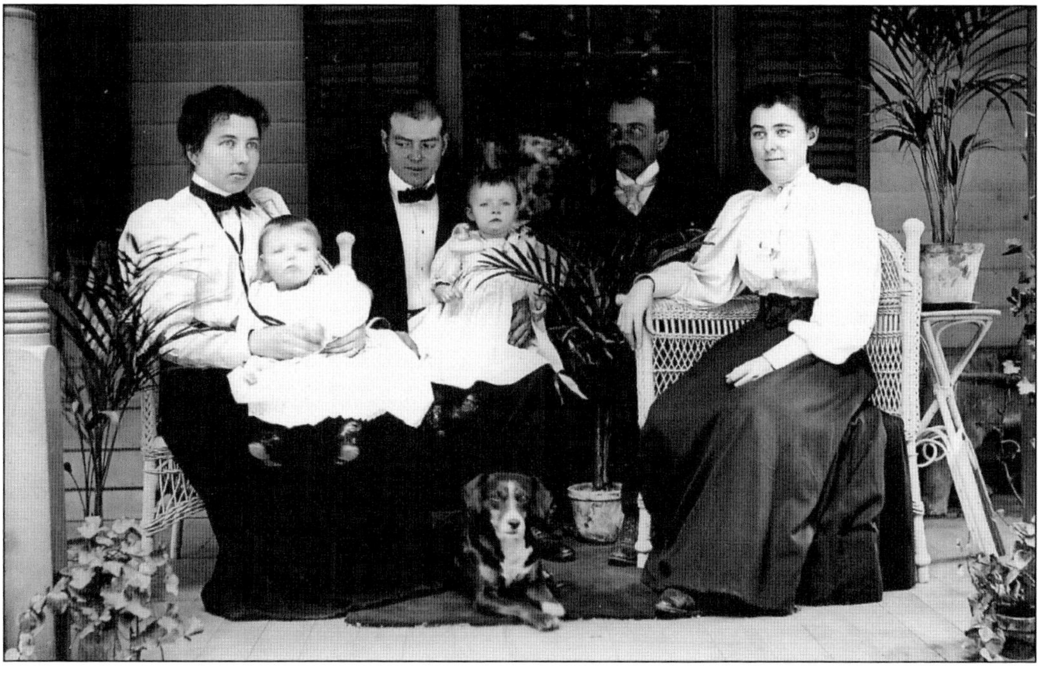

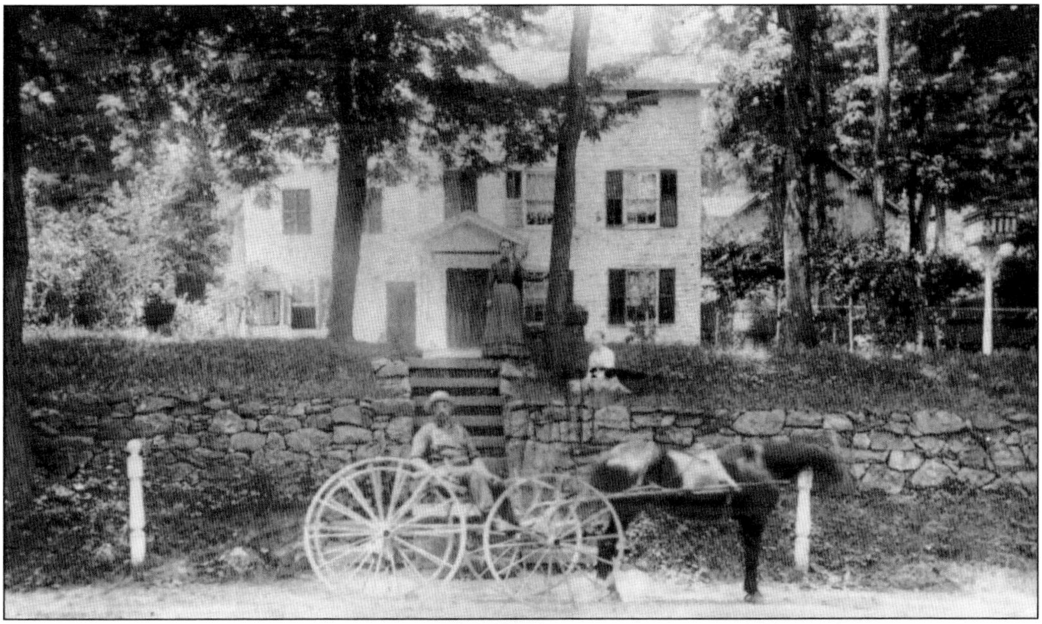

Seen above, Henry Clay Thorne, liveryman and undertaker, stops his wagon on Main Street in front of his house around 1890. The woman is probably his wife, and the girl their daughter Gertrude. Henry's father Leonard had been a partner of John Willis at the Roslyn gristmill. Henry Clay Thorne ran his livery business on upper Main Street until his death in 1916. A very fancy Greek Revival temple-front birdhouse stands on the front lawn on the far right. At right, Eveleen Rogers, Henry Clay Thorne's granddaughter, stands in front of the same elegant birdhouse around 1920. (Courtesy of RLS.)

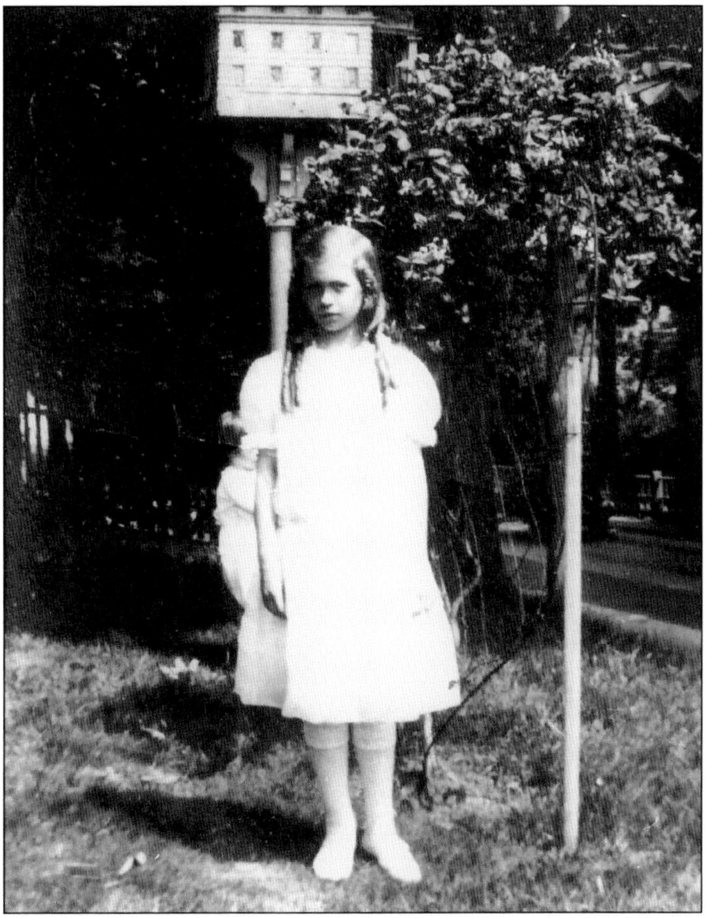

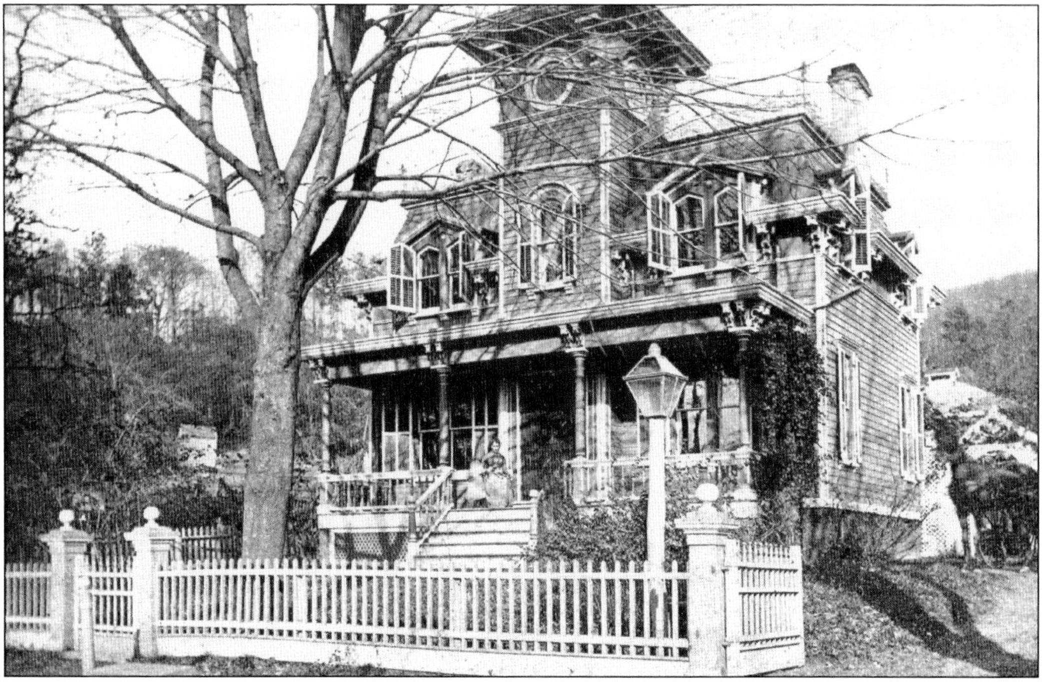

In May 1877, the Roslyn *Tablet* noted that carpenter James K. Davis's brand-new East Broadway house was "the prettiest place in Roslyn," and that it was "better to be born lucky than rich." Above, on the porch stands Davis's young wife Eliza, daughter of the Mansion House proprietor John Charlick. In addition to being a builder, Davis was a general entrepreneur and active in civic affairs. He owned an icehouse and a meat market, was a director of the Bank of Hempstead Harbor, postmaster, president and member of the board of education, a director of the Bryant Library, a Freemason, and a life member of Roslyn Rescue Hook and Ladder Company No. 1. For relaxation, he drove in the trotting races at the Mineola Fairgrounds. Below, around 1905, the builder's son Frederick Coles Davis shows off a fine horse in front of the barn. (Courtesy of RLS.)

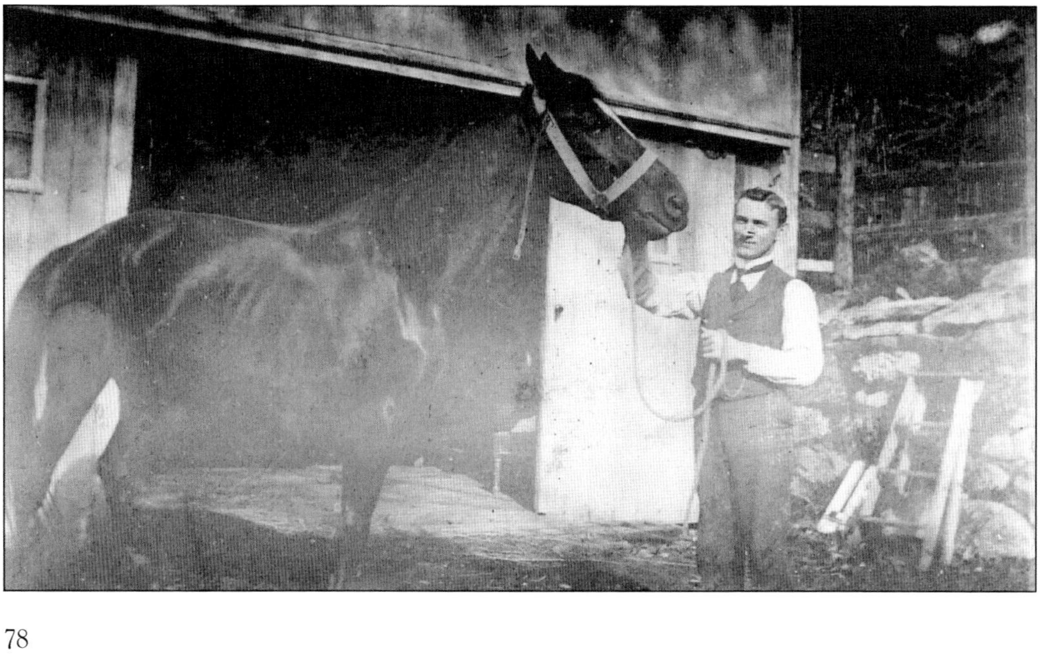

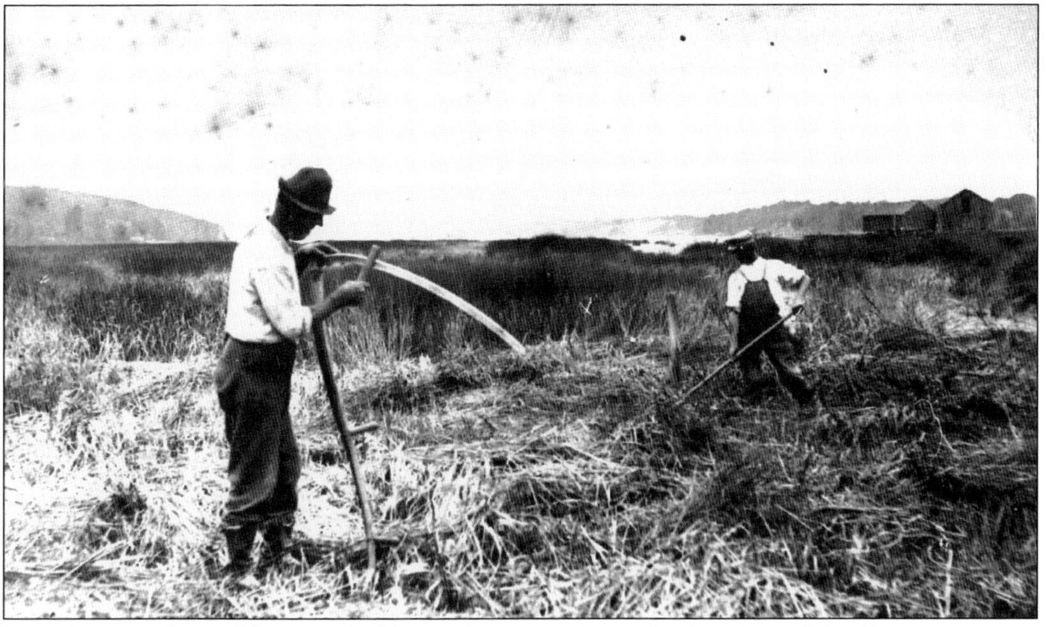

It is photographs and historic buildings that remind people that Long Island's economy was once based on agriculture, shellfisheries, and sandpits. Wealth came from the land, the marshes, and the sea. Roslyn village was settled because it offered waterpower to grind grain into flour and a harbor for shipping products to market. In the 1880 photograph by Rachel Hicks above, men scythe salt hay in the wetlands on the edges of Hempstead Harbor for use as bedding for livestock. The *c.* 1940 photograph below shows Roslyn farmer Leon Rushmore atop a truckload of his produce bound for New York City. Rushmore also operated a popular farm stand on Roslyn Road. (Above, photograph by Rachel Hicks, courtesy of the Nassau County Museum Collection, Long Island Studies Institute; below, courtesy of the Nassau County Museum Collection, Long Island Studies Institute.)

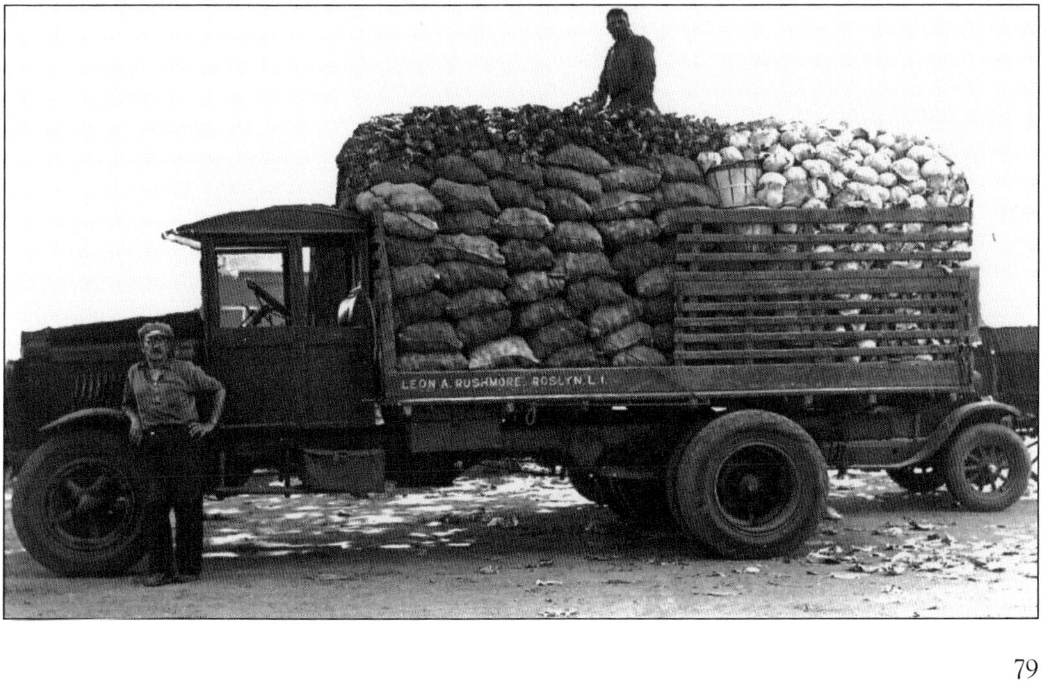

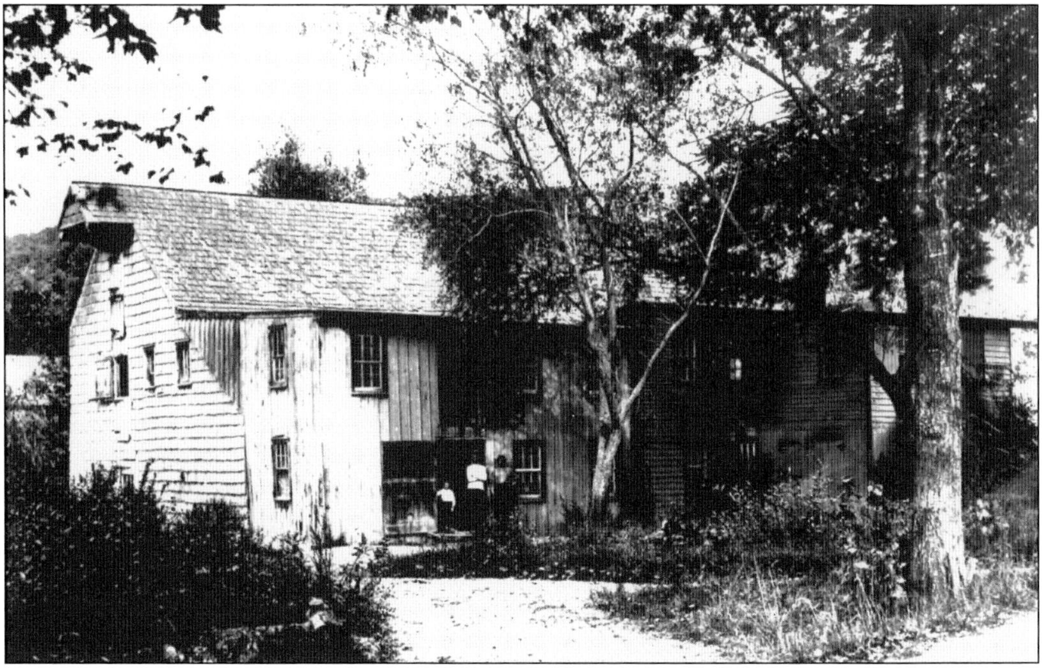

From earliest days through the early 20th century, Roslyn industry flourished. There was a gristmill, a paper mill, sawmills, and a silk mill. At first the mills needed falling water, but by the later 19th century, steam power increased their capacity and made them more dependable. Here Roslyn's longest-lived and most important mills are shown near the end of their operating days. Above, the gristmill appears early in the 20th century during Isaac Hicks's ownership. Workers relax in a shady doorway at the northwest corner of the building. Below, the last shift of paper mill operatives stands in front of the building around 1885, a few years before Myers Valentine's death brought production to a halt. (Above, courtesy of the Nassau County Department of Parks, Recreation and Museums, Cedarmere, Harold Godwin's gristmill file; below, courtesy of Ian Zwerdling.)

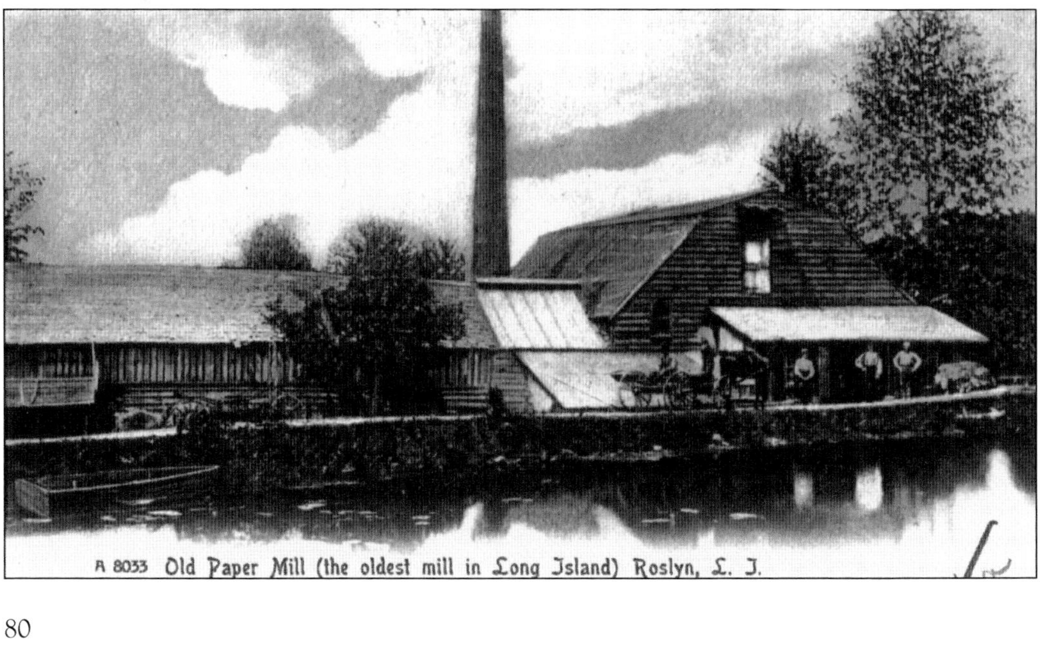

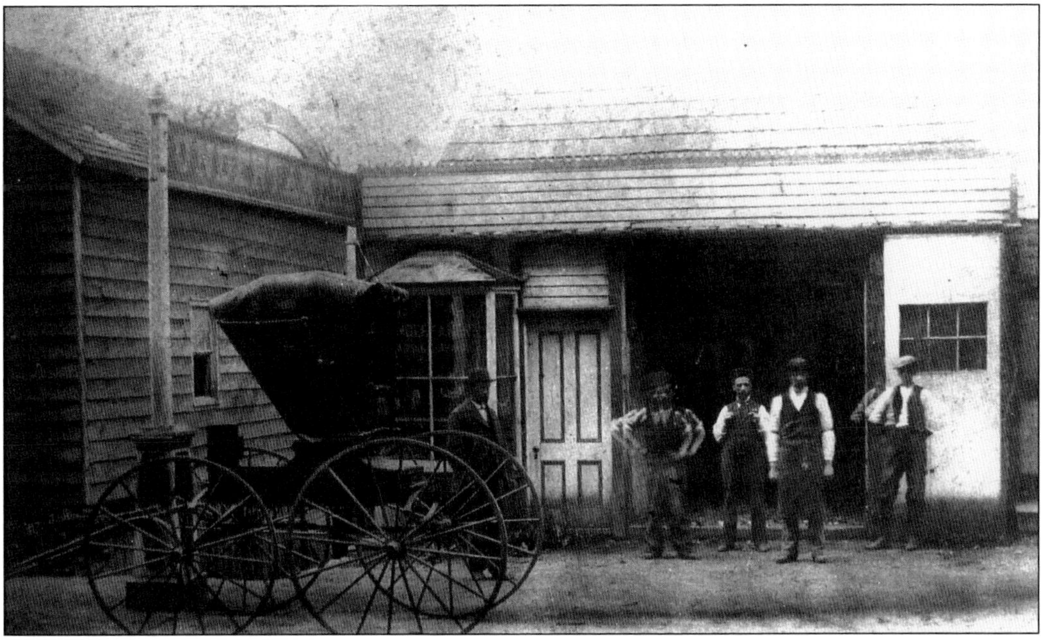

Many Roslynians worked in the transportation trades. By the heyday of photography, shipping had yielded some of its volume to a variety of land-based modes. In the upper photograph, the employees of Henry Clay Thorne's livery business pose with a buggy at their Main Street headquarters. A tall, freestanding archway sign on posts reads "H. C. Thorne, Undertakers." While livery stable and funeral home may seem like strange partners, both enterprises required a fleet of well-appointed vehicles and the horses to pull them. The lower view, taken around 1910, features a shiny New York and North Shore Traction Company trolley car with its driver and conductor on Main Street. (Courtesy of RLS.)

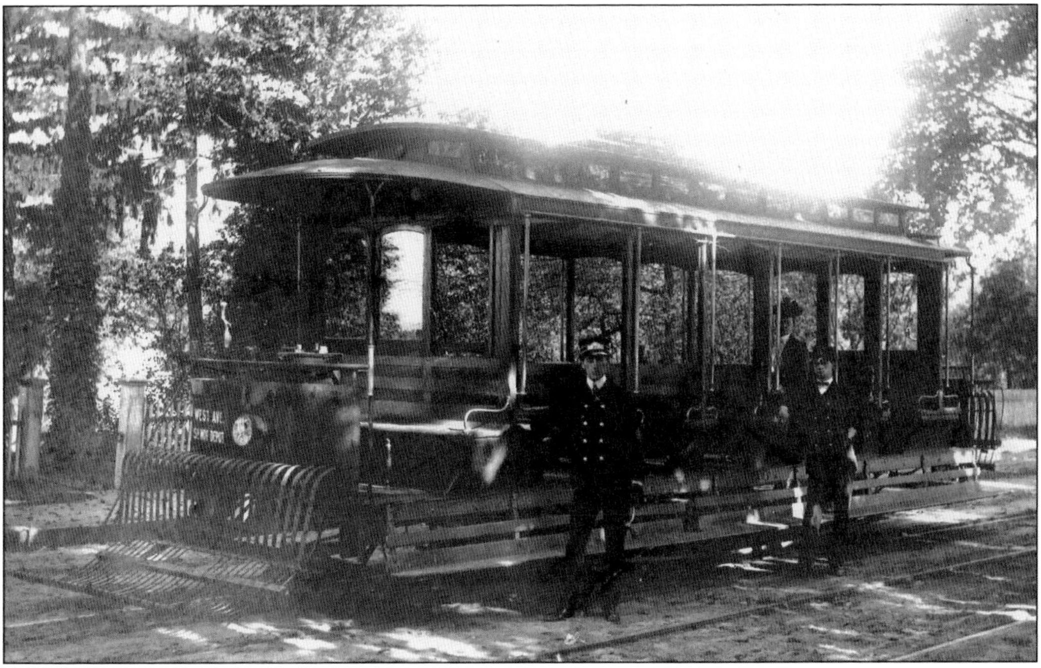

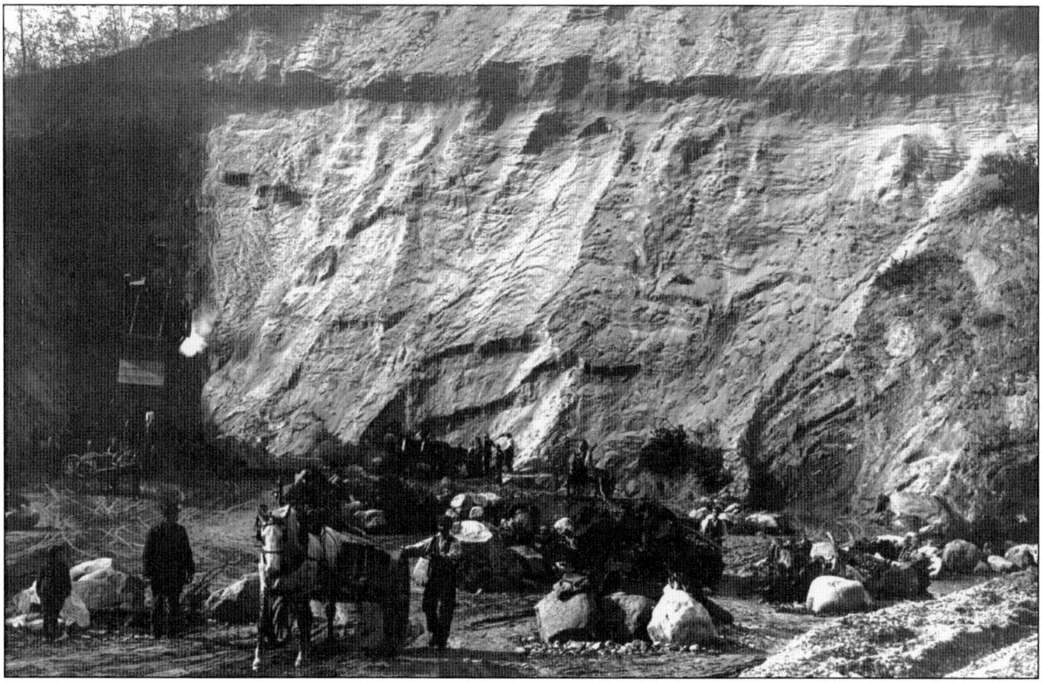

The last important commercial use of Hempstead Harbor was sand mining, which began near the end of the 19th century. The sand was loaded on scows drawn to New York by tugboat, to go into the skyscrapers and infrastructure that transformed the city. Above, in 1897, men scoop away a hill with steam shovels and heavy horse-drawn carts. Below, sand barges lie in Roslyn Creek. Sand mining silted up the harbor, so that by 1900, steamboats could no longer use it. So, as the 20th century opened, waterborne transportation slipped into the past along with the stagecoach and the harbor sloop, giving way to the trolley, the train, and the automobile. (Above, courtesy of the Suffolk County Historical Society, Hal B. Fullerton Collection; below, courtesy of the Queens Borough Public Library, Long Island Division, Illustrations Collection–Roslyn.)

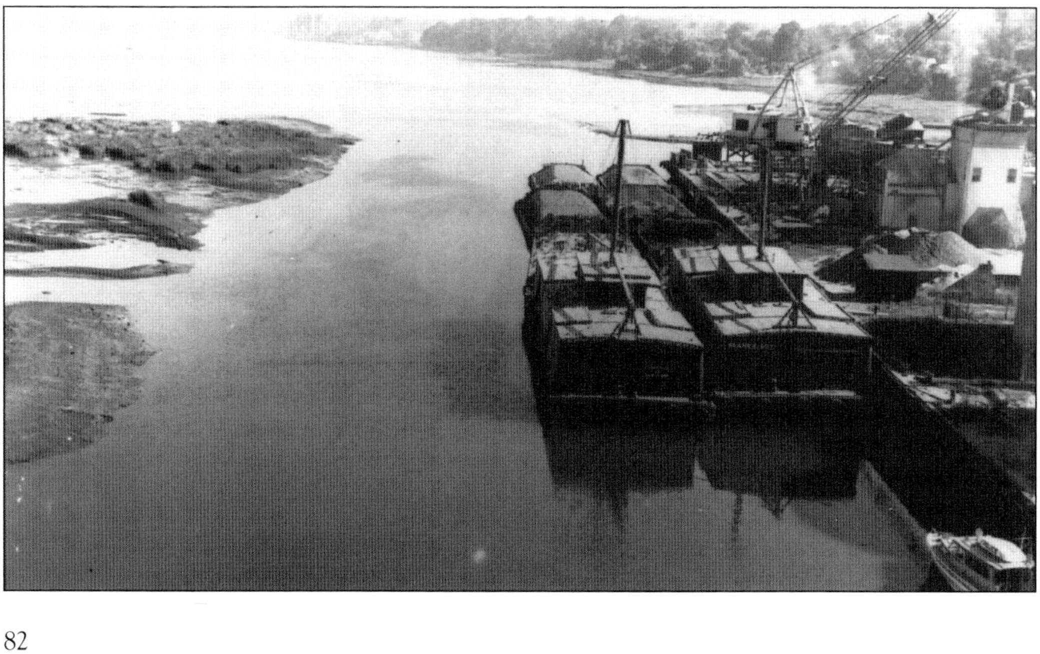

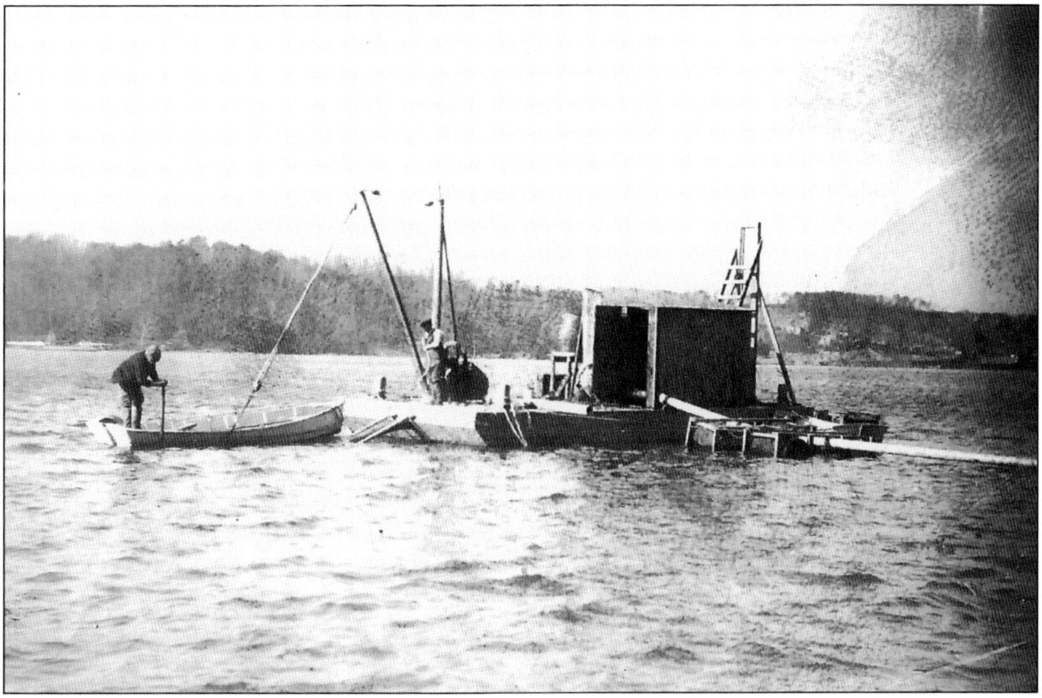

The harbor was used for pleasure long after commercial uses ended. Sailboats and motorboats moored in the summer behind the Grist Mill Tea House. People fished off the milldam. Up at Cedarmere, William Cullen Bryant's grandson Harold Godwin dredged a channel (above) so pleasure boats could come in to the old steamboat landing. He also moored a houseboat in the bay and formed an association to use it. Below, an entrepreneur called Captain George kept rowboats behind the gristmill, renting them to anglers from New York who came out on the milk train. Early in the morning, the captain towed strings of rowboats out into the harbor, and he went back for them in time for the evening train. (Courtesy of Nassau County Department of Parks, Recreation and Museums, Cedarmere.)

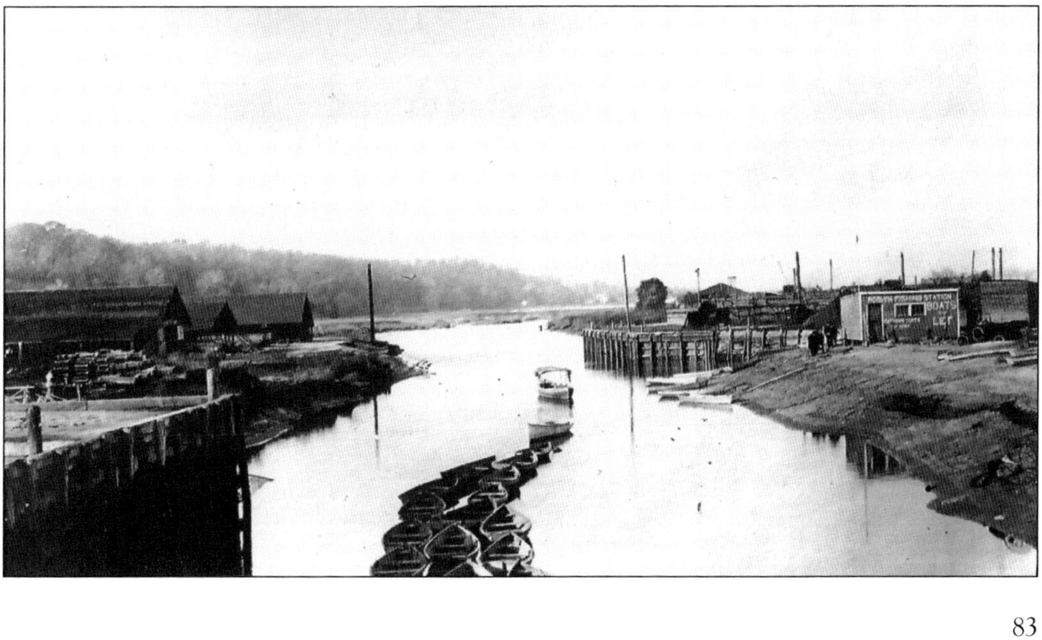

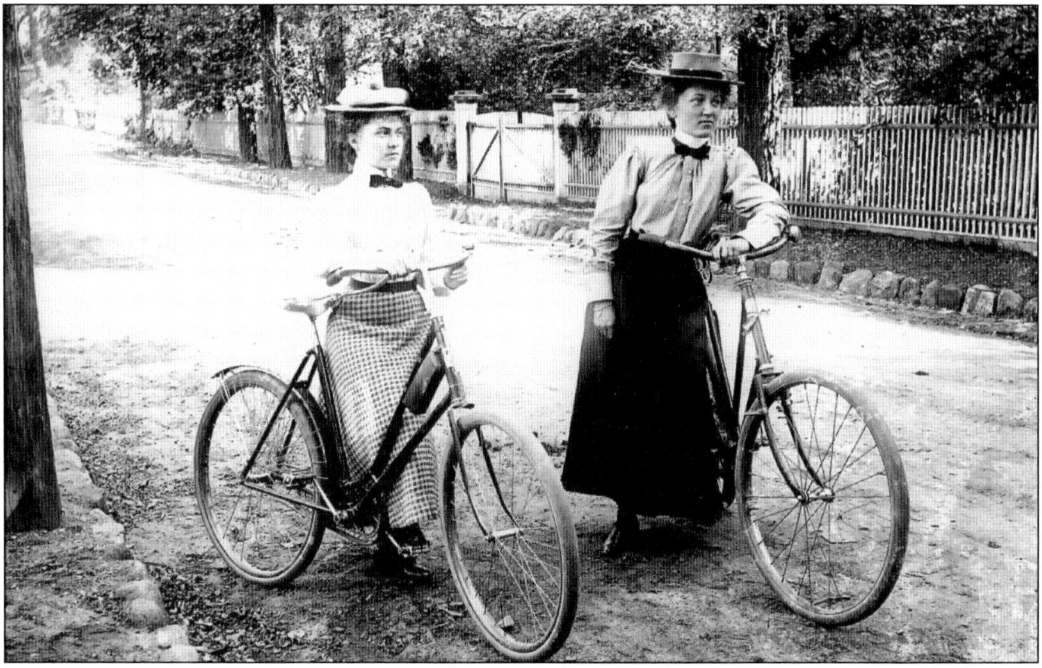

The 1890s bicycle craze began an era of rapid change. On bicycles, people went where and when they liked, exhilarated by the speed. Soon they demanded more and better roads; when the private automobile came in, drivers added their voices, and the world began to change. Here on Main Street, girls pose near Kirbys Corners. (Courtesy of RLS.)

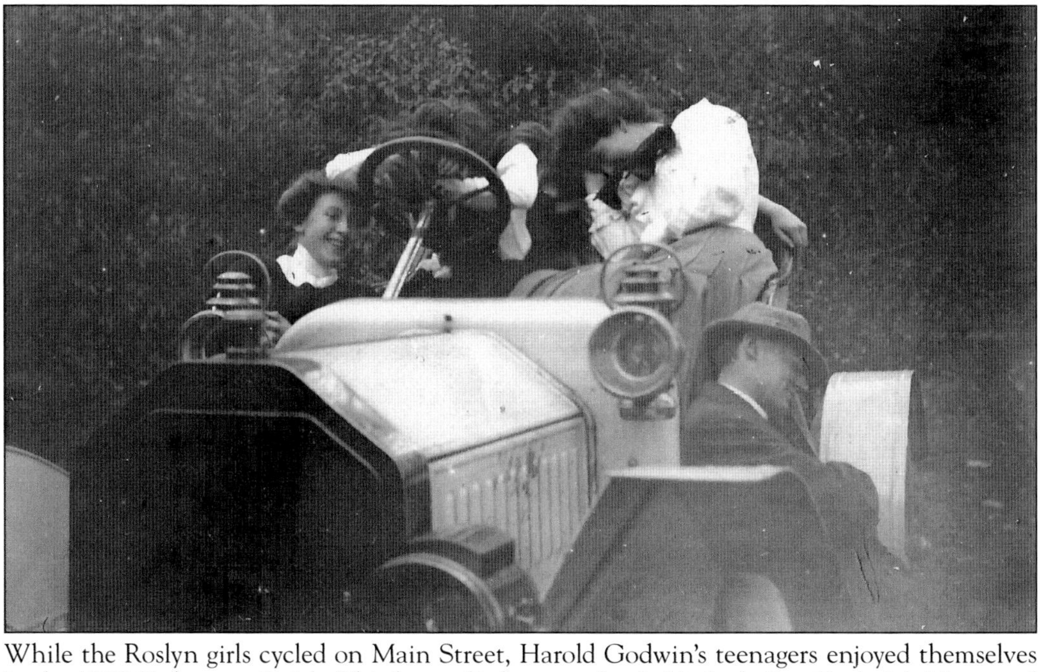

While the Roslyn girls cycled on Main Street, Harold Godwin's teenagers enjoyed themselves in the 1908 Cedarmere Buick. This happy little group (probably including Frederick Marquand Godwin with his sisters Frances and Elizabeth Love) is doing more laughing than driving. (Courtesy of the Nassau County Department of Parks, Recreation and Museums, Cedarmere.)

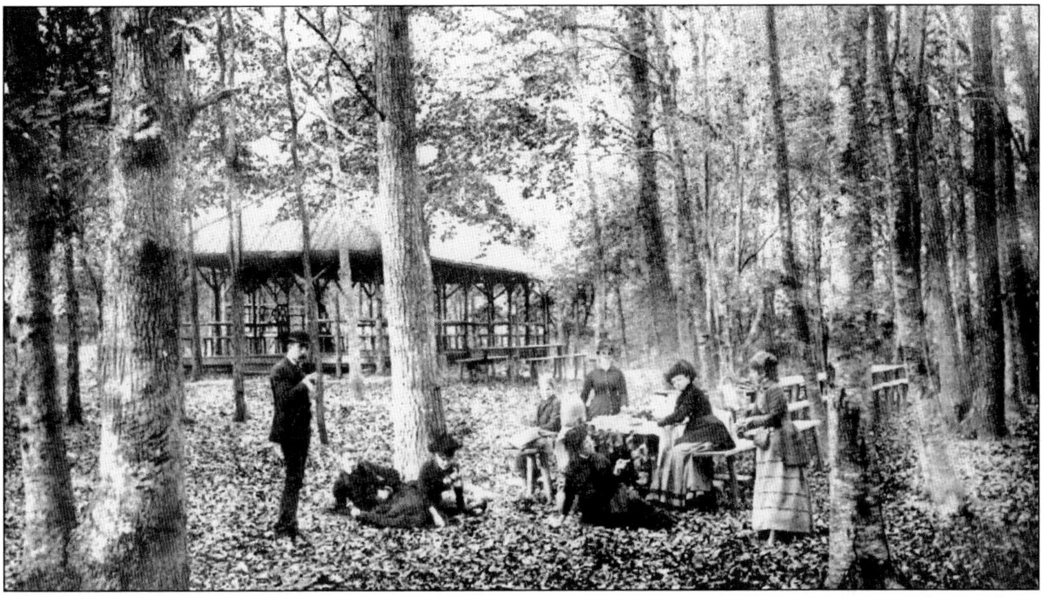

Stephen Taber's Harbor Hill observation tower and pavilion were new when this group of picnickers visited in 1875. Harold Godwin, far left, is joined by friends and family: Fanny Godwin White, Mrs. Thomas Clapham and her son Griffith, Mr. and Mrs. Taylor, Ashton Crosby Clarkson, and several others who are unidentified. When Clarence and Katherine Mackay closed Harbor Hill to recreation, most Roslynians felt personally deprived. (Courtesy of the Bryant Library Local History Collection, Roslyn.)

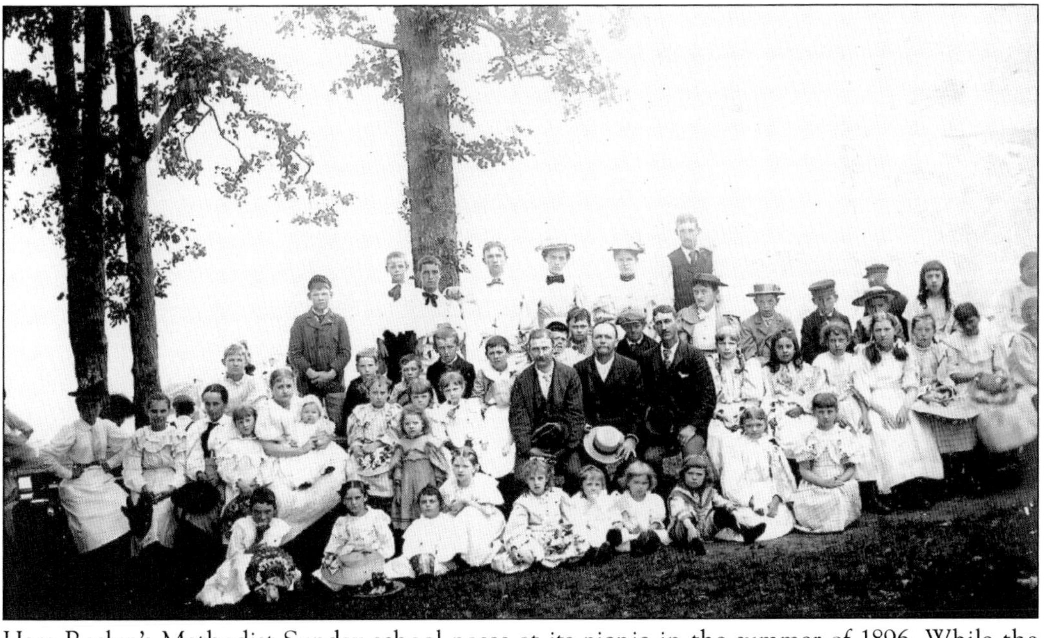

Here Roslyn's Methodist Sunday school poses at its picnic in the summer of 1896. While the location is not known, the students are handsomely dressed for a warm day. Many of the girls wear or hold beautifully trimmed straw hats; a few of the boys sport boaters. More than 50 students, from babies to young adults, have turned out for the picnic. (Courtesy of the Nassau County Department of Parks, Recreation and Museums, Cedarmere.)

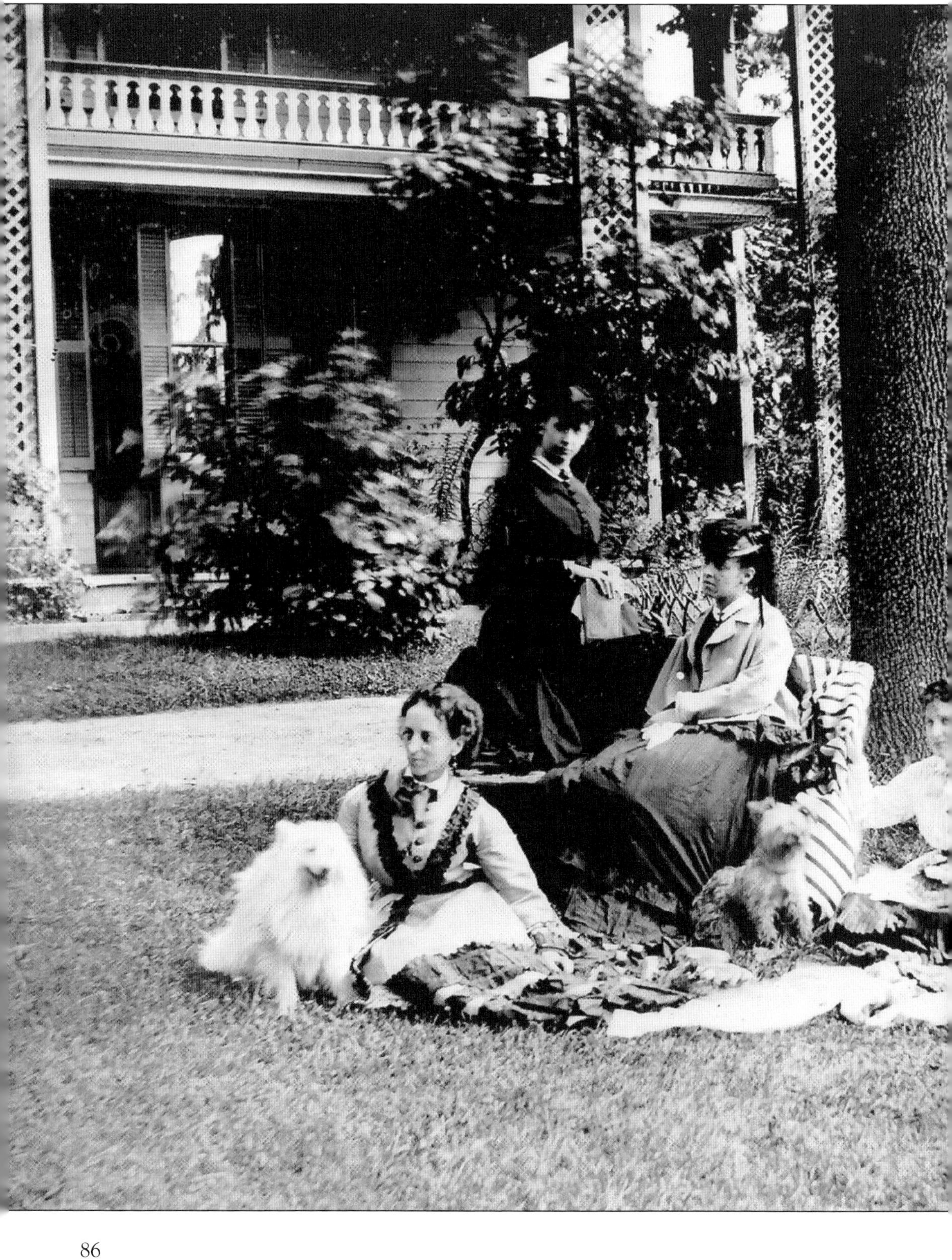

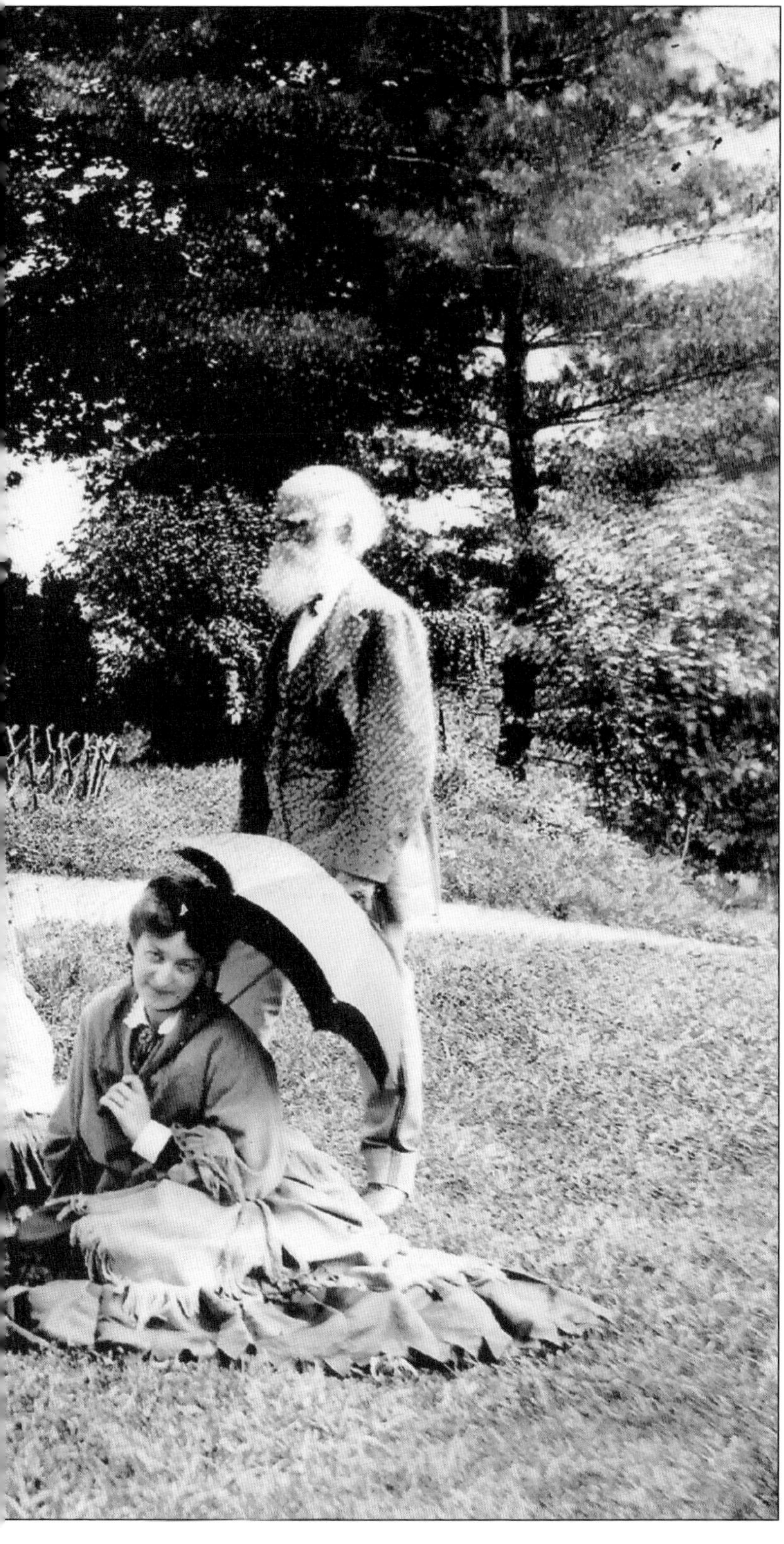

Even the most distinguished Roslynians had time for summer picnics in the mid-1870s. William Cullen Bryant (standing at right), enjoys an afternoon outdoors with his daughter Julia (at left, with dog) and friends at Cedar Mere. (Courtesy of the Bryant Library Local History Collection, Roslyn.)

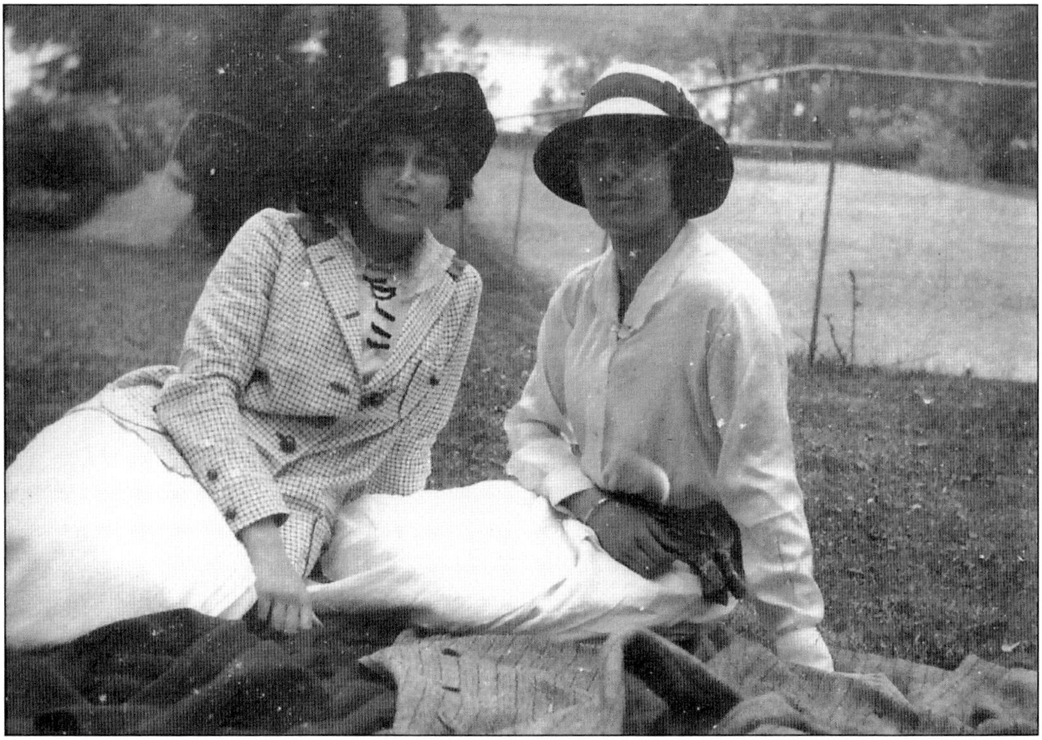

Above, William Cullen Bryant's great-granddaughter Love Godwin (right) enjoys an afternoon beside the lake at Cedarmere with her friend Mary Canfield in 1913. Below, a group of Godwins and their company picnics on a Roslyn Road. (Courtesy of the Nassau County Department of Parks, Recreation and Museums, Cedarmere.)

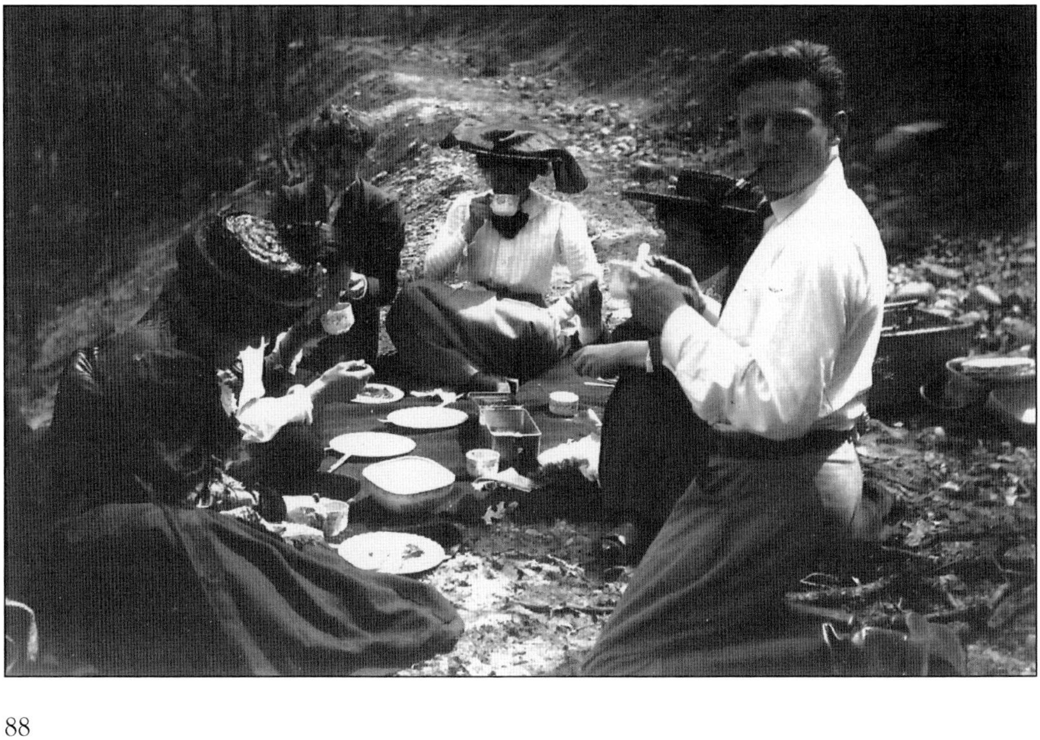

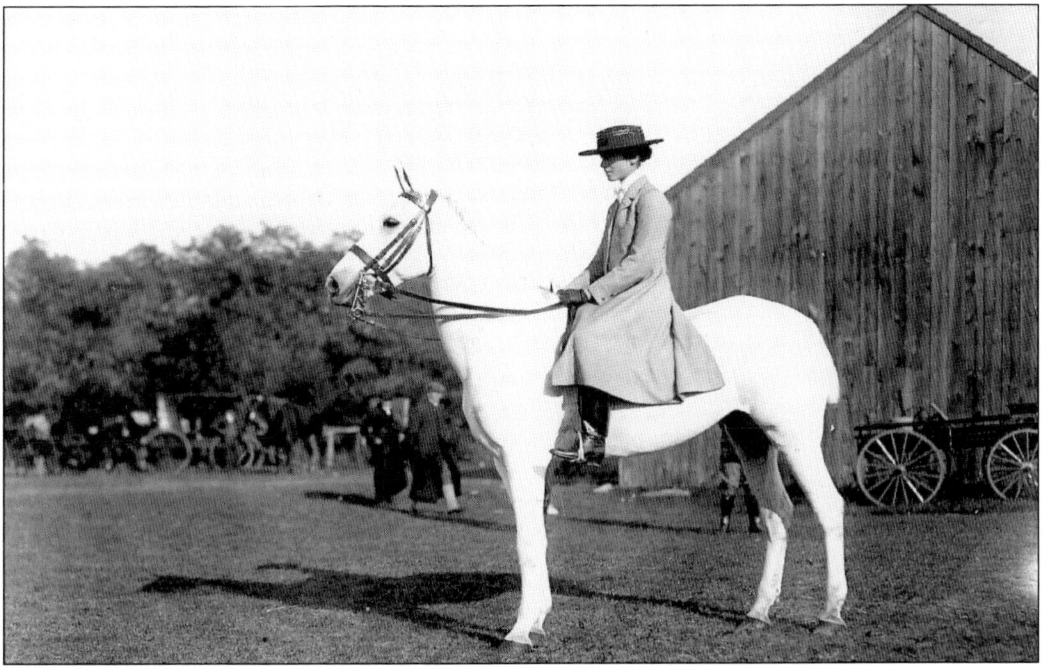

Harold Godwin's wife Elizabeth Love Marquand is elegantly mounted at the Piping Rock Club in 1884 (above). The North Shore was a rider's paradise before post–World War II development: a network of trails ran through forests, farms, and estates from the Queens border to Oyster Bay. Another, shaggier horse pulls the buckboard taking Priscilla Pearsall and friends to her Roslyn Harbor home in 1890. (Above, courtesy of the Nassau County Department of Parks, Recreation and Museums, Cedarmere; below, courtesy of the Nassau County Museum Collection, Long Island Studies Institute.)

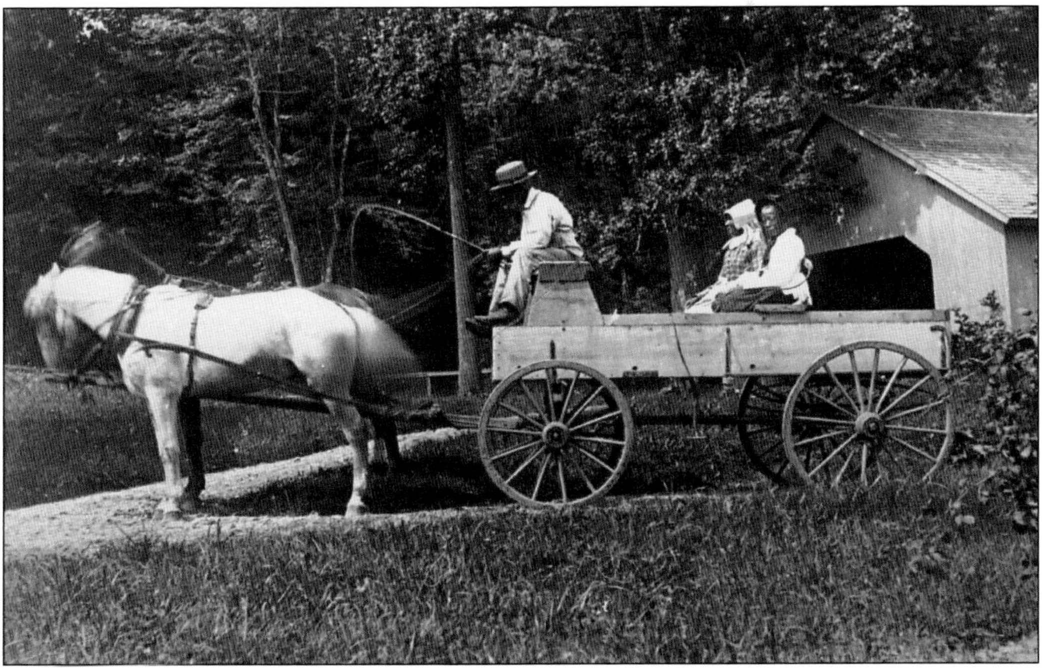

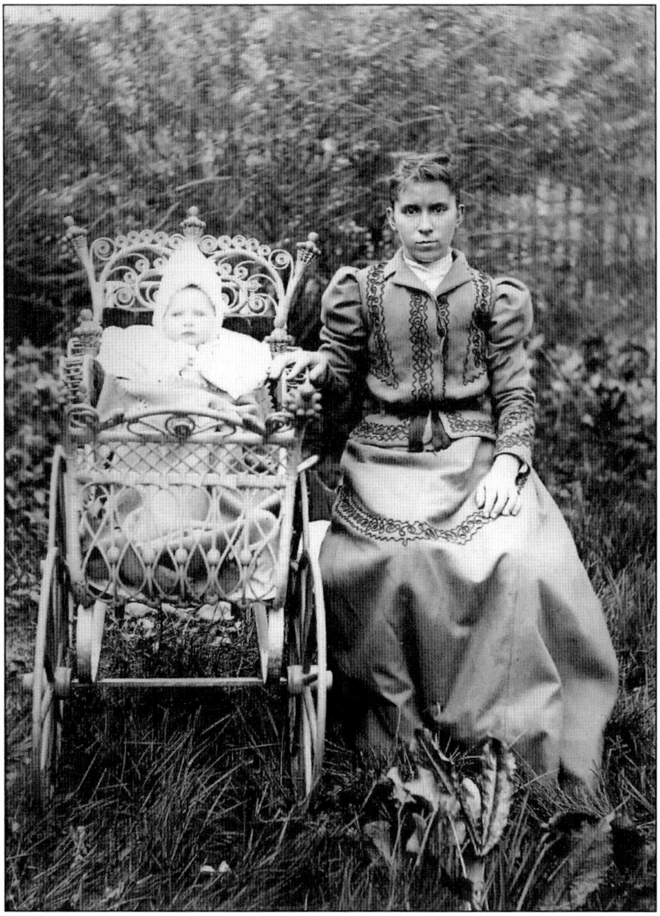

At left, Isaac Henry Kirby's wife and their baby enjoy an afternoon outdoors around 1905. The elaborate rattan scrollwork on the baby buggy echoes Mrs. Kirby's dress embroidery, while the tall grass at her feet suggests that the power lawn mower was still in the future. This young family lived in the 1680s Van Nostrand–Starkins house, now a museum. Below, photographer William Pickering's children Arthur and Annie fish and pick up shells on a west shore beach around 1905. (Left, courtesy of RLS; below, courtesy of John and Michelle Santos.)

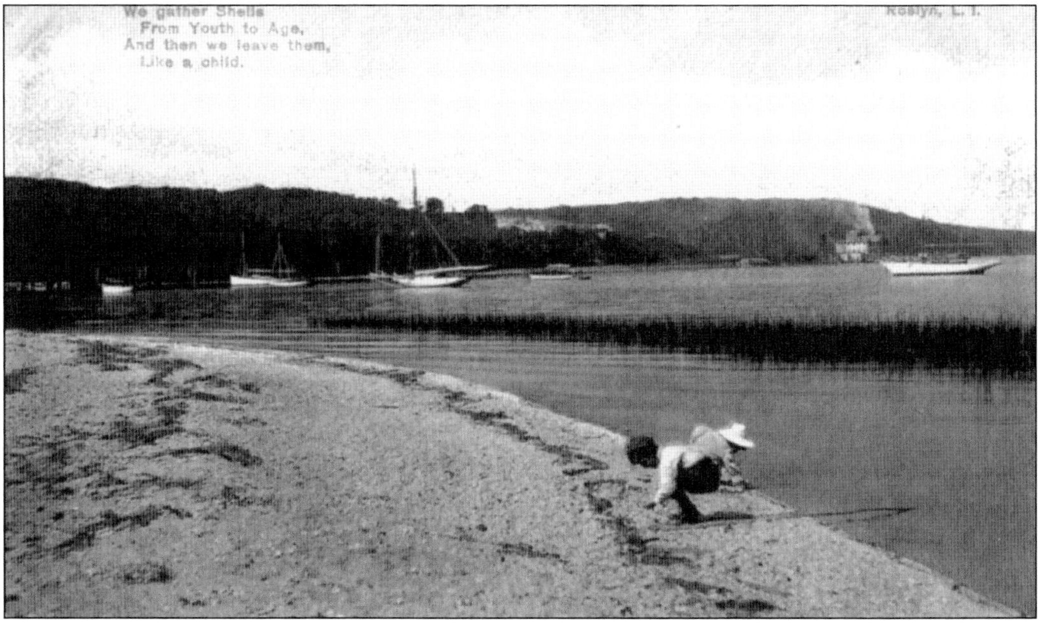

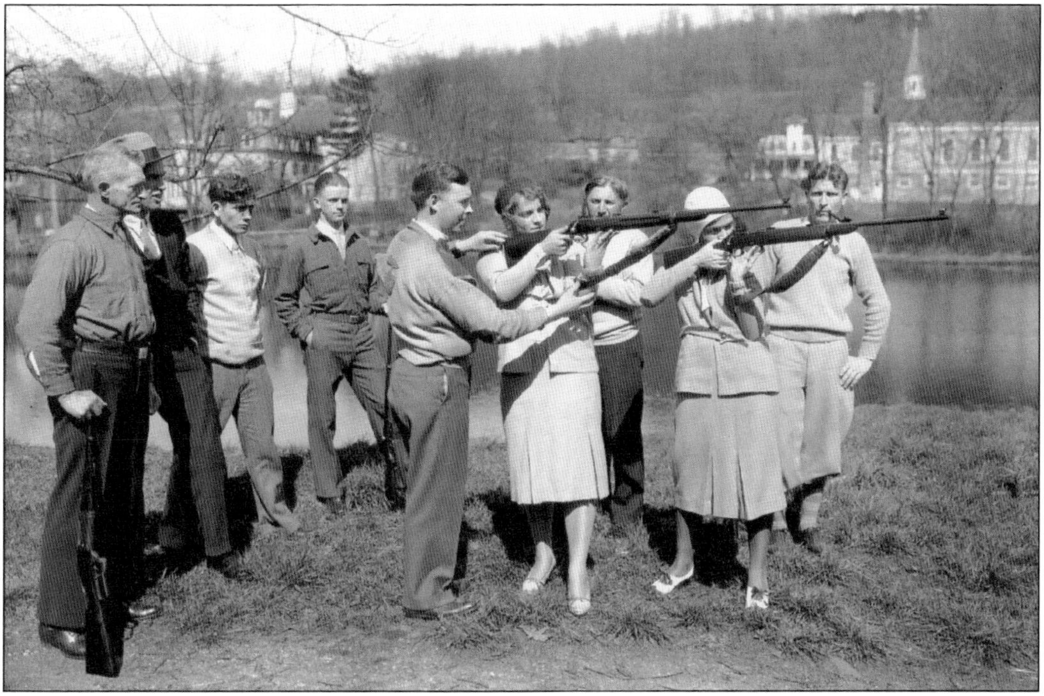

Roslynians went out for sports of all kinds. Seen above, the Roslyn Rifle and Revolver Club has a field day in the park in 1930. Male members stand watching while the women get some coaching. Clarence Mackay was a nominal member of this club. Below, croquet players assemble with their equipment around 1905 at Kirbys. (Above, courtesy of the Queens Borough Public Library, Long Island Division, Joseph Burt Photographs; below, courtesy of RLS.)

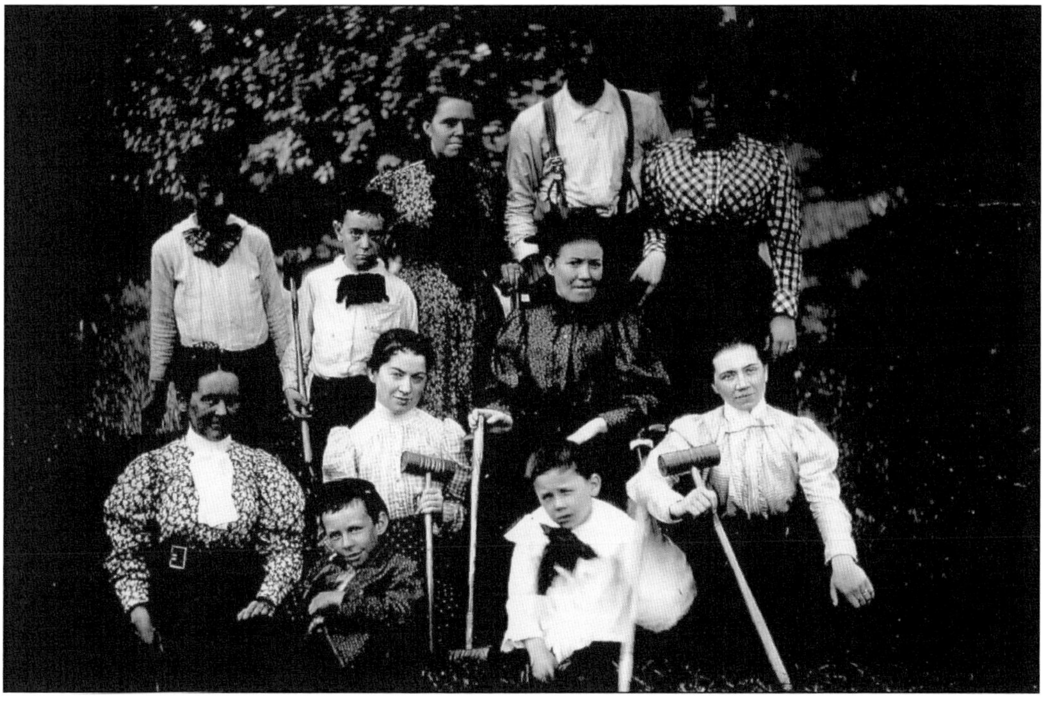

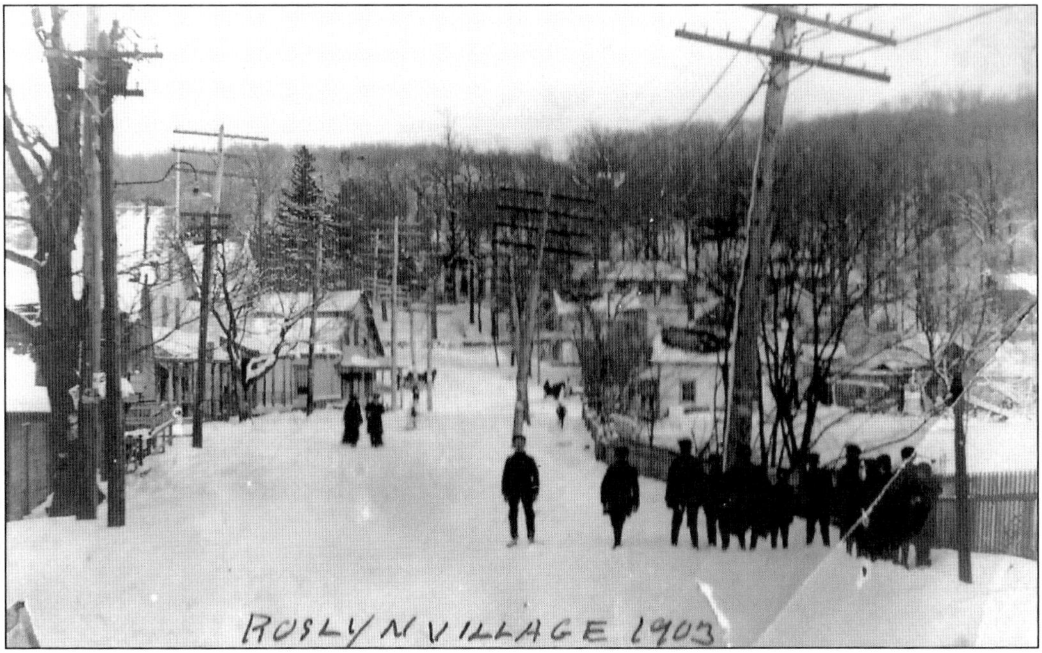

Roslynians enjoyed winters as well as summers. Seen above, boys cluster at the west end of the milldam in 1903 to stomp around in a fresh snowfall. The Conklin lumberyard office is the farthest building on the left, Silver Lake is at the right. Below, men cut ice on Silver Lake around 1906. The Conklin office roof shows behind the buildings at the right, while the store at the far left, run by Thomas Fagan, had just been built. (Courtesy of RLS.)

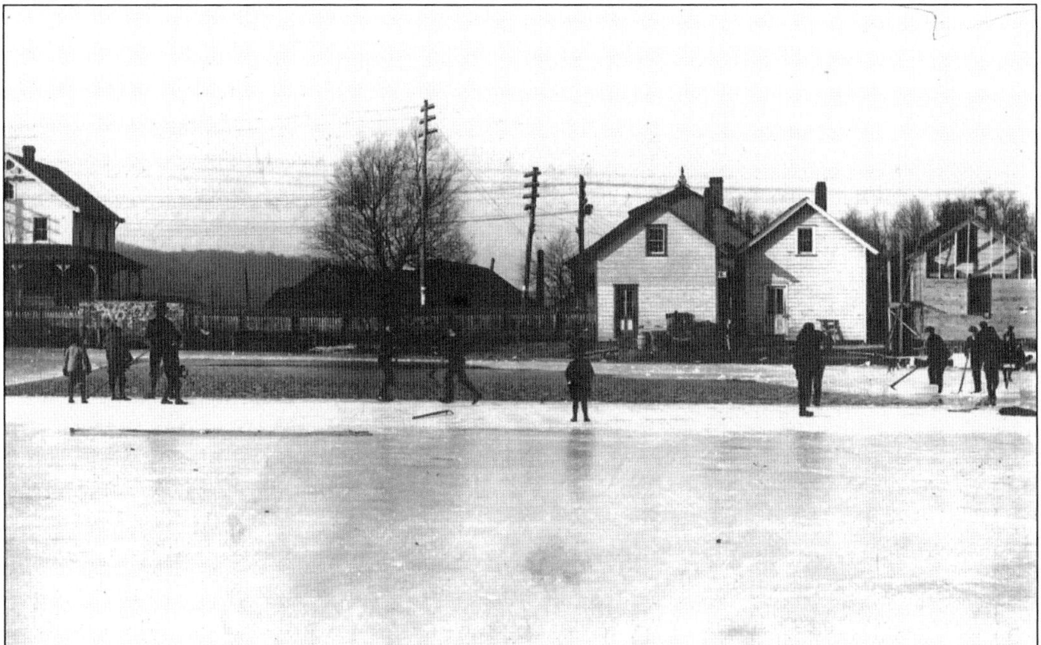

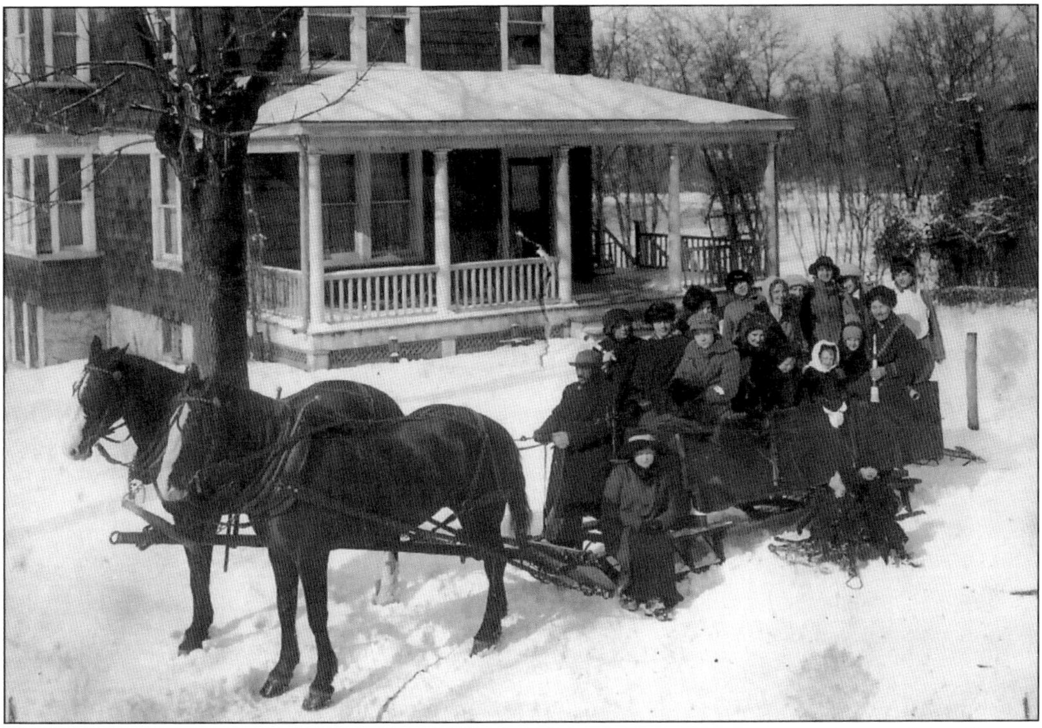

In the upper *c.* 1910 photograph, a sled packed with young people pauses in front of the George Conklin house on East Broadway. One of Roslyn's several icehouses at this time stands behind this house on the shore of Silver Lake. Below is a timeless view of eel spearing and skating on Hempstead Harbor, taken in 1920. (Courtesy of RLS.)

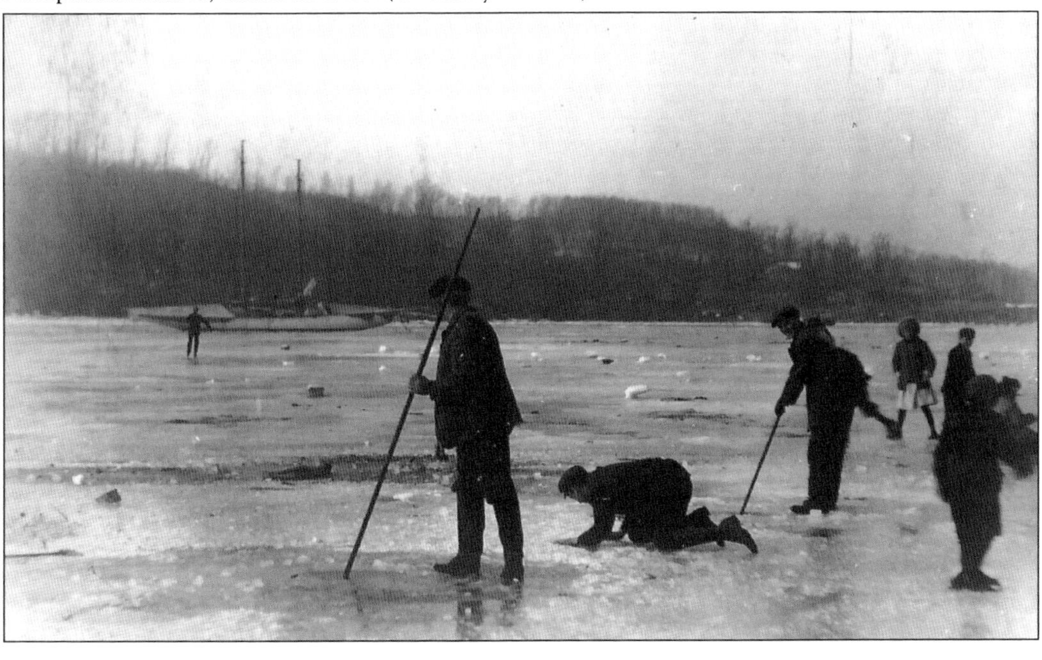

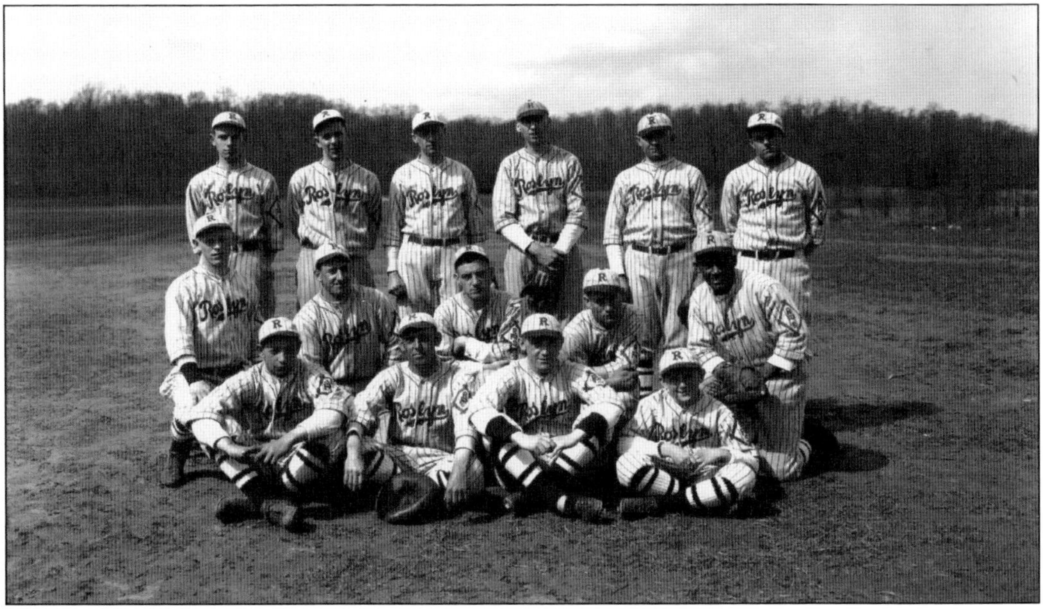

The famous Roslyn Red Sox baseball team, above, poses for newspaper photographer Joe Burt in the 1920s. In 1923, the Roslyn High School girls' basketball team (below) included Fran and Mary O'Reiley, Bess McCue, Fran Pfister, Anne Peterson and Agnes Maverick. (Above, courtesy of RLS; below, courtesy of the Queens Borough Public Library, Long Island Division, Joseph Burt Photographs.)

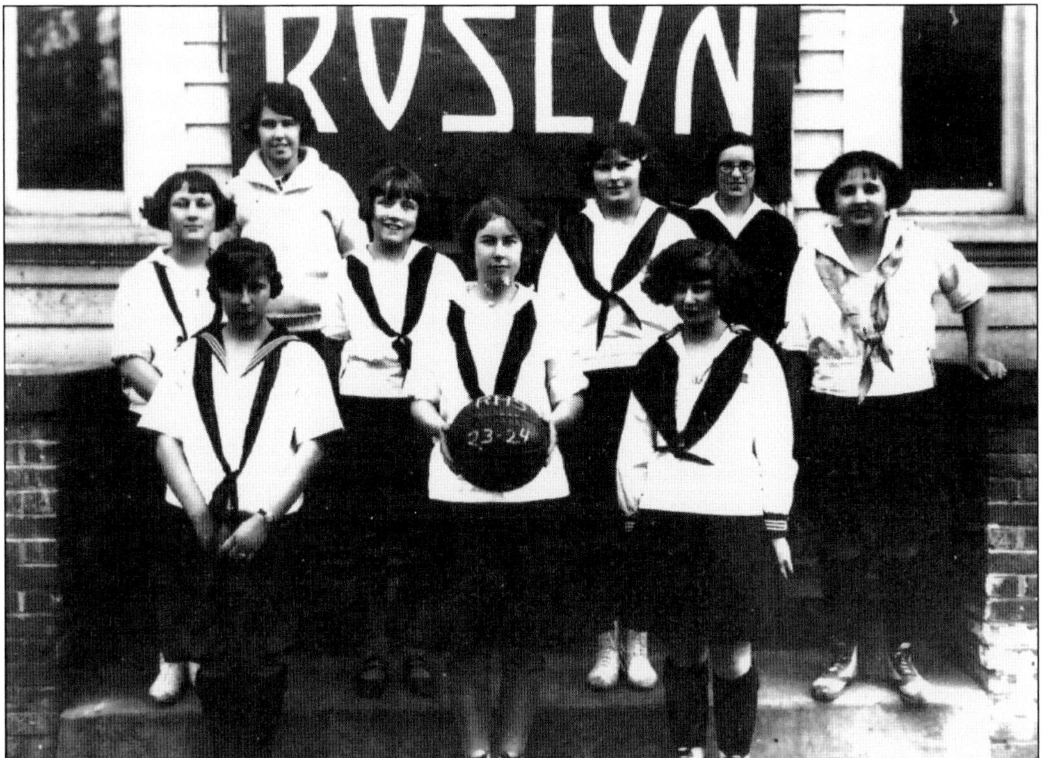

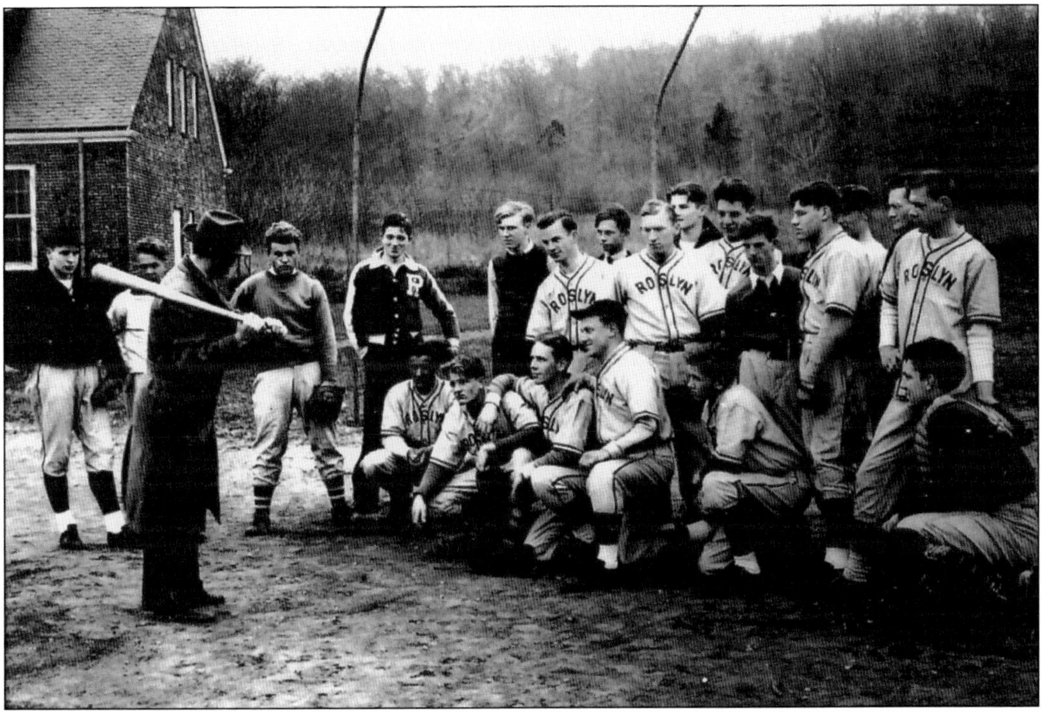

Above, the high school boys' baseball team watches a batting demonstration around 1940. At right, four men in bathing costume soak up the sun in 1910. (Above, courtesy of RLS; below, courtesy of the Nassau County Department of Parks, Recreation and Museums, Cedarmere.)

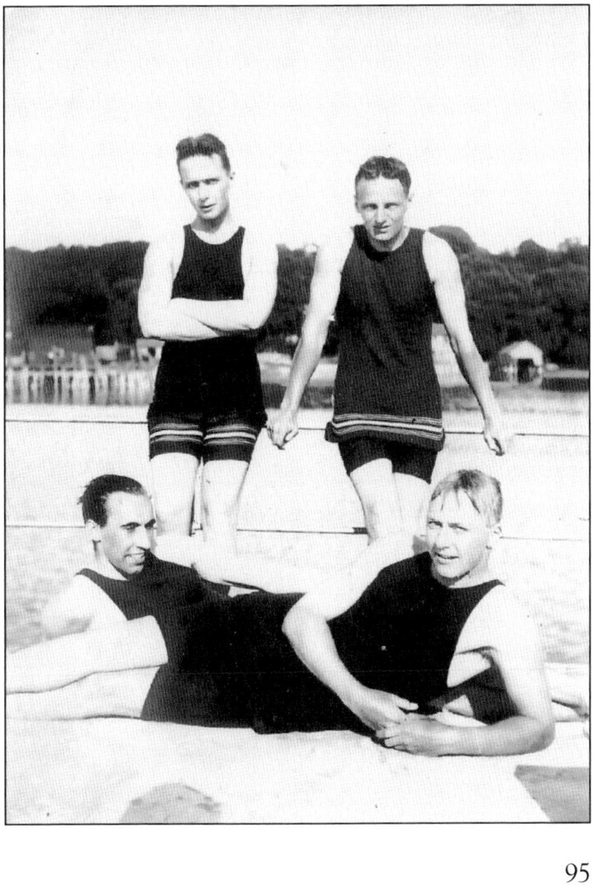

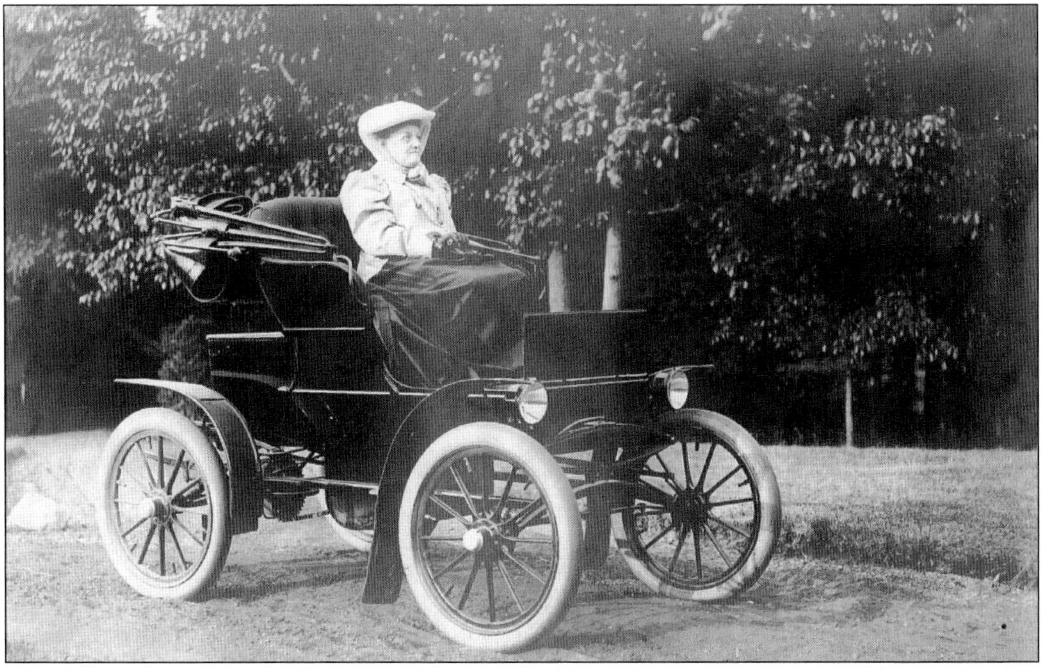

The first cars came to Roslyn around 1903; Harold Godwin's sister Fanny, wife of Alfred L. White (above), was the first woman driver in town. She drove her electric automobile until one day, entering the barn, she could not stop the car and it plowed through the rear wall. She never drove it again. The Godwins and Goddards were early car enthusiasts. Harold Godwin had a White Steamer. Conrad Goddard's first car, a 1904 Orient Buckboard, looked like a wagon, and went 23 miles an hour. Below, a car of the same vintage labors up the West Turnpike Road (Old Northern Boulevard), passed by a man-drawn peanut wagon. (Above, courtesy of the Nassau County Department of Parks, Recreation and Museums, Cedarmere; below, courtesy of RLS.)

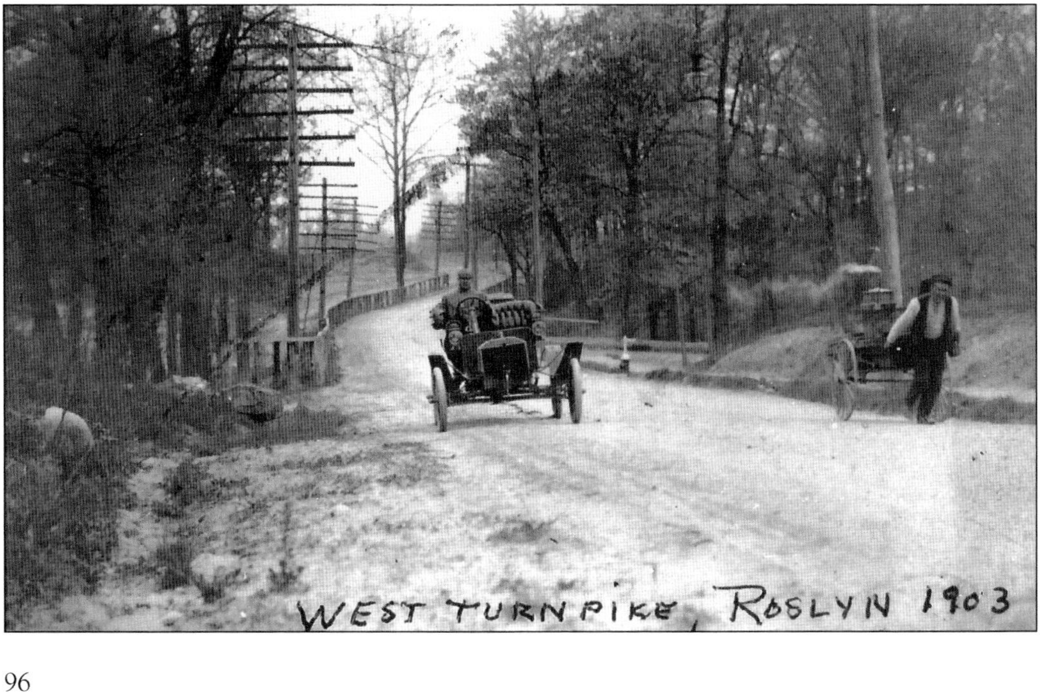

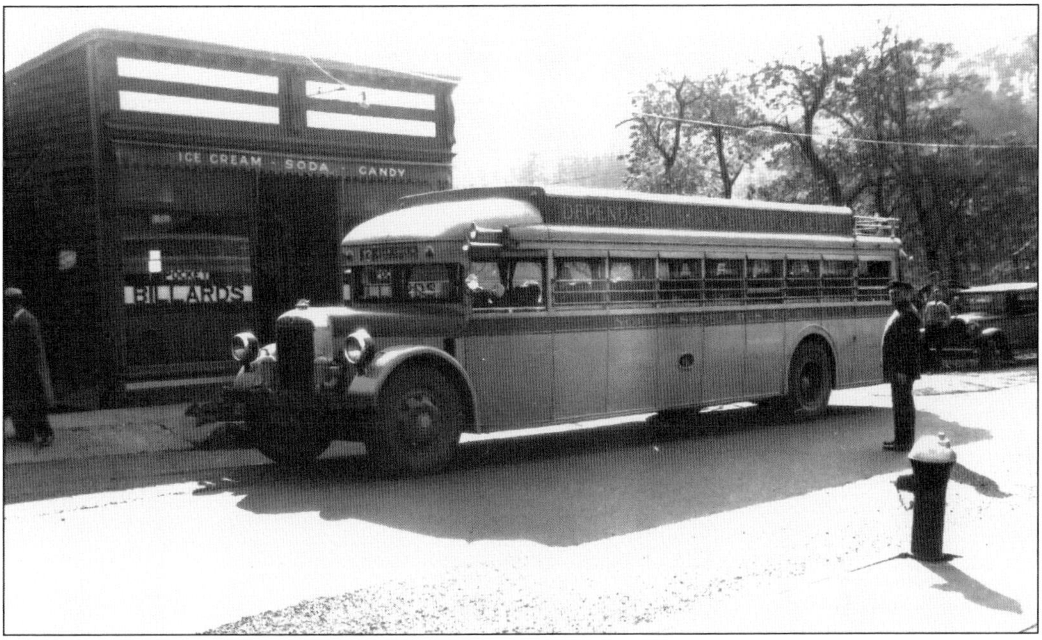

The trolleys, introduced in 1907, were short-lived; Roslyn's last one ran in 1920. Costs rose, fares did not, so when a strike cut off cheap coal, the company failed, to be replaced by the North Shore Bus Company's interurban bus. Here, in the 1930s, the bus stops in front of a milldam candy store. (Courtesy of the Queens Borough Public Library, Long Island Division, Illustrations Collection–Roslyn.)

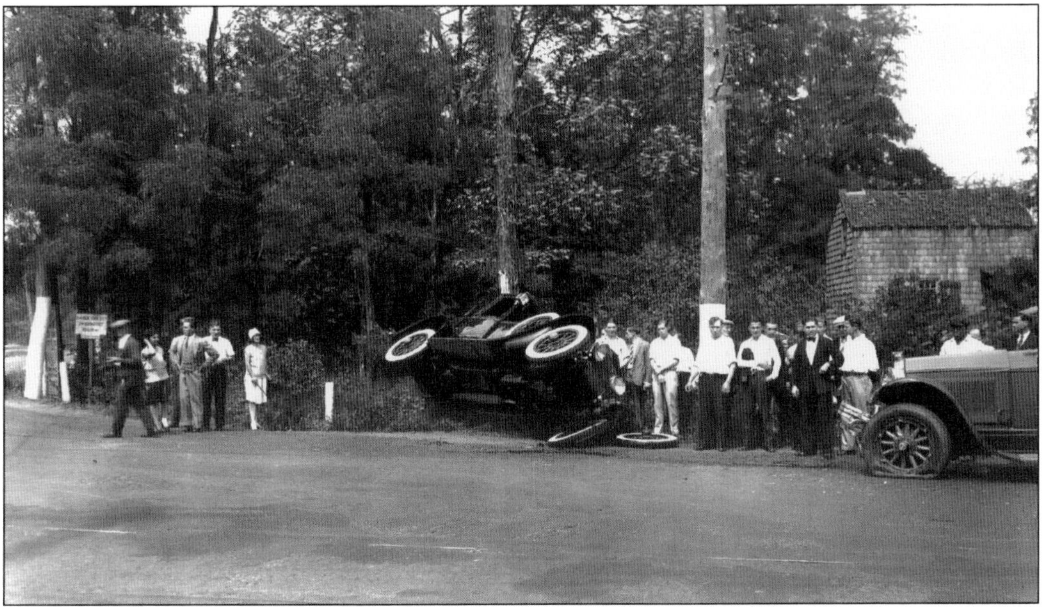

People were not blasé about car wrecks in the 1930s, as this crowd attests. Photographer Joseph Burt arrived in time to catch the overturned vehicle before it was hauled out of the ditch. It happened on Northern Boulevard (25A) at Willis Avenue. A telephone pole, a tree, and several fence posts are whitewashed for motorist safety. (Courtesy of the Queens Borough Public Library, Long Island Division, Joseph Burt Photographs.)

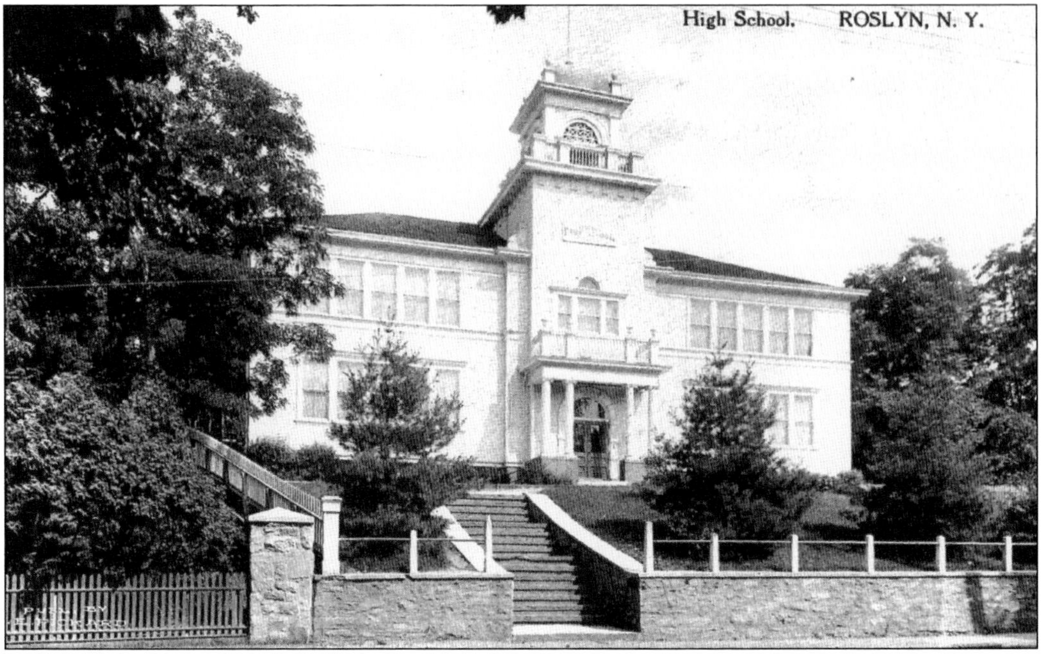

Roslyn's village school stood on School Street (beyond the east end of the milldam) from as early as 1790 until 1927. The fine building (above) with its Palladian window and central tower, replaced an older school that burned in 1897. A defective furnace caused this one's destruction 30 years later. Below, the Roslyn High School class of 1910 reveals a formal dress code. (Above, courtesy of John and Michelle Santos; below, courtesy of RLS.)

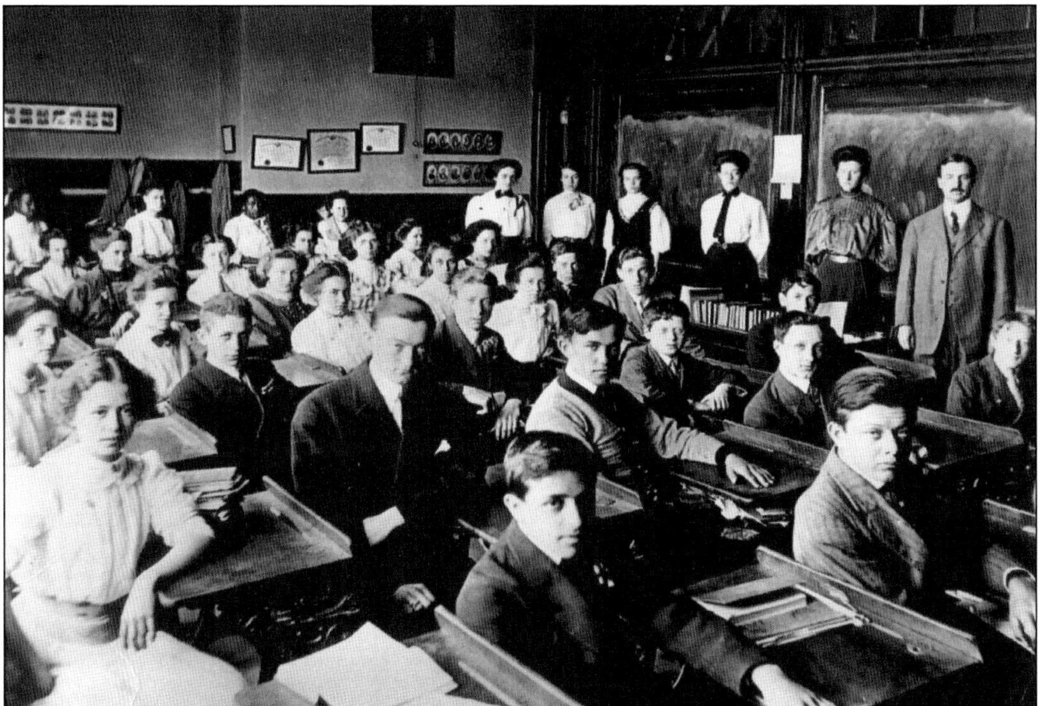

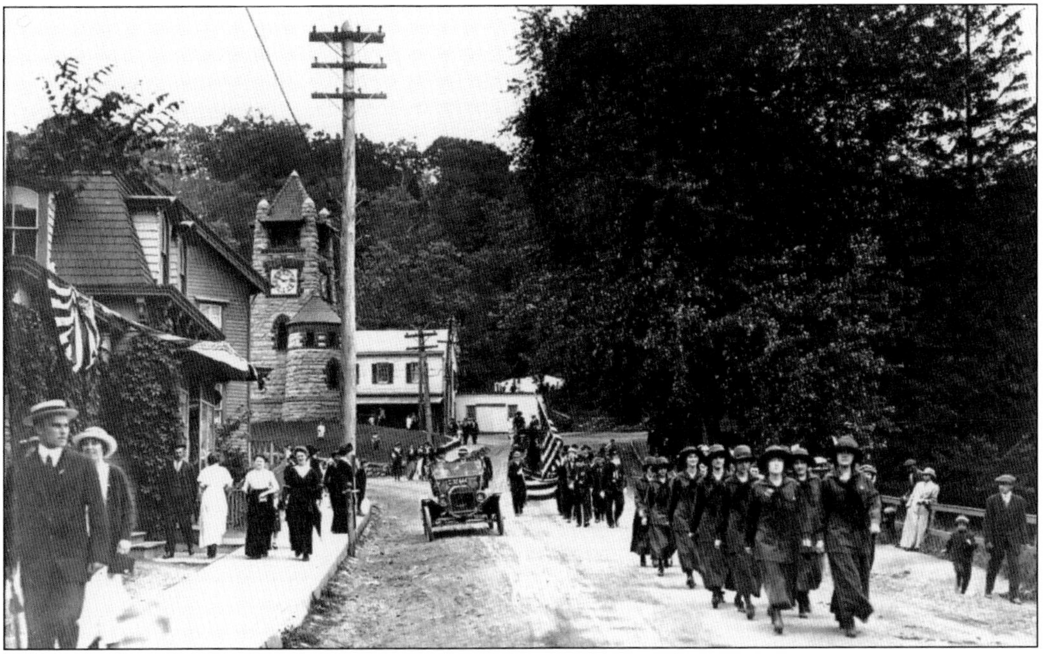

To be a Girl Pioneer in 1911, a girl had to be 12 years old, have 50¢ in the bank, and pass certain simple tests. The Pioneers aimed to instill in girls "an enthusiasm for efficient work and joyous recreation." They enjoyed cultural, civic, and charitable activities, and their motto was "I Can." Roslyn's girls were organized around 1913 by Grace Hicks. Above, the Pioneers march east on the milldam, perhaps to the cemetery, on Memorial Day in 1914. Roslyn's girls did not become Scouts until 1929. Roslyn's Troop No. 1 was one of the first Boy Scout troops in the country. For many years the master was Ed Pietsch. Below, Troop No. 1 poses during its encampment in the summer of 1918. (Above, courtesy of the Nassau County Museum Collection, Long Island Studies Institute; below, courtesy of RLS.)

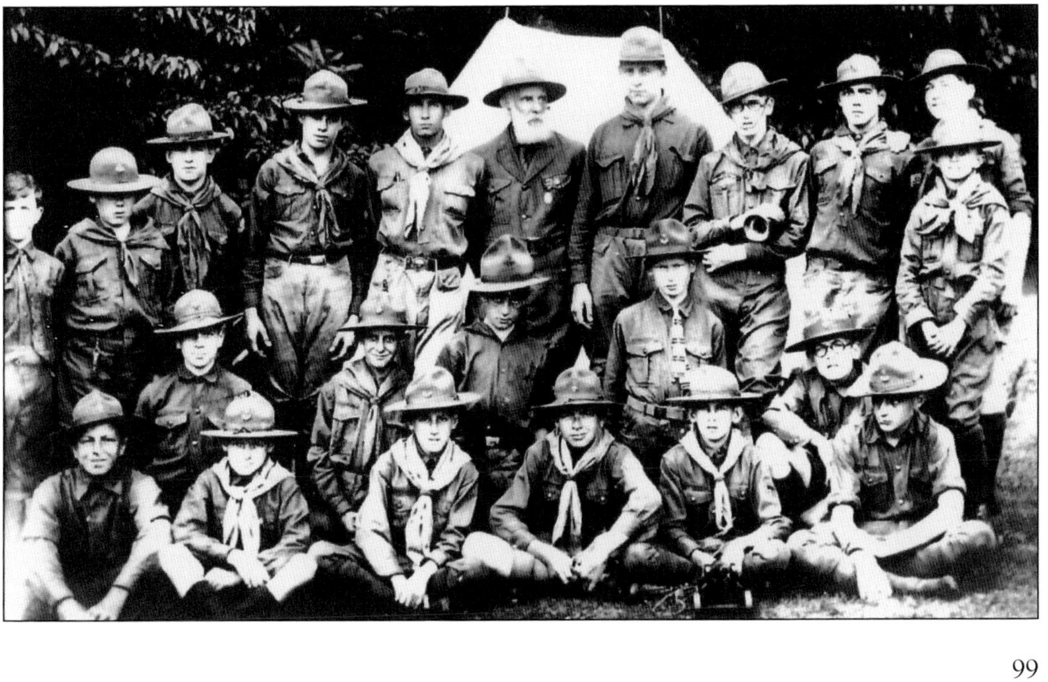

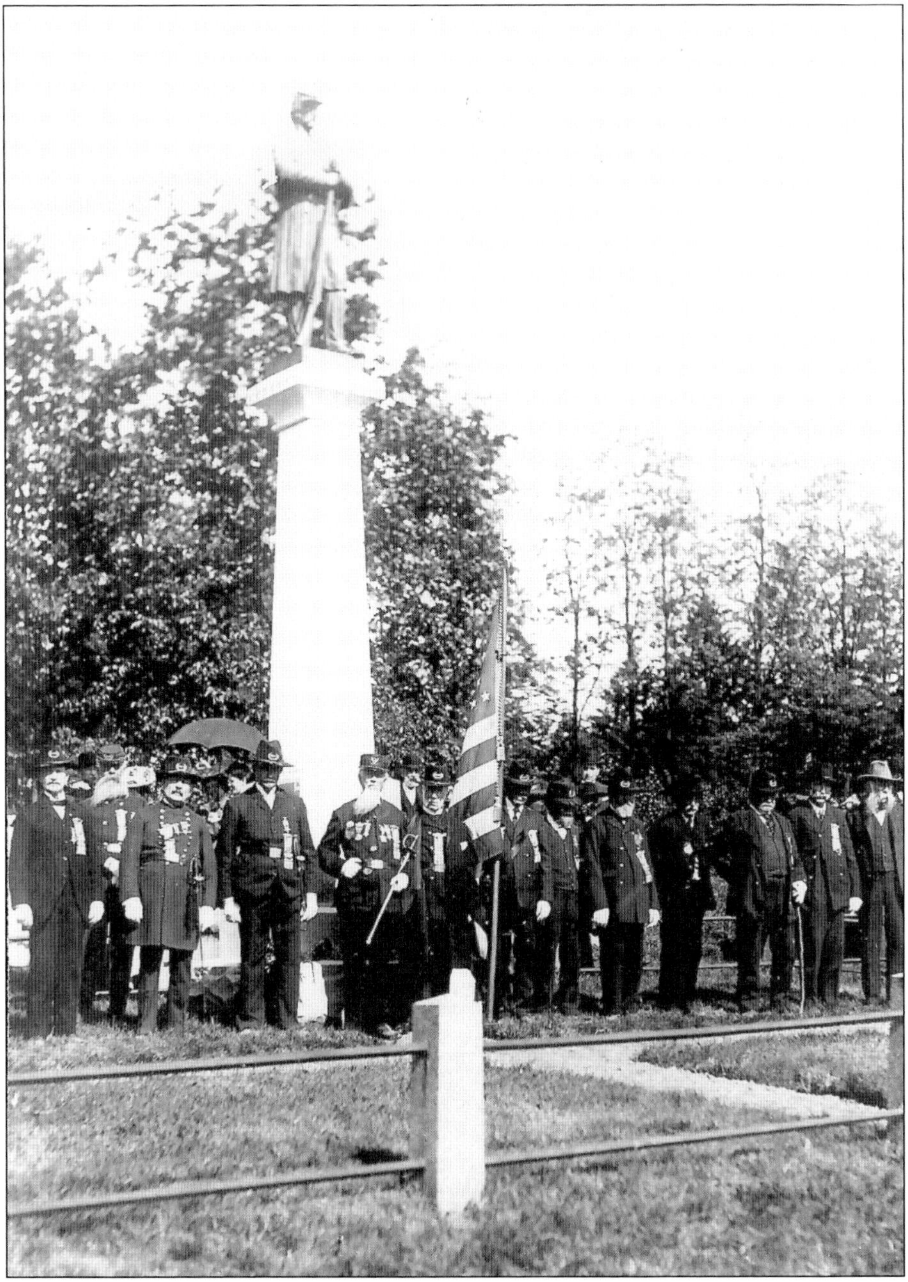

After the Civil War, Union veterans established the Grand Army of the Republic (GAR) to commemorate the war and raise monuments to the dead. Roslyn's Post No. 643 was formed in 1891; many of its members had served in the Roslyn company organized by Benjamin Willis. The post held an annual remembrance ceremony on Memorial Day, which remains a solemn Roslyn event. In 1902, the GAR raised a life-sized bronze soldier on a 14-foot granite plinth in the Roslyn Cemetery. The statue was stolen in 1992, and in 2005 a replacement, copied from one in Brooklyn's Greenwood Cemetery and financed by contributions, was installed. Here Memorial Day observances in 1915 are attended by Civil War veterans. The last veteran died in 1934. (Courtesy of RLS.)

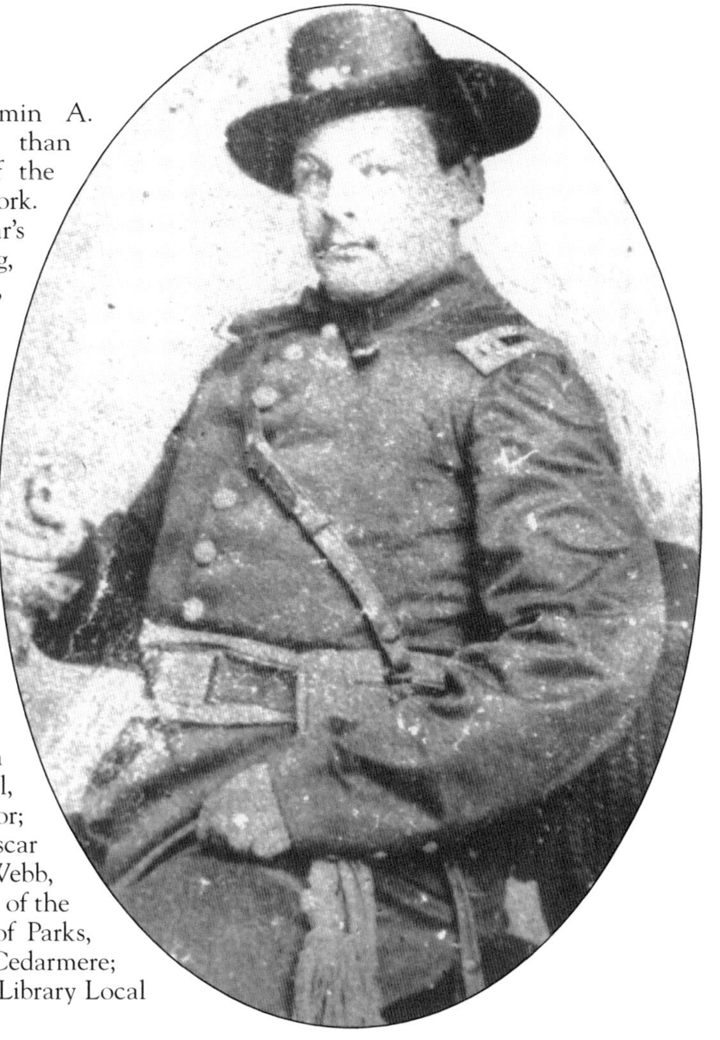

In 1862, 22-year-old Benjamin A. Willis (right) raised more than 100 men for Company H of the 119th Regiment of New York. They fought in some of the war's worst battles: Fredericksburg, Chancellorsville, Gettysburg, Lookout Mountain, and Missionary Ridge. In an 1863 letter, Willis described "heart-rending scenes of carnage." Only 57 of his men survived the war. Willis later practiced law and served two terms in Congress. Below, Roslyn's World War I veterans were honored. They include Bert Hicks (left), William Eastman (right), and Tom Kennely (top). From left to right are (first row) Elmer Brand, J. Breen, William Daly, J. Peel, Floyd Hill, unidentified, and R. Traynor; (second row) Joe Purick, Oscar Smith, George Murphy, T. Webb, and H. Hicks. (Right, courtesy of the Nassau County Department of Parks, Recreation and Museums, Cedarmere; below, courtesy of the Bryant Library Local History Collection, Roslyn.)

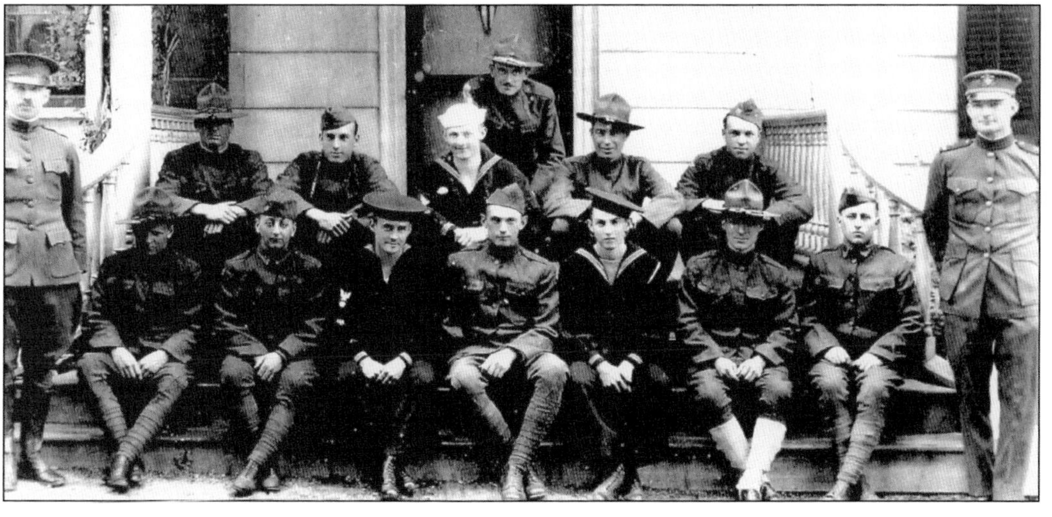

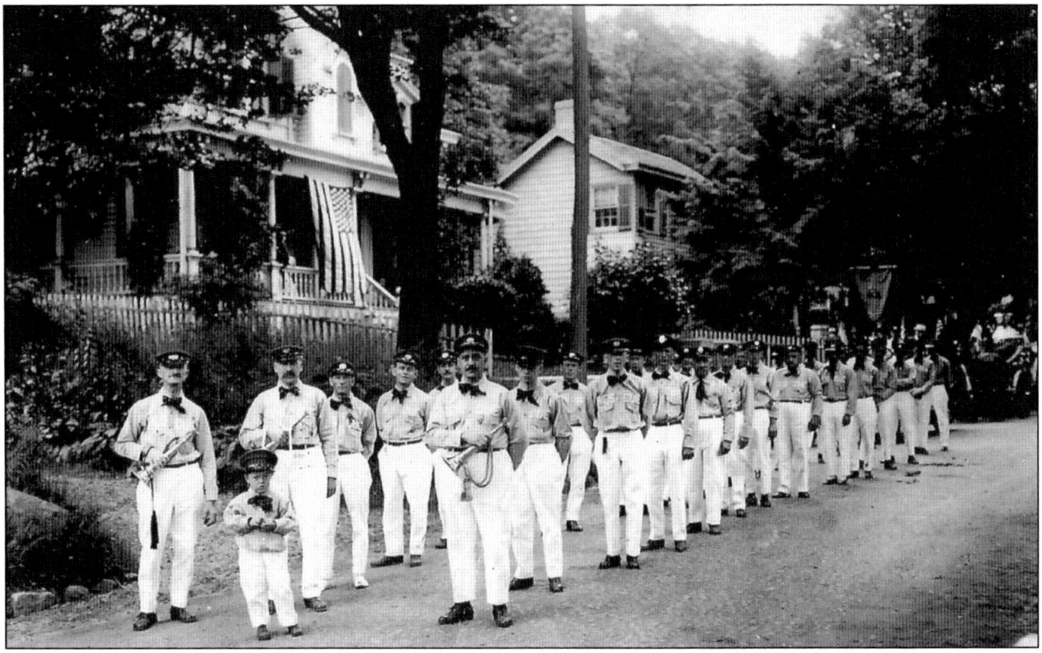

Roslyn Rescue Hook and Ladder Company No. 1 was the first local fire company, founded in 1852. In the early 20th century, it was the "kid glove company," comprising the most successful local businessmen and influential politicians. The photograph above shows the men mustered for Memorial Day in 1905. The original truck house stood beside what is now the Washington Manor; in 1879, it was "walked" across the milldam to its present site on School Street. In 1903, Clarence Mackay gave Roslyn Rescue the fine Silsby Steamer shown below in front of the Bell House on Bryant Avenue. The newspaper opined that if this engine had been on hand a year earlier, Cedarmere might have been saved. (Courtesy of RLS.)

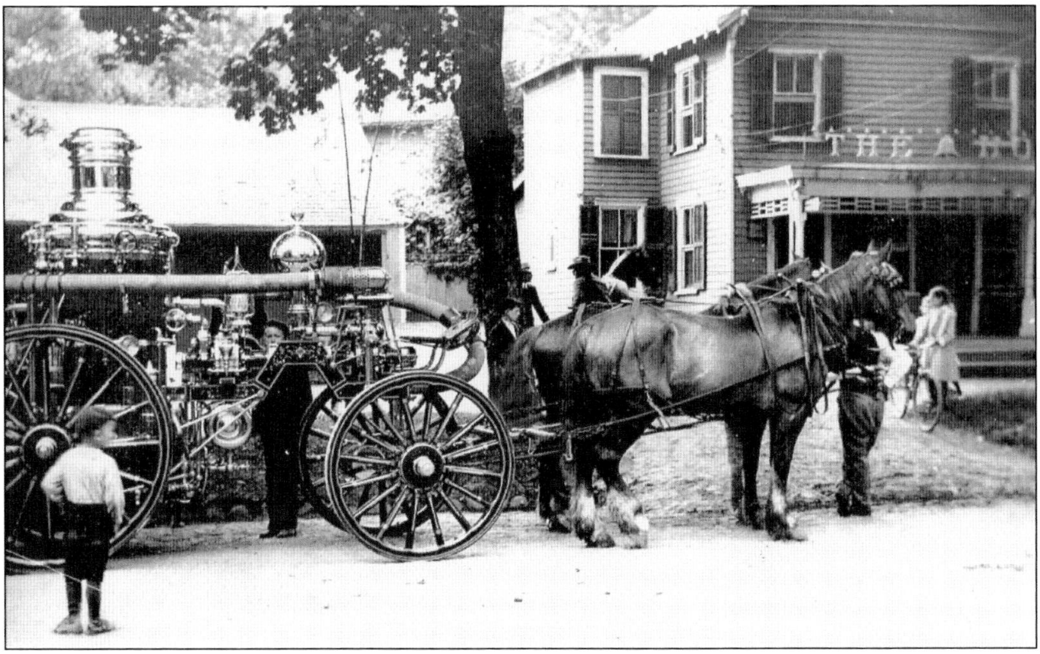

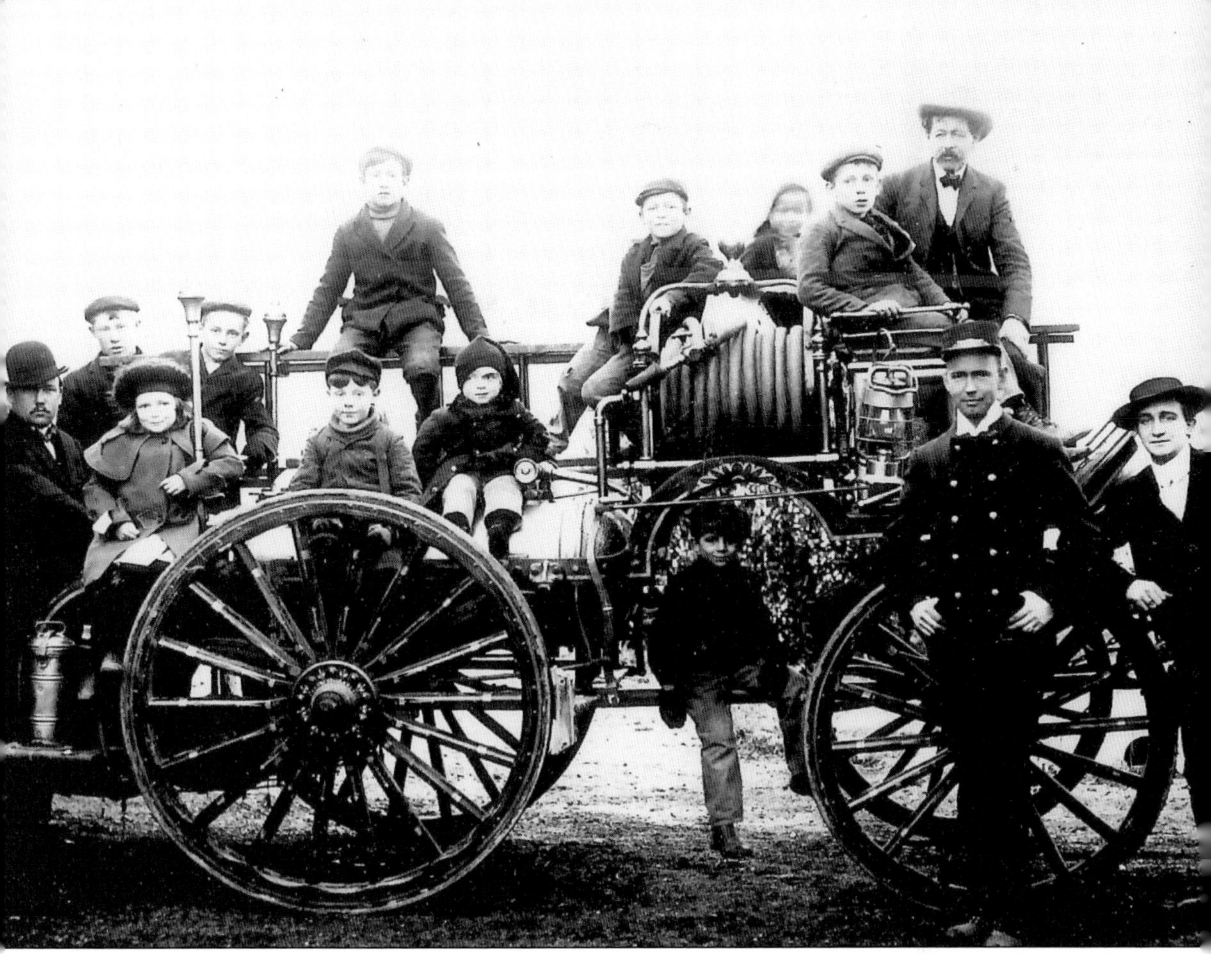

The Roslyn Highlands Hook and Ladder, Engine and Hose Company No. 1, formed in 1905, served the developing Roslyn Heights and Roslyn Estates areas. The 1907 Garden Street firehouse was a center of community life, used for plays, dances, movies, and dinners. The church used it for programs, the school used it for classrooms, and for years it was the polling place as well. Here photographer William Pickering's children pose with firemen on the horse-drawn chemical cart that was bought in 1905 for $1,000 from a Staten Island manufacturer. Outside the current (1951) firehouse, the original fire bell stands as a memorial to fallen members. (Courtesy of RLS.)

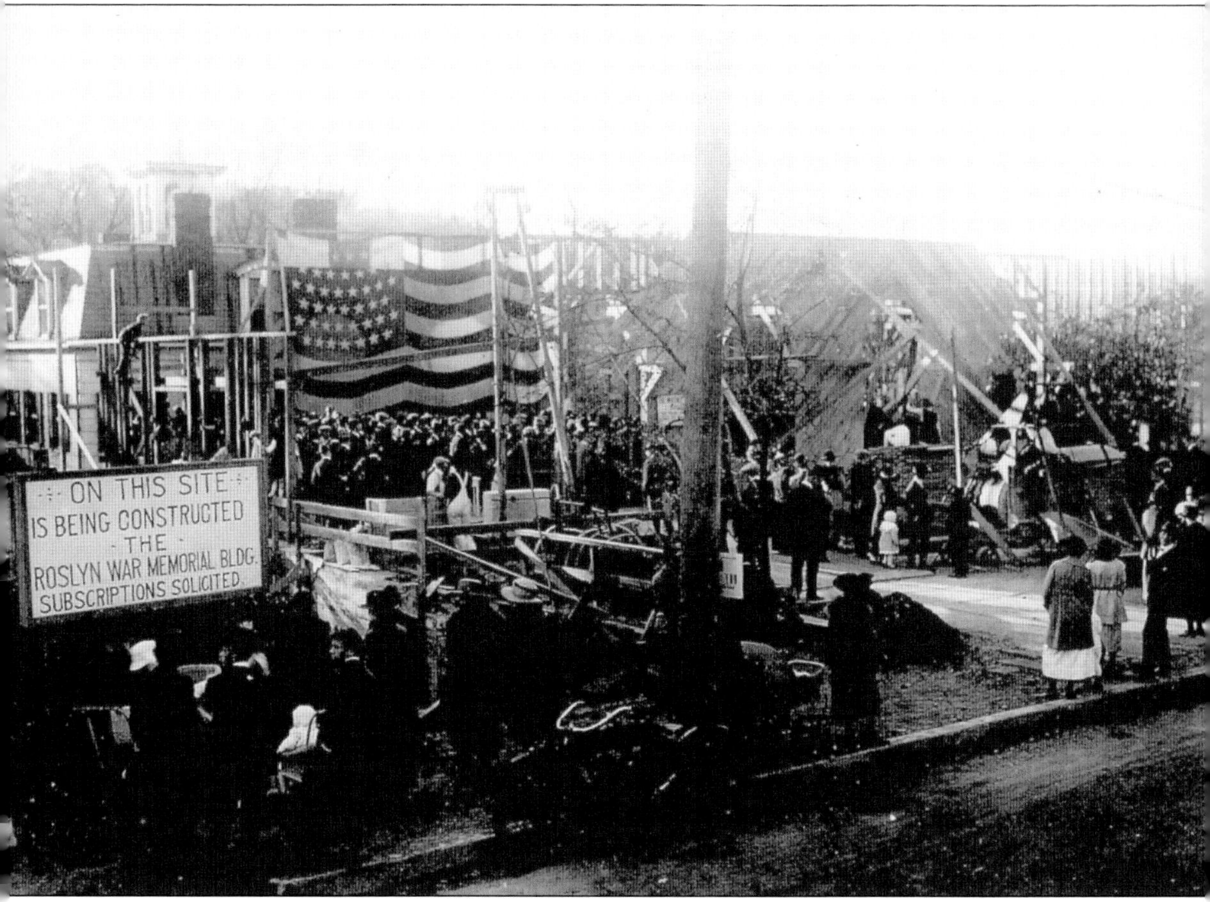

In 1919, the Roslyn Neighborhood Association began a memorial to Roslyn's World War I servicemen. Harold Godwin's son Frederick Marquand Godwin designed it as a community center, which was quickly funded and built, and it was dedicated in 1921. Here the cornerstone is laid in 1919. The building had a rifle range, bowling alley, basketball court, and pool tables. In its theater, the Works Progress Association (WPA) staged Long Island's federal theater project. Today the building houses the Bryant Library. (Courtesy of the Bryant Library Local History Collection, Roslyn.)

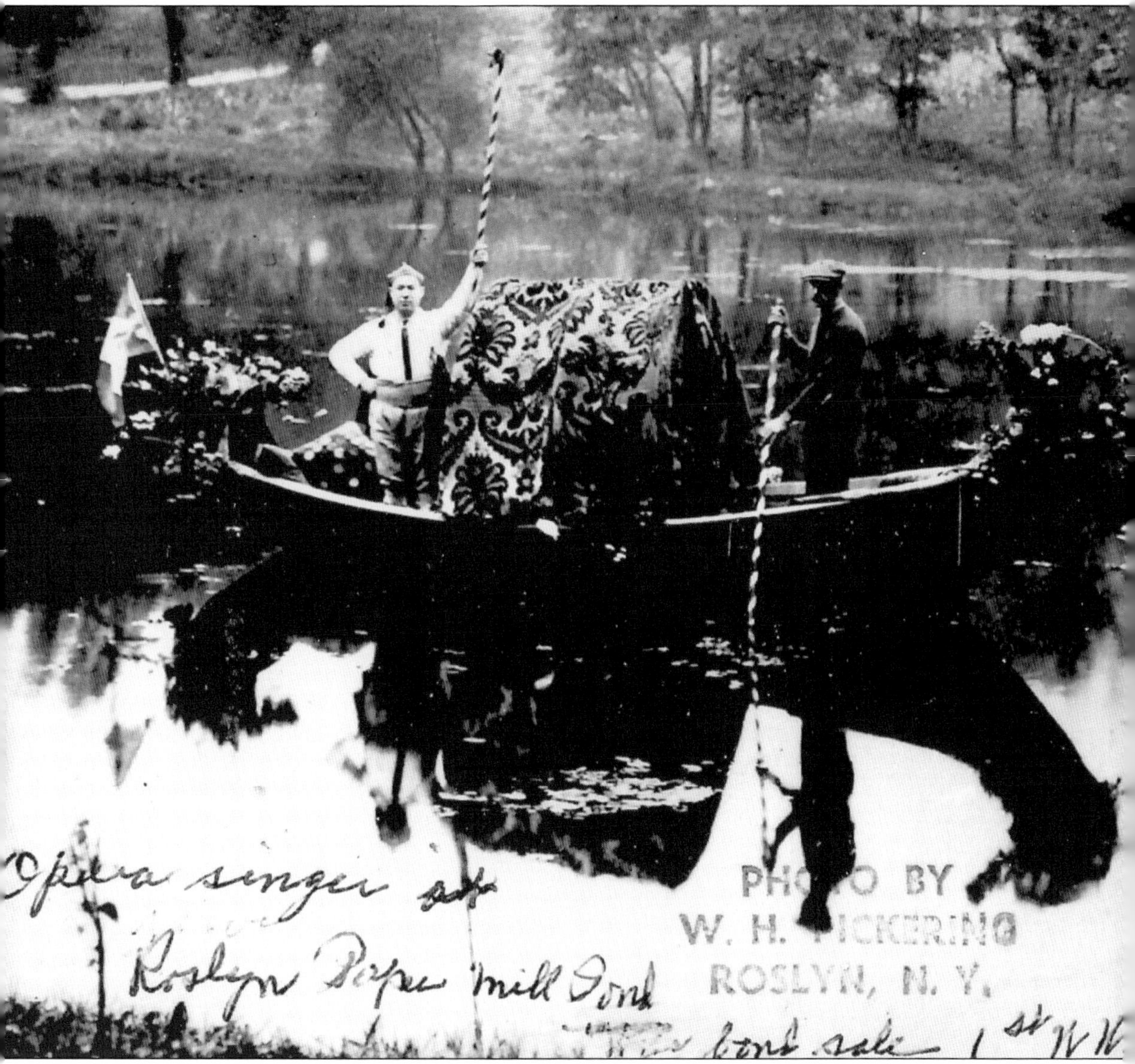

The war memorial's dedication on October 2, 1921, was an extravaganza due to the generosity of the Mackays, who provided the entertainment. The United States Marine Band played, and the tenor Giovanni Diaz sang an aria from *Tosca* and some Spanish songs. Diaz appears above on a gondola on Silver Lake. The commander of the American Legion, headquartered in the paper mill replica in the park, accepted a bronze memorial tablet bearing 242 servicemen's names. Later that memorable afternoon, another concert was held at Harbor Hill. (Courtesy of RLS.)

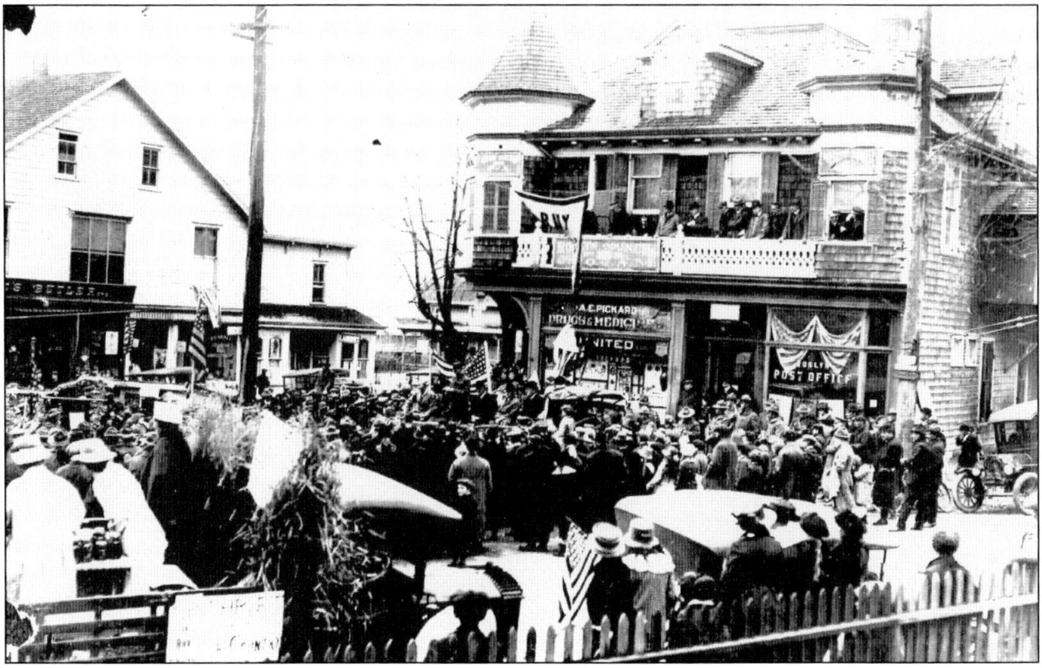

The World War I era brought intense local and national spirit to Roslyn; organizations and individuals were deeply patriotic and committed to community improvement. Throughout the war years, Roslynians rallied to support the war effort and to buy Liberty Bonds. Here, in 1917 or 1918, hundreds are gathered with bunting and flags at the plaza in front of the post office and Pickard's drugstore. (Courtesy of RLS.)

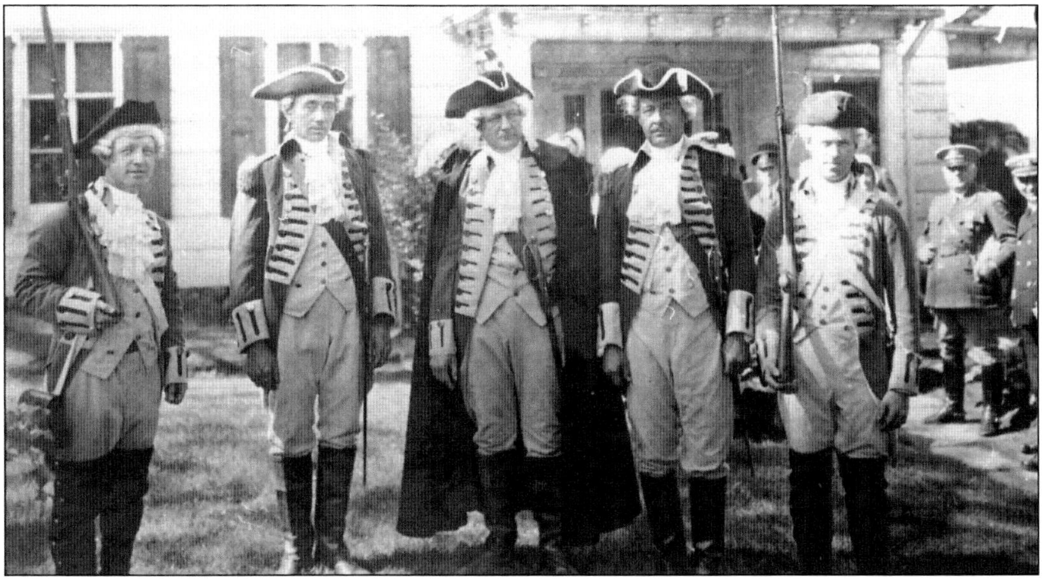

Roslyn has never forgotten the long-ago day when George Washington paid a visit. Hendrick Onderdonk was honored then, and the house the nation's first president entered is venerated yet today. As the Washington Manor restaurant, it features Colonial atmosphere and fare and occasionally hosts a reenactment, like the one shown above in 1933. (Courtesy of the Nassau County Museum Collection, Long Island Studies Institute.)

Six

COUNTRY LIFE AND SUBURBS

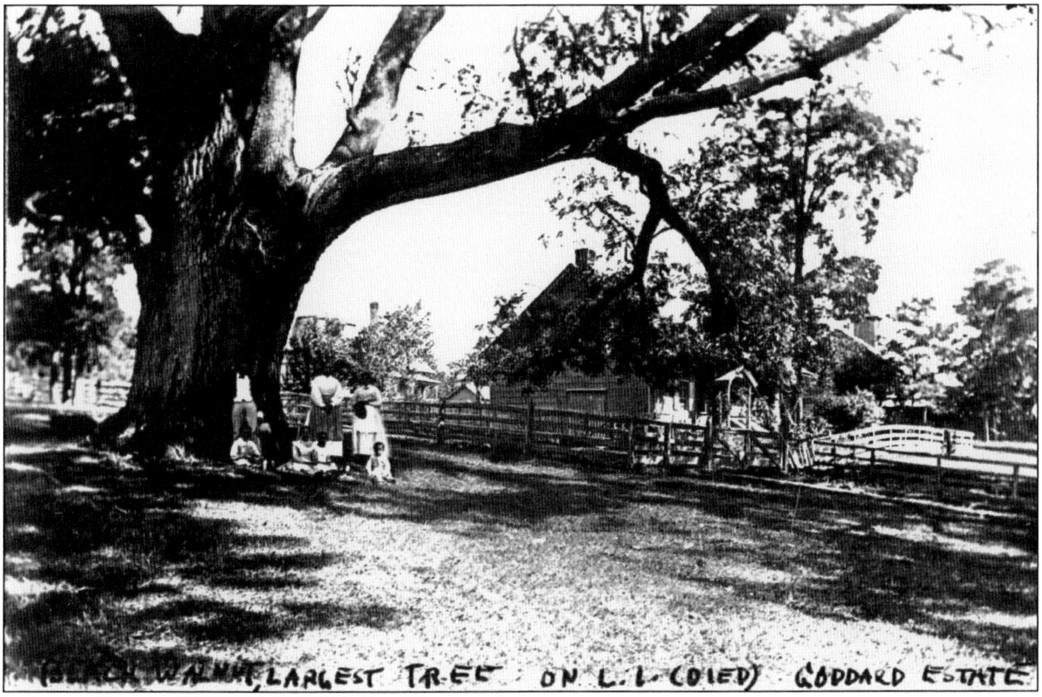

Roslyn has attracted country houses since William Cullen Bryant came to Cedar Mere in 1843. Bryant created a rural retreat by purchasing hundreds of acres; along with the land came houses, including the *c.* 1740 Mudge farmhouse, the site of a 1775 Royalist assault. Here the Eatos, an African American family, picnic around 1885 under Long Island's largest black walnut tree, now gone. (Courtesy of the Nassau County Museum Collection, Long Island Studies Institute.)

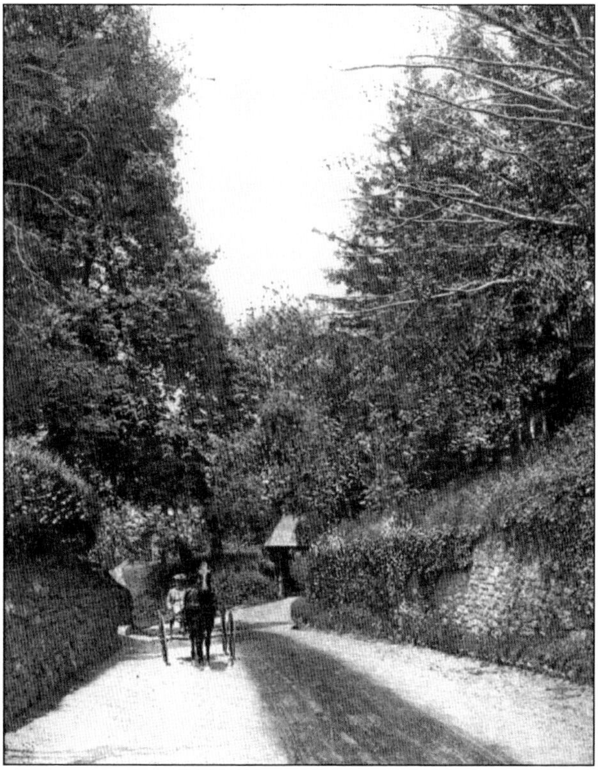

Early-20th-century Roslyn Harbor was a rolling, rural place studded with Quaker farmhouses and the more stylish houses and cottages designed by William Cullen Bryant's architect friends. Bryant Avenue, shown here around 1900, was—and is—its major thoroughfare, running parallel with the eastern shore of Hempstead Harbor. (Courtesy of John and Michelle Santos.)

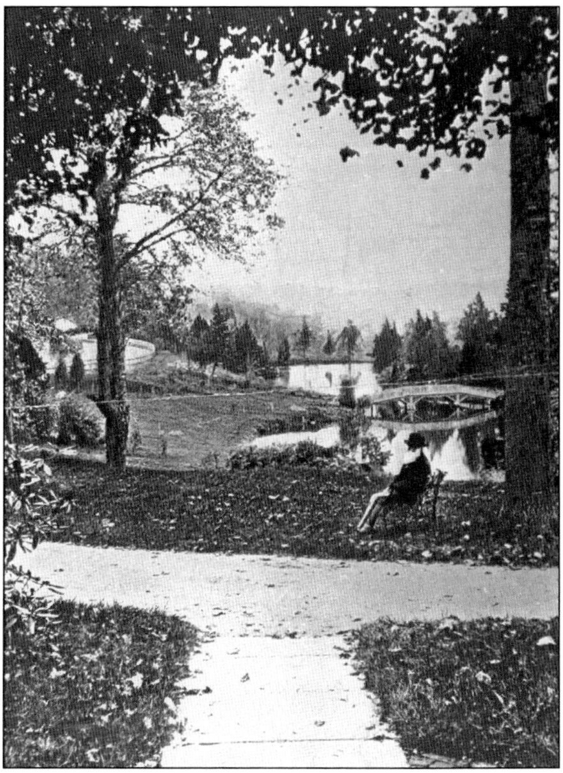

William Cullen Bryant, aged 76 in 1870, sits in his favorite spot outside Cedar Mere's front door overlooking the pond (or mere), its rustic bridge, and Hempstead Harbor beyond. The elements of this scene survive to this day and are among the most beautiful features of Roslyn. (Courtesy of the Nassau County Museum Collection, Long Island Studies Institute.)

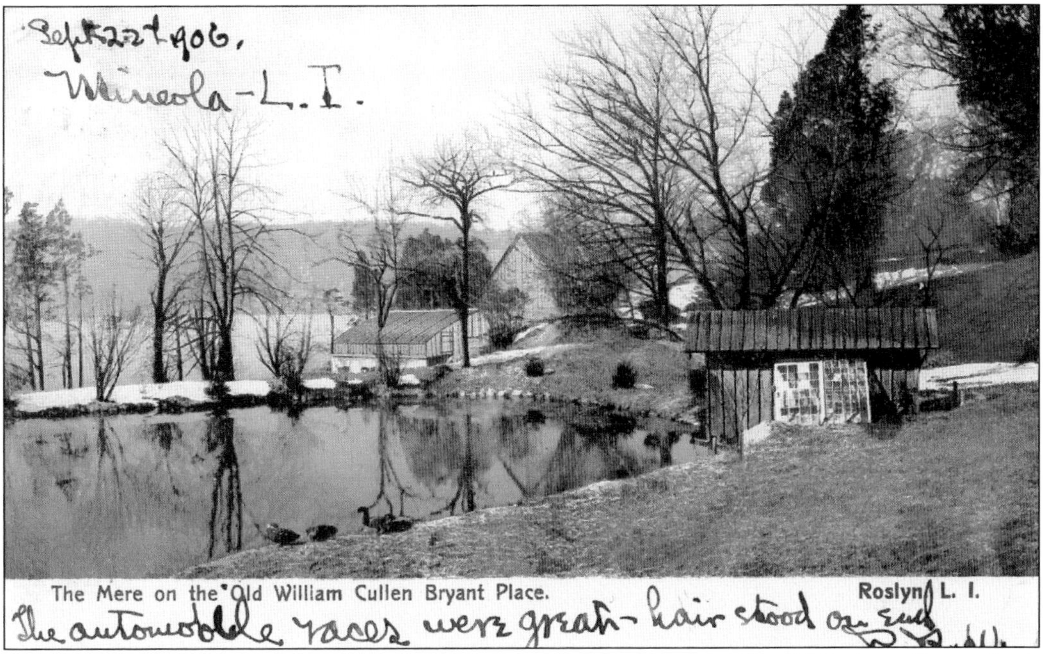

Bryant enjoyed planning his gardens and grounds, as did his grandson Harold Godwin. Bryant built the little punt house on the lake around 1861, and Godwin put the cold frame on its south side. Godwin also built the greenhouse (center of view) in 1905, replacing Bryant's forcing shed. Below, Harold Godwin's wife Elizabeth Marquand stands, around 1905, on the rustic bridge that crossed the lower end of the pond from 1876 until 1916. (Above, courtesy of John and Michelle Santos; below, courtesy of the Nassau County Department of Parks, Recreation and Museums, Cedarmere.)

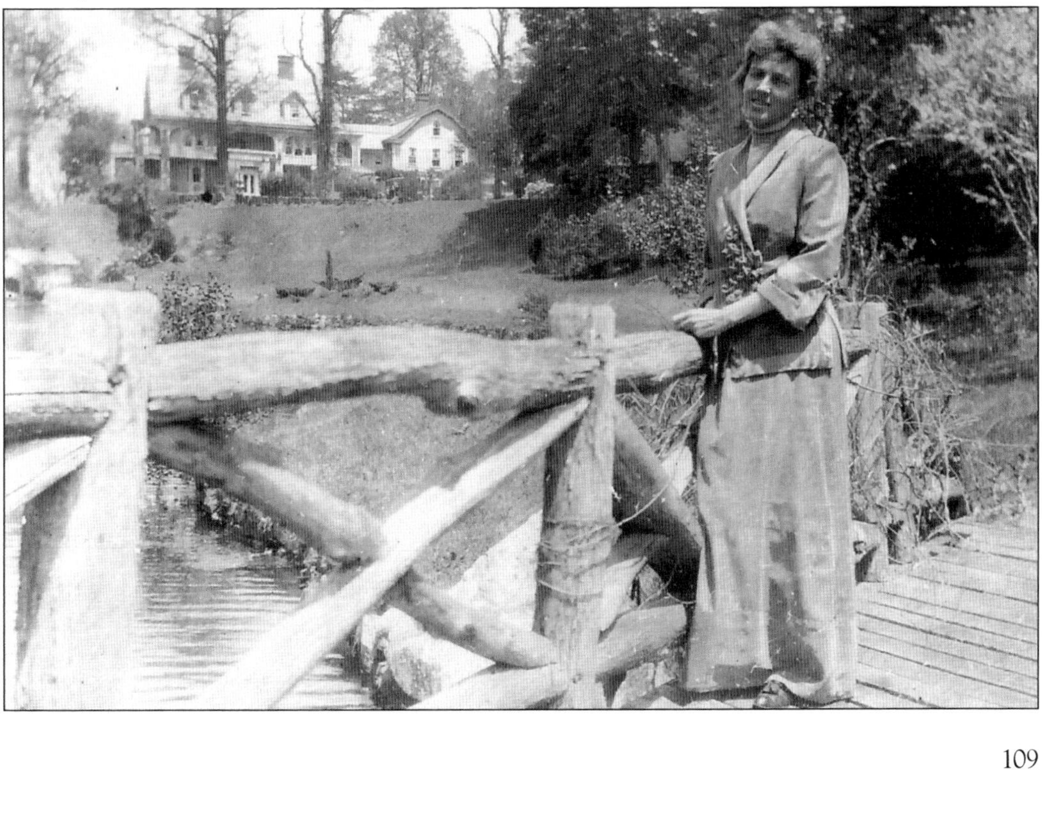

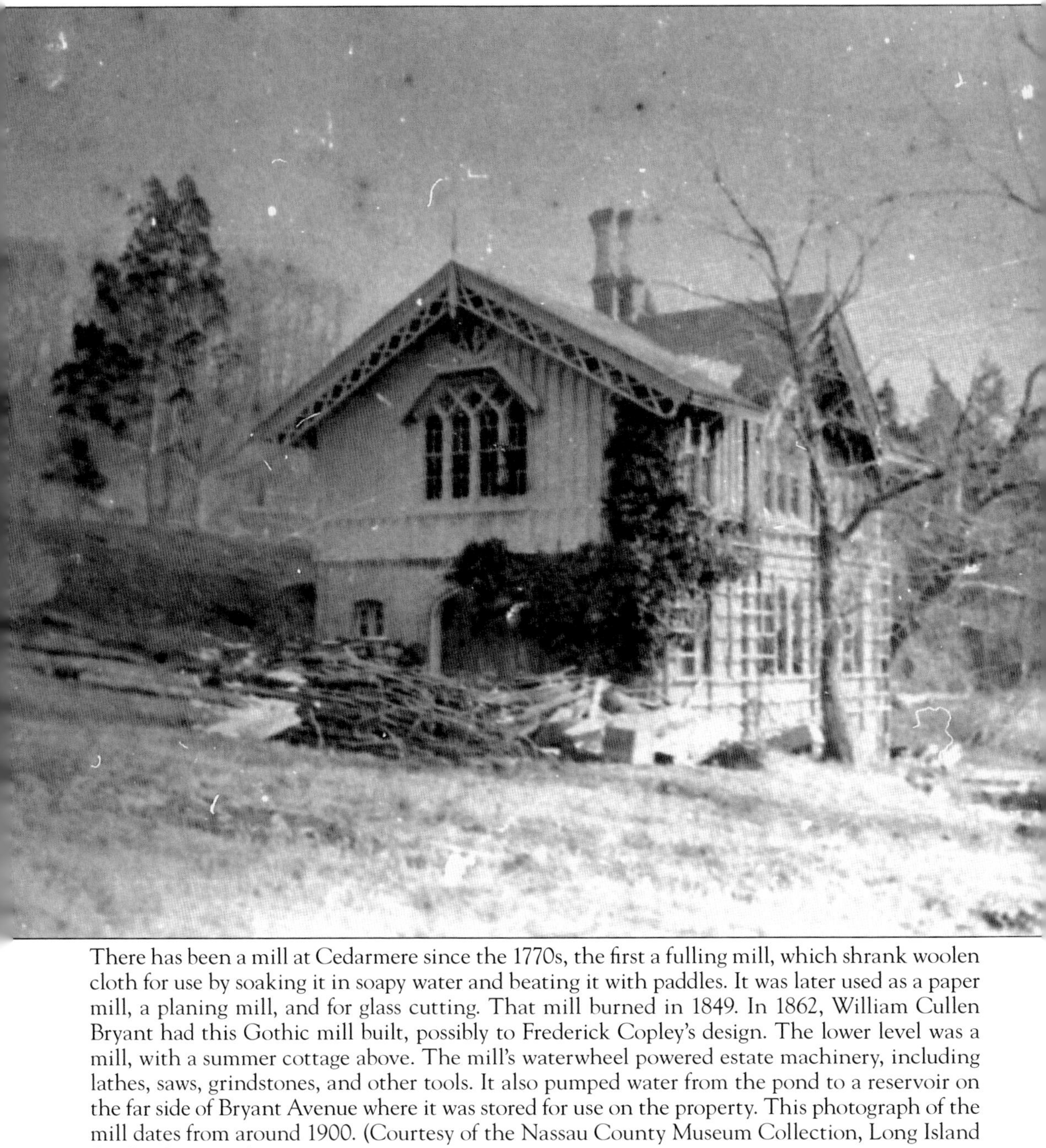

There has been a mill at Cedarmere since the 1770s, the first a fulling mill, which shrank woolen cloth for use by soaking it in soapy water and beating it with paddles. It was later used as a paper mill, a planing mill, and for glass cutting. That mill burned in 1849. In 1862, William Cullen Bryant had this Gothic mill built, possibly to Frederick Copley's design. The lower level was a mill, with a summer cottage above. The mill's waterwheel powered estate machinery, including lathes, saws, grindstones, and other tools. It also pumped water from the pond to a reservoir on the far side of Bryant Avenue where it was stored for use on the property. This photograph of the mill dates from around 1900. (Courtesy of the Nassau County Museum Collection, Long Island Studies Institute.)

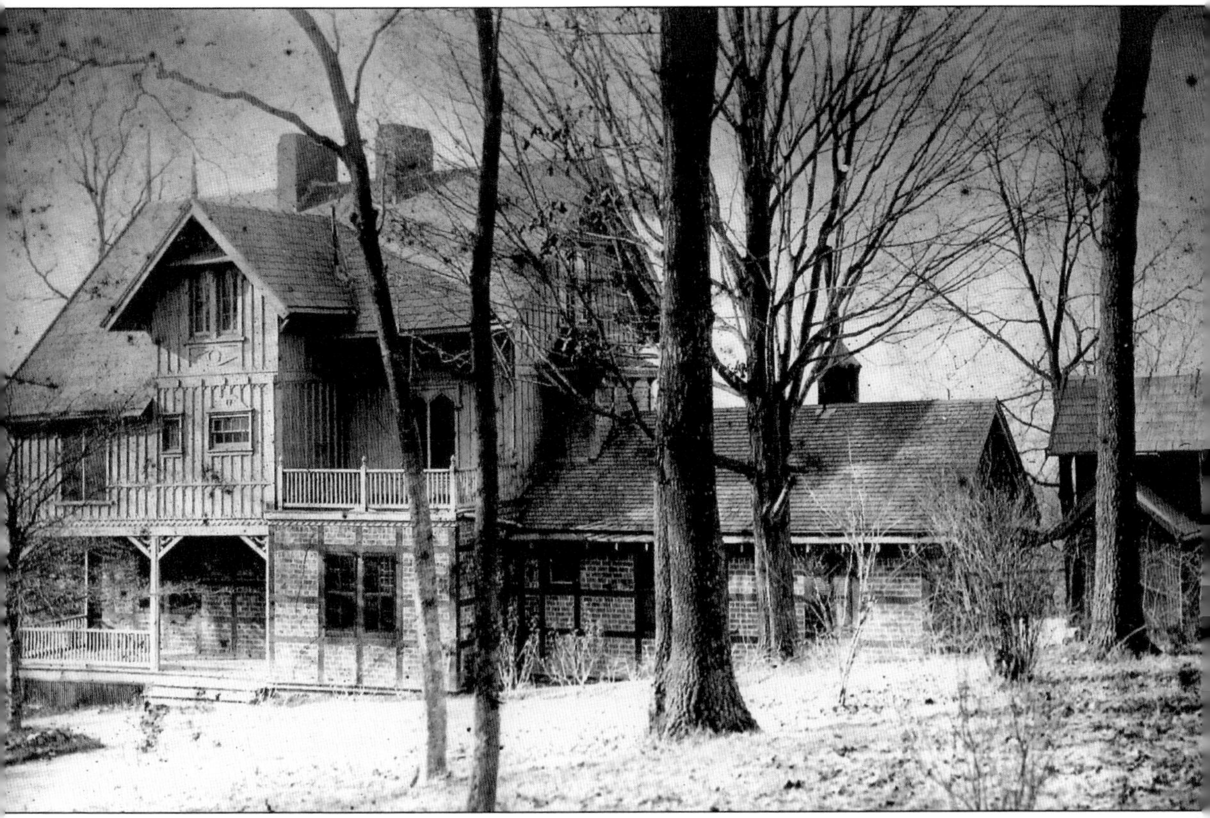

Bryant built many houses for relatives, employees, and visiting friends. Designed by Frederick Copley in 1862, this pretty Gothic Revival house was published that year as "a gardener's cottage" in *Woodward's Country Homes*. Bryant regarded the cottage as the home of his friend Jerusha Dewey, sister of the Reverend Dr. Orville Dewey. Later two spinster cousins of Bryant's wife Fanny lived in it. (Courtesy of RLS.)

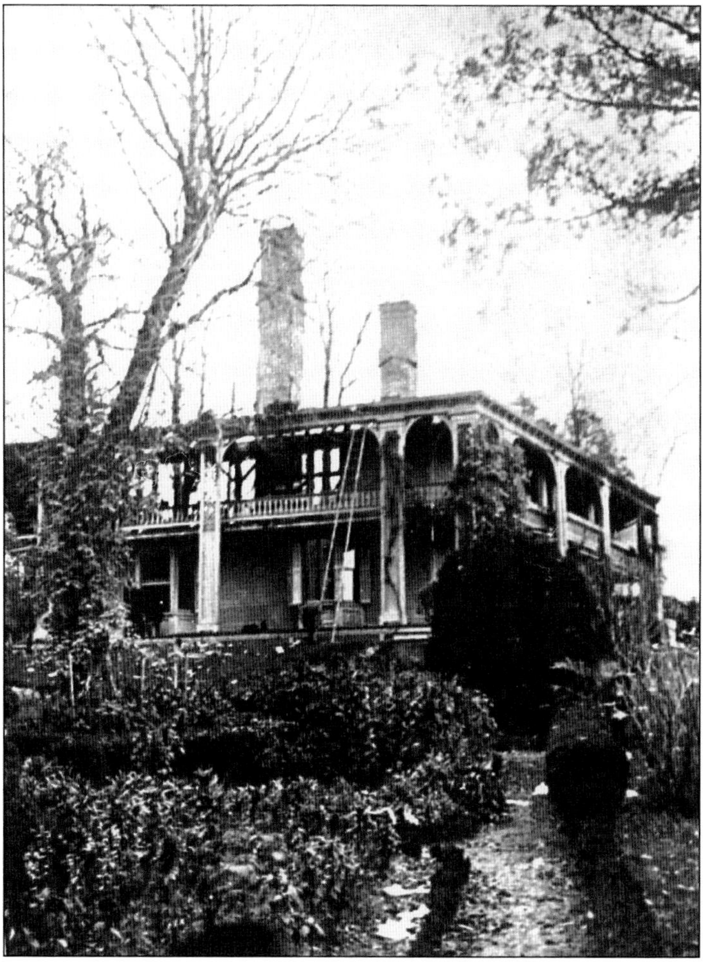

On the afternoon of November 15, 1902, a fire broke out in the servants' wing at Cedarmere. Roslyn Rescue Hook and Ladder raced to the scene, but by dark most of the house was gone. Harold Godwin, examining the ruins, admired the "thought and knowledge" that had gone into the original Quaker farmhouse. He noted the huge oak plates that bore the floor weight and the chimneys, still perfect after a century of use and a major fire. He rebuilt the house much as it had been, but modernized it for comfort and fireproofing. The Godwins lived in the rebuilt house (below) until Elizabeth Love died in 1975. (Courtesy of the Nassau County Museum Collection, Long Island Studies Institute.)

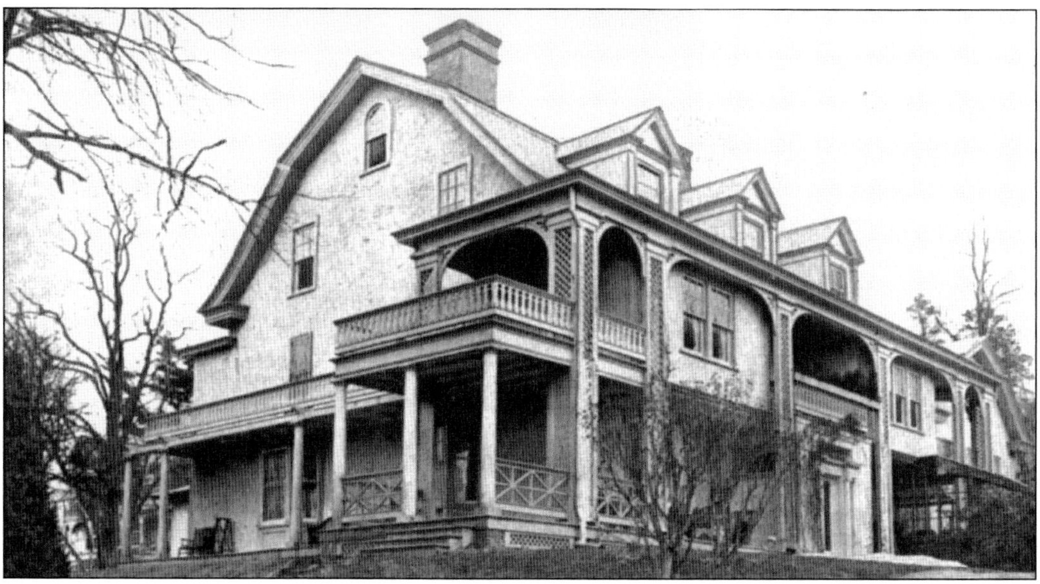

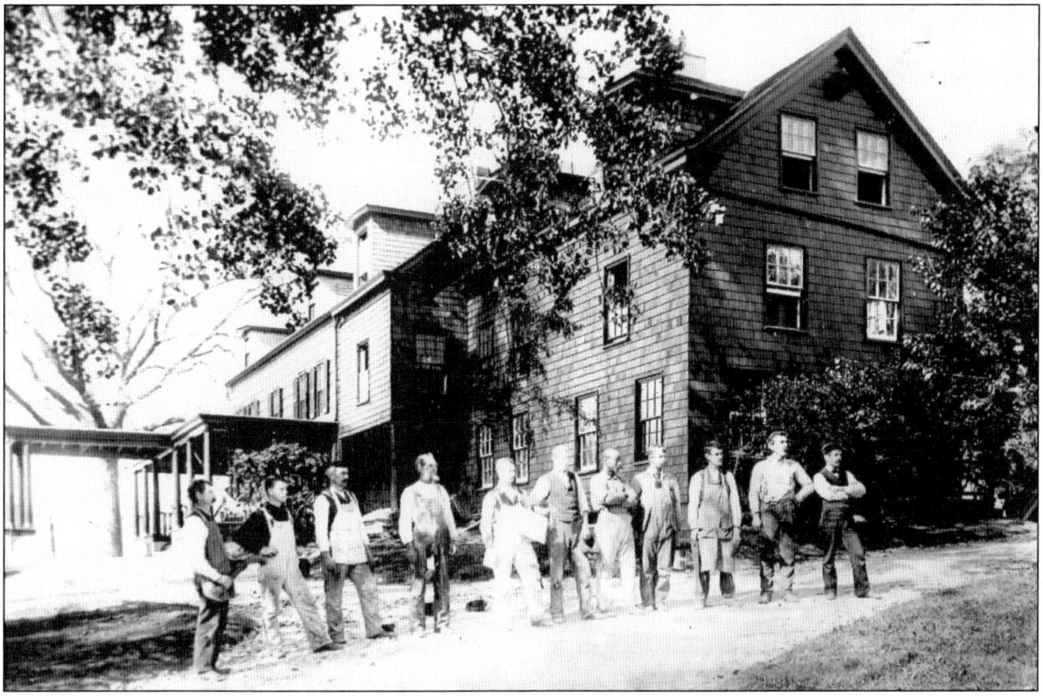

Roslyn estates employed local craftsmen and gave rise to new businesses. Above, a crew of 11 carpenters pauses in 1893 near the porte cochere (left) they have just built at the great old Roslyn Harbor house Willowmere for Ellen and Gen. Elijah Ward. Below, laborers from Hicks Nurseries in Westbury transplant a mature beech tree at a Roslyn estate. Henry Hicks transformed his father's fruit-tree nursery that catered to farmers into a specialized concern that moved large specimen trees for estate landscaping. (Above, courtesy of RLS; below, courtesy of the Nassau County Museum Collection, Long Island Studies Institute.)

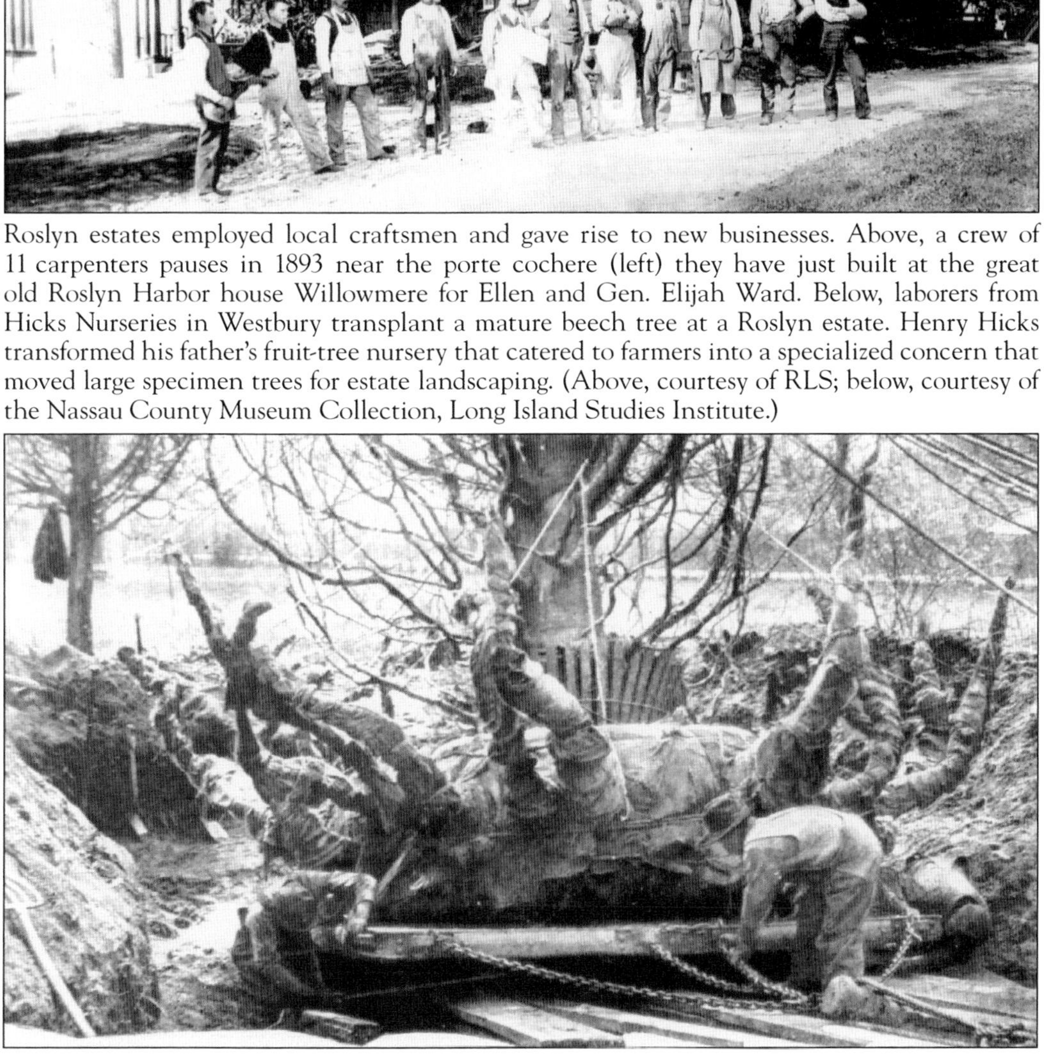

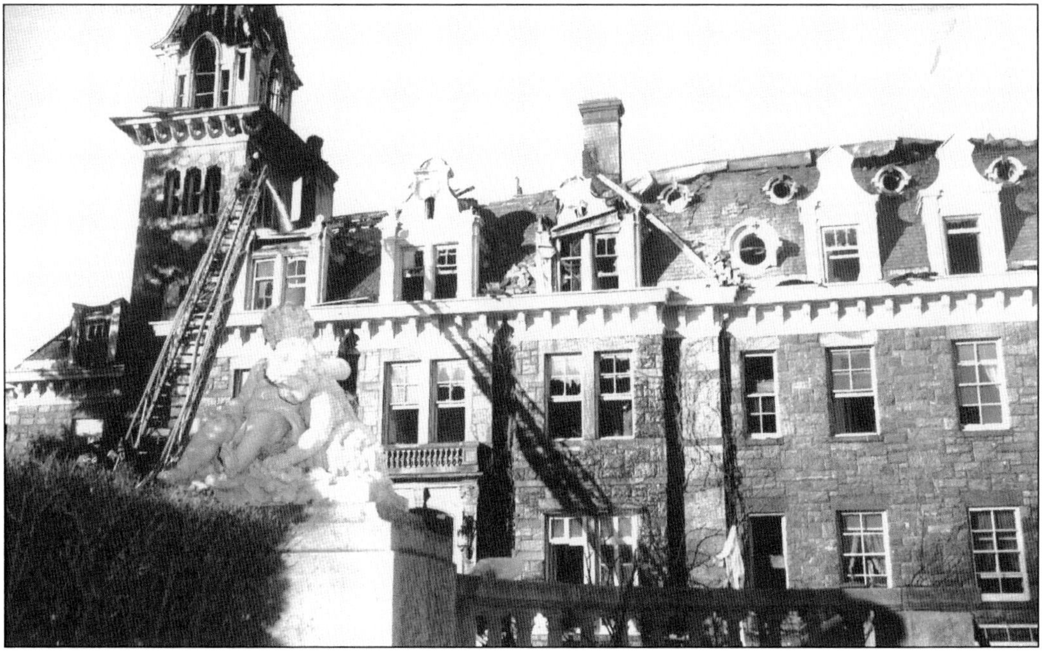

In the mid-1870s, Thomas Clapham of Connecticut sailed around Hempstead Harbor looking for a house site. Deciding on Stephen Taber's land, Clapham paid a stiff price and in 1867 engaged prominent New York architect Jacob Wrey Mould to build the Italianate villa he named Stone House. Around 1885, Clapham lost his fortune and moved to a cottage on his property. In 1906, New York department store magnate Benjamin Stern bought the property and rebuilt it as a French chateau with gardens, greenhouses, and gate lodge. In 1960, the house was consumed by a fire (above); a 1963 restoration (below) resulted in a much smaller house. (Above, courtesy of the Queens Borough Public Library, Long Island Division, Illustrations Collection–Roslyn; below, courtesy of RLS.)

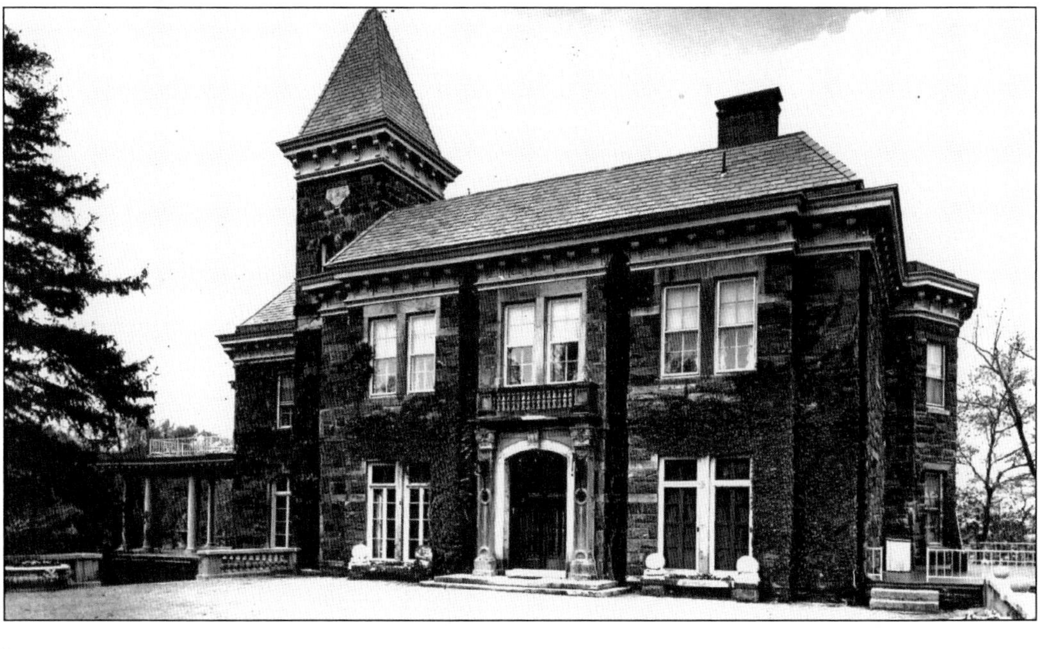

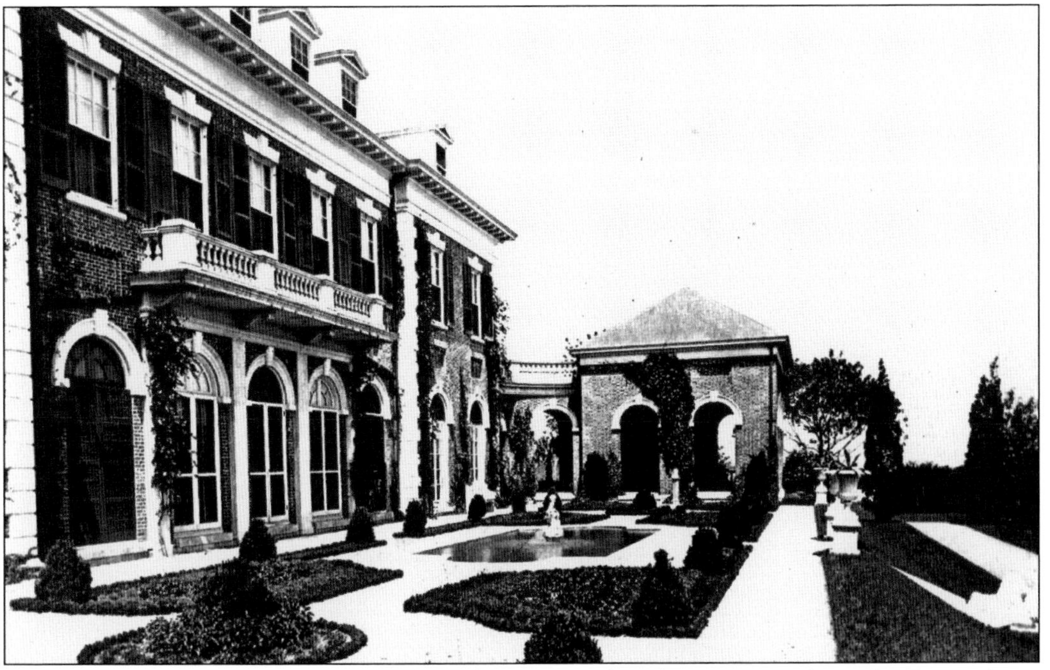

Around 1890, writer and editor Lloyd Stephens Bryce bought 200 acres from the Bryant heirs and engaged controversial New England architect Ogden Codman to design him a country house. Codman, who with Edith Wharton wrote *The Decoration of Houses*, insisted on the Georgian Revival style. Contractor James K. Davis of East Broadway built the house. In 1917, the estate was purchased for Childs Frick, paleontologist and son of coke-and-steel magnate Henry Clay Frick. It was Childs Frick's idea that the Village of Roslyn Harbor be incorporated. He and his wife Frances had the Bryce house remodeled and named Clayton. In 1930, the Fricks had landscape architect Marion Cruger Coffin develop a plan for elaborate formal gardens. In 1969, after Childs Frick's death, the property became the Nassau County Museum of Art. The image above was taken around 1895, whereas the one below is from the 1930s. (Courtesy of RLS.)

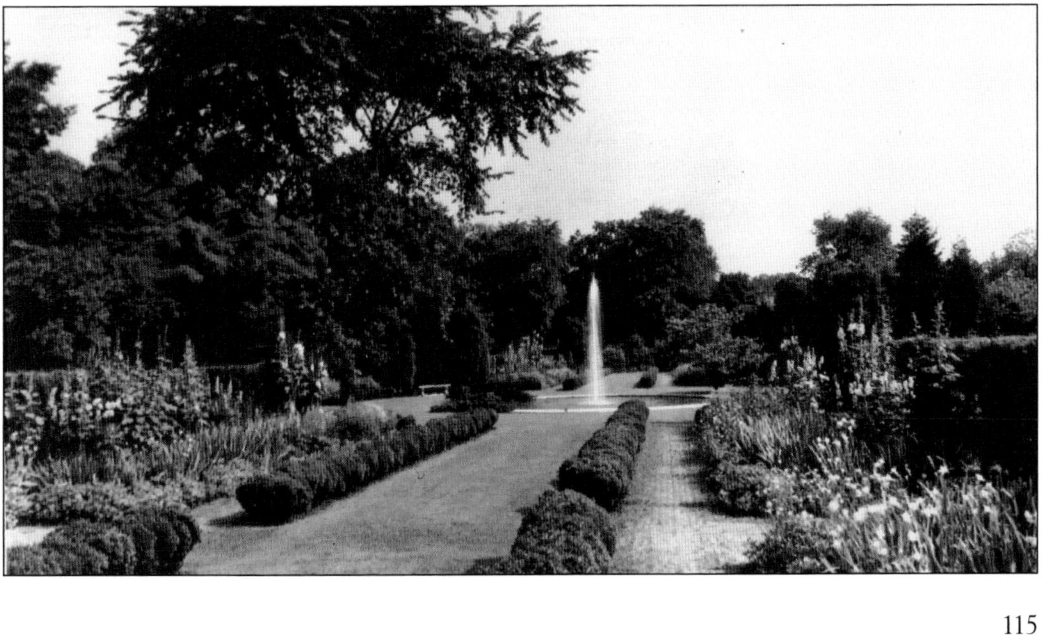

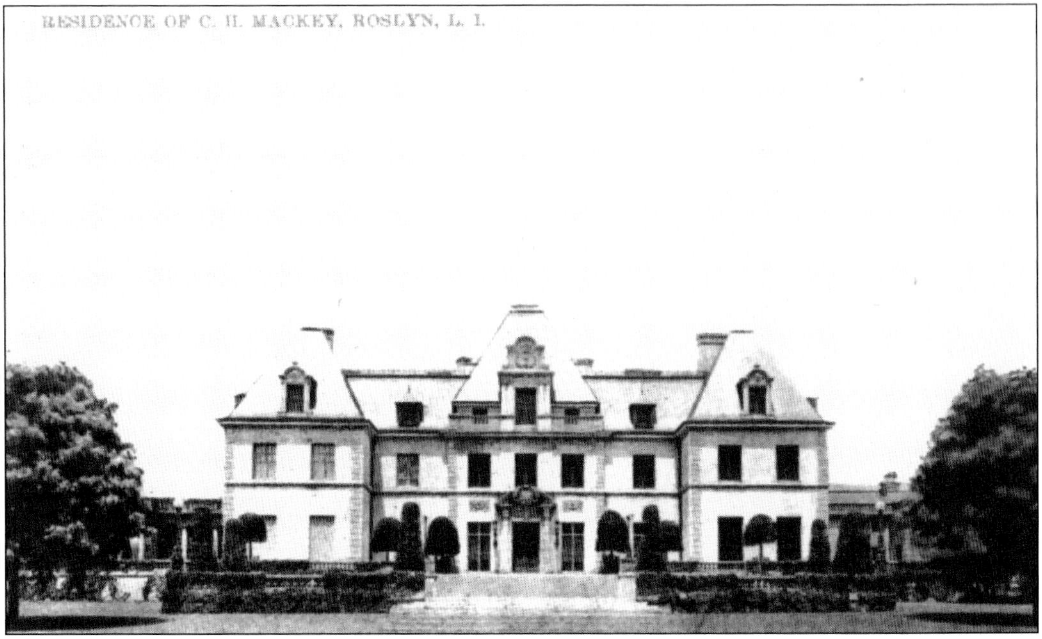

In 1898, financier Clarence H. Mackay, son of silver mogul John W. Mackay, married Knickerbocker debutante Katherine Duer. As a wedding present, his parents gave them 500 acres including Harbor Hill. The Mackays meant their country house to impress. They engaged architect Stanford White and directed him to base the design on the French Renaissance chateau Maisons-Lafitte. They got a pale-toned limestone house of 50 rooms centering a vast complex that included stables and garages, casino, dairy and poultry houses, kennels, farmhouses, barns, greenhouses, cottages, and more. The mansion was approached through a gate lodge that echoed the high-roofed pavilions of the main house. It opened to a mile-long drive that curved through a landscape designed by Guy Lowell. (Courtesy of John and Michelle Santos.)

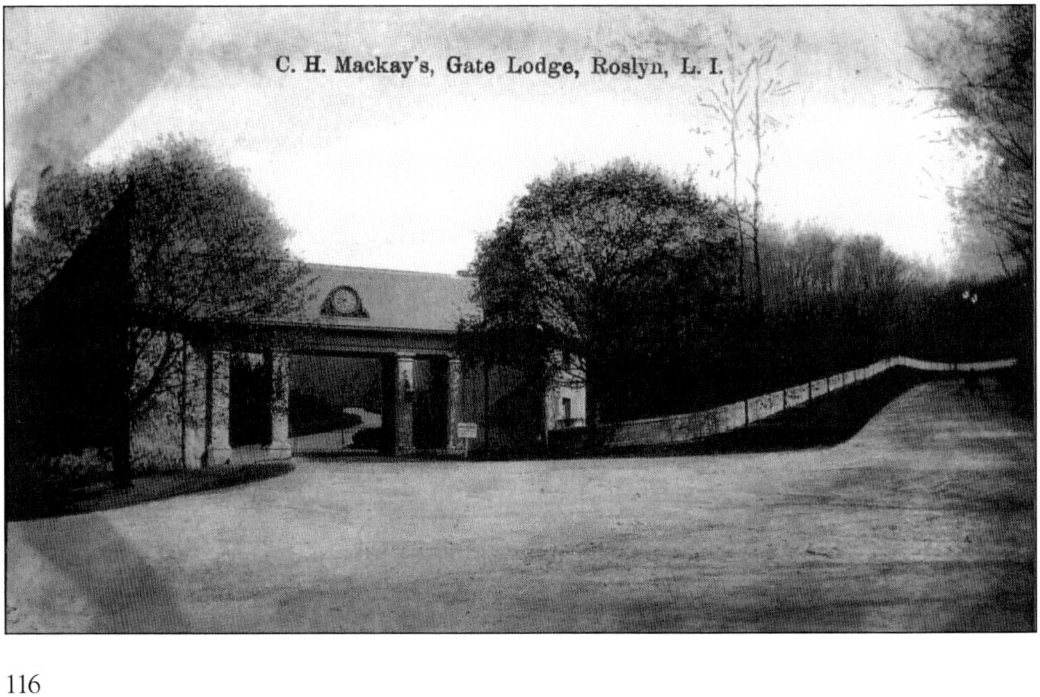

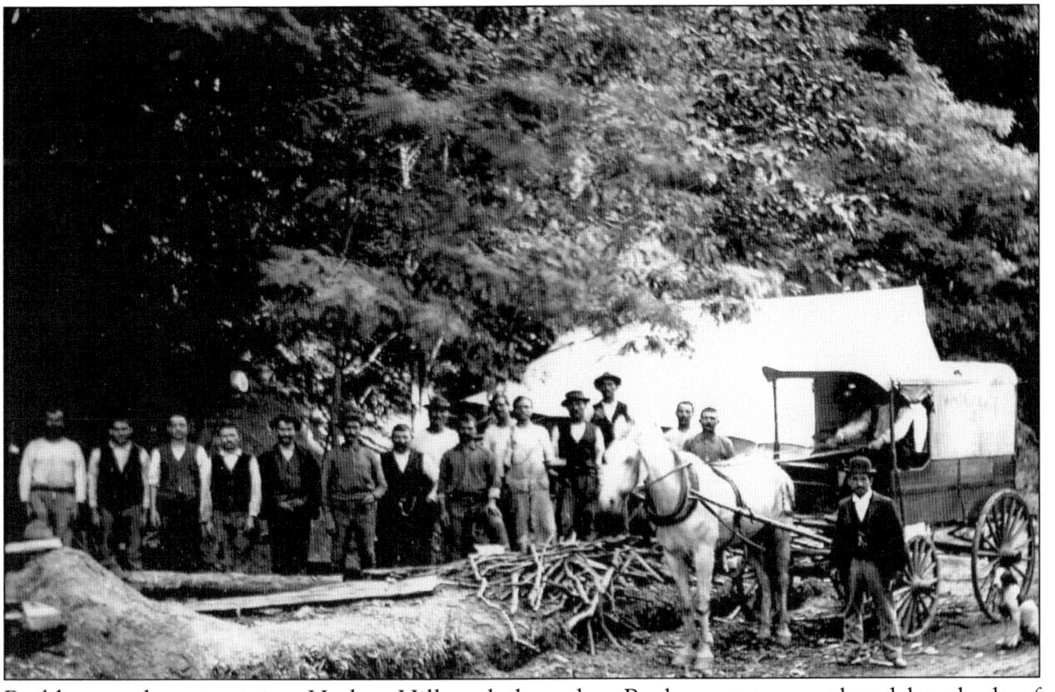

Building and maintaining Harbor Hill and the other Roslyn estates employed hundreds of people and machines. The year 1902 was spent getting the site ready to build the house. Water was a challenge: the Mackays had to put in a pumping station near Roslyn Creek, then pipe water through the village and up the hill to a water tower. Seen around 1902, the crew of 16 men (above) appears to be trenching for the water pipes, while the steamroller (below) works on the network of roads that linked the far-flung corners of the estate. (Courtesy of RLS.)

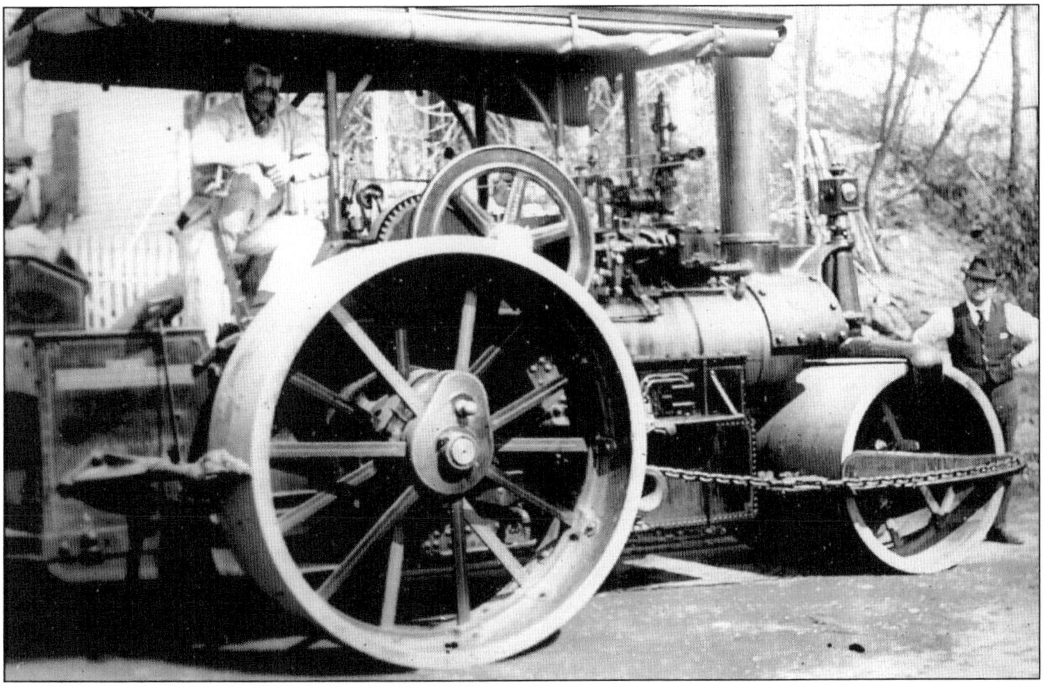

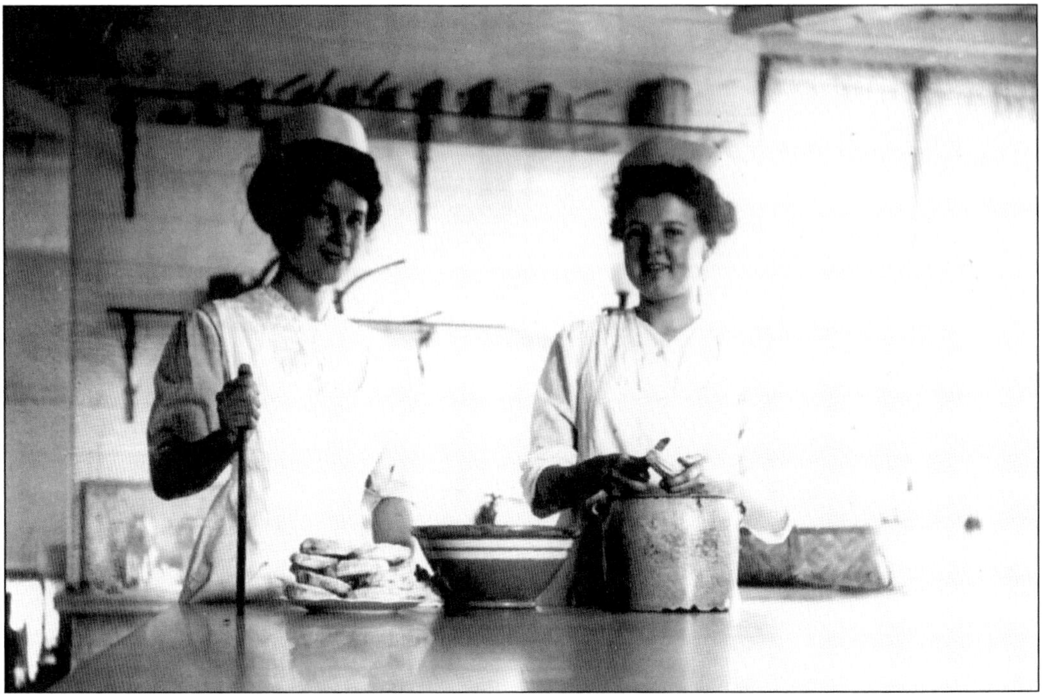

At its peak, Harbor Hill employed around 180 men and women, some Roslyn residents and some hired from other large households. The upper servants lived with their families in cottages on the estate. The kitchen was the fiefdom of a chef, sous-chef, icebox man, and waitresses. Kitchen helpers Lizzie Proudfoot (left) and Minnie Steel are shown above in 1909. The footmen, seen below around 1904, wore brown uniforms to answer the door, wait on the table, clean the dishes, clear up after meals, polish the silver, and help the valet maintain Clarence Mackay's wardrobe. The footmen may be Louis Hall, Charles Podevin, John Fraser, and Jack Bremerer. (Above, courtesy of the Bryant Library Local History Collection, Roslyn; below, courtesy of RLS.)

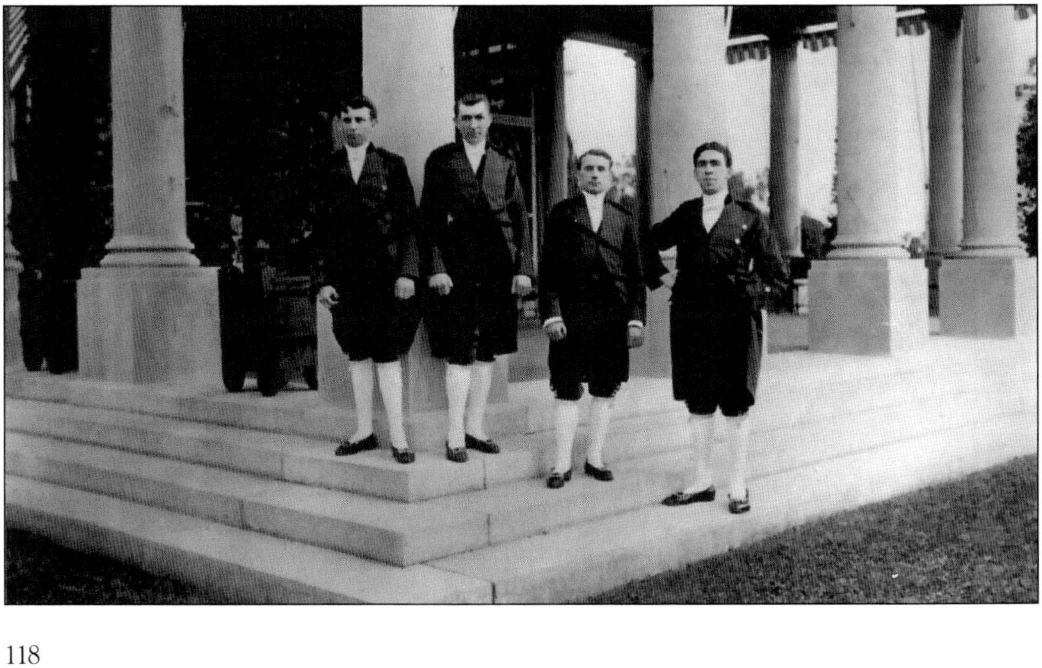

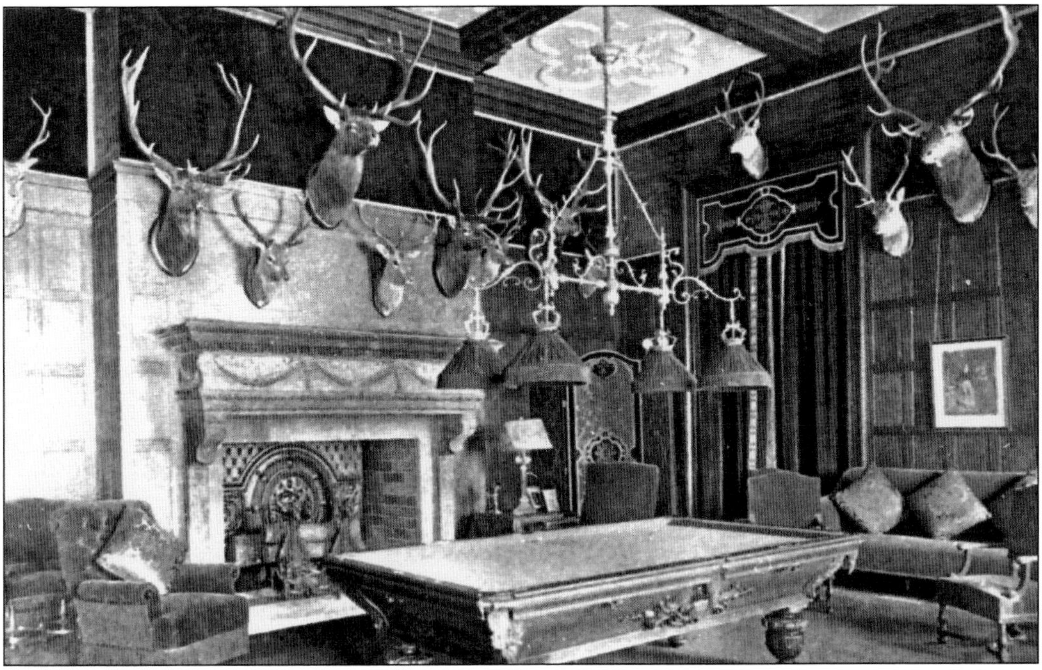

Harbor Hill originally contained this billiard room, but Katherine Mackay soon decided they needed a library. She had Stanford White dismantle the billiard room: dispatching the antlers, altering the paneling, reworking the antique mantel, and hanging tapestries. Clarence H. Mackay used the new room to display his art collection. Below, the stable complex designed by Warren and Wetmore is a Chateauesque structure with twin turrets. The stable head lived on the second floor, which also had sitting and dining rooms for the farm staff. The farm buildings were not meant to be practical: they were picturesque landscape objects, sited so the Mackays would neither hear nor smell them. (Courtesy of the Nassau County Museum Collection, Long Island Studies Institute.)

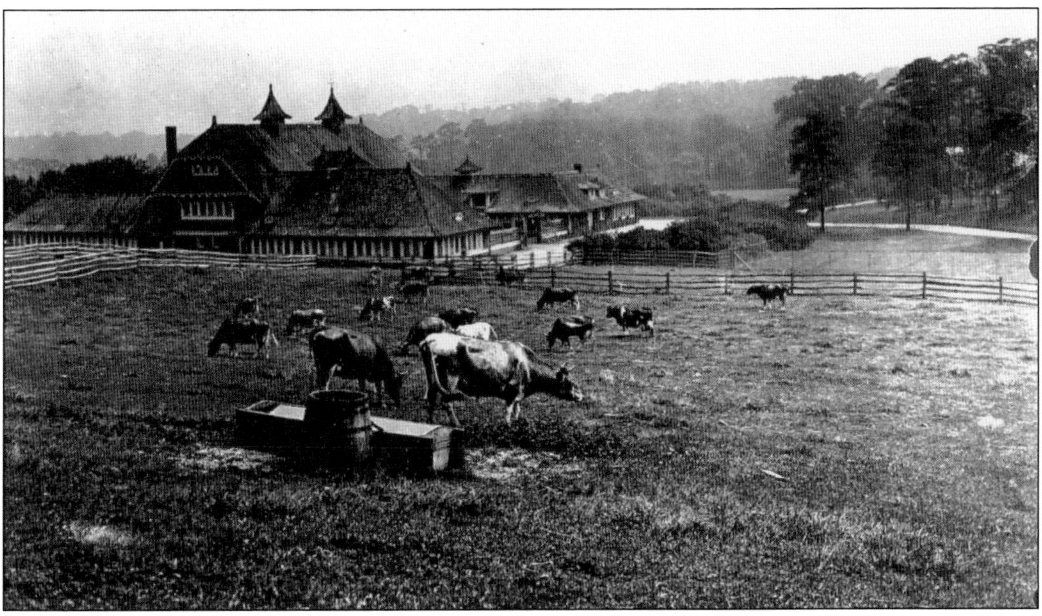

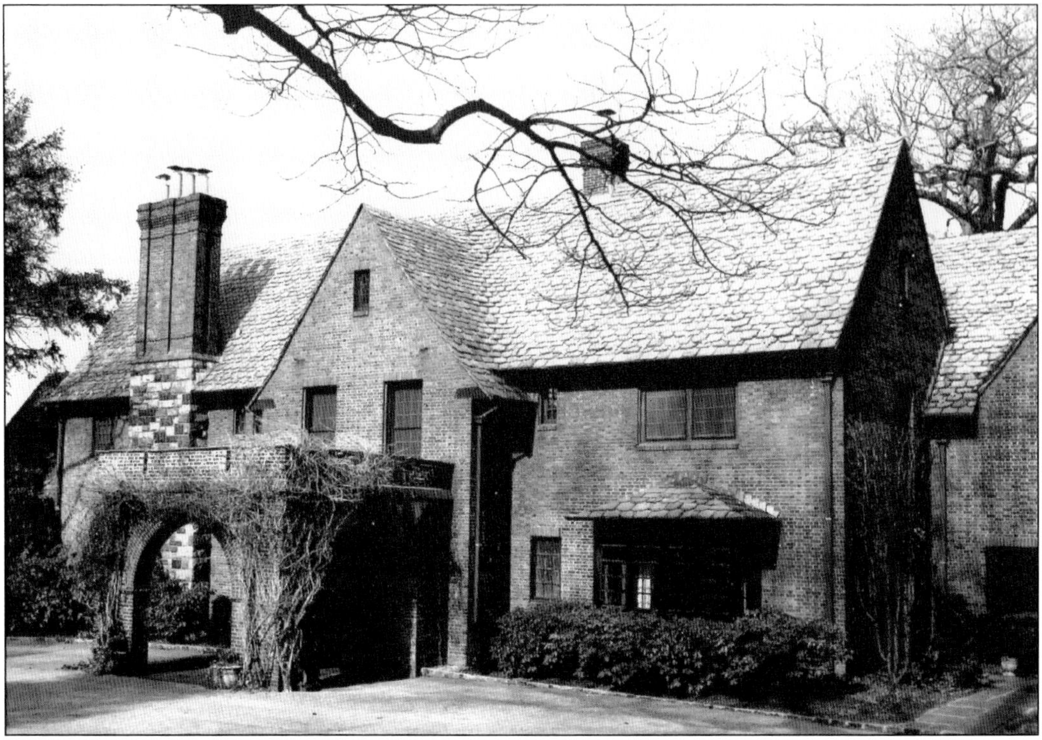

Arthur Williams built two large houses in Roslyn Harbor, first Greenridge on Bryant Avenue (above) in 1916, then after having lived there only four years, Brook Corners (below) on Glenwood Road in 1920. A vice president at the New York Edison Company, Williams retired at age 50 to turn his attention to house building, charitable work and clubs, and to founding the village of Roslyn Harbor. Greenridge is a fine example of Stockbroker Tudor, with its brick walls and steep slate roofs. Brook Corners is a sprawling Mediterranean-villa structure with stuccoed walls and pantiled roofs. It is now the Swan Club restaurant. (Courtesy of RLS.)

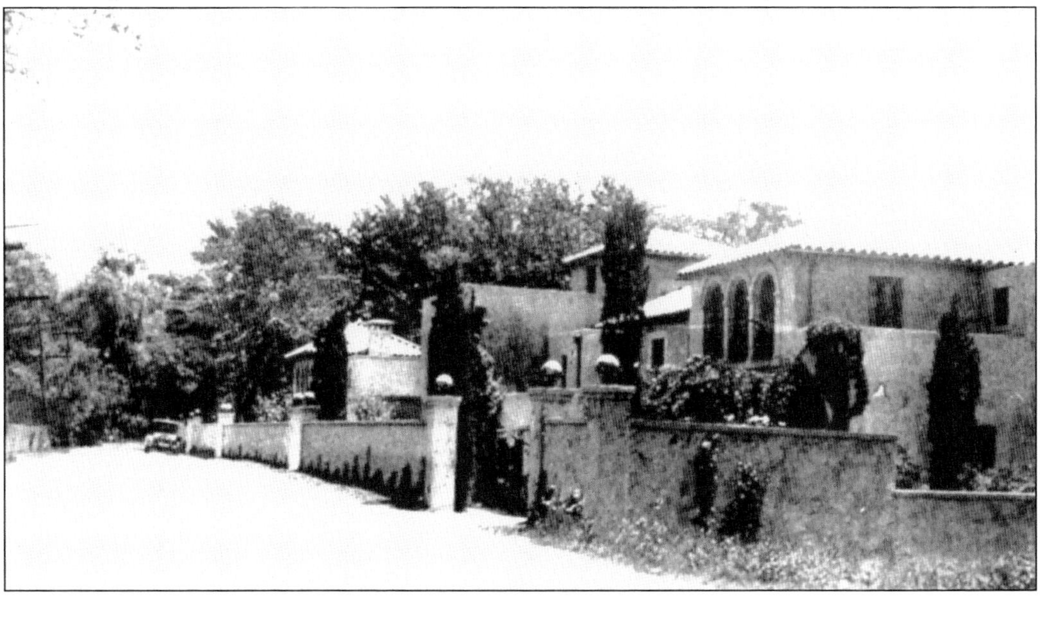

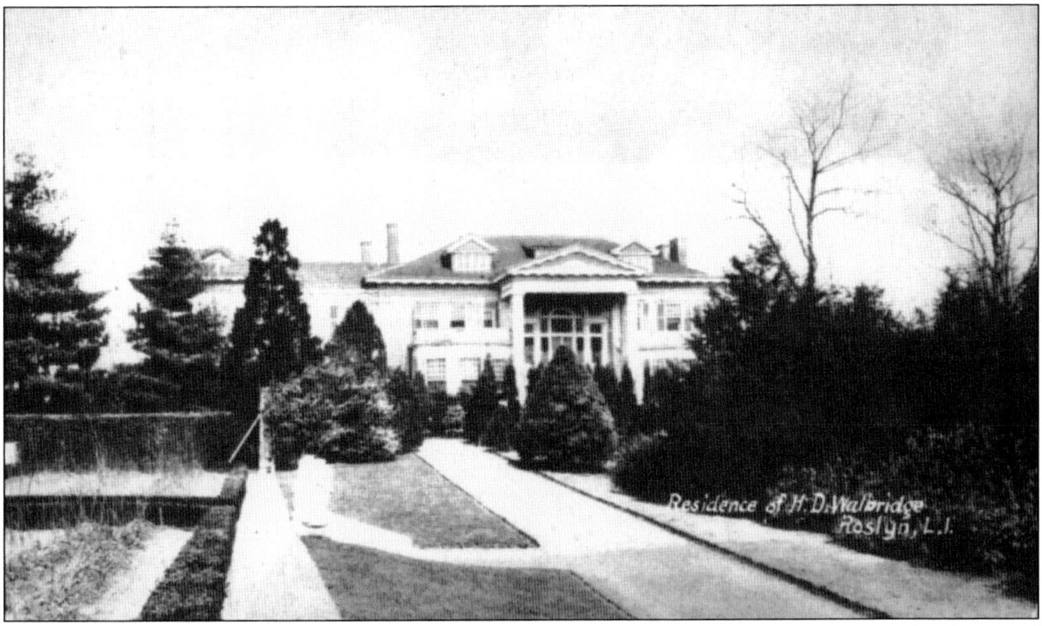

The Colonial Revival house above was built around 1900 for Walter G. Oakman to the design of architect Grosvenor Atterbury. It, along with farm buildings including the stable (below), stood on nearly 200 acres between West Shore Road and Mineola Avenue. Oakman was chairman of the Guaranty Trust Company. After he died in 1922, the estate went to Henry D. Walbridge, who was a trustee of Harold Godwin's gristmill museum. After Roslyn Creek was dredged in 1929, the Walbridges built a yacht boathouse there. The estate was demolished for development in 1946. (Above, courtesy of the Queens Borough Public Library, Long Island Division, Postcard Collection; below, courtesy of RLS.)

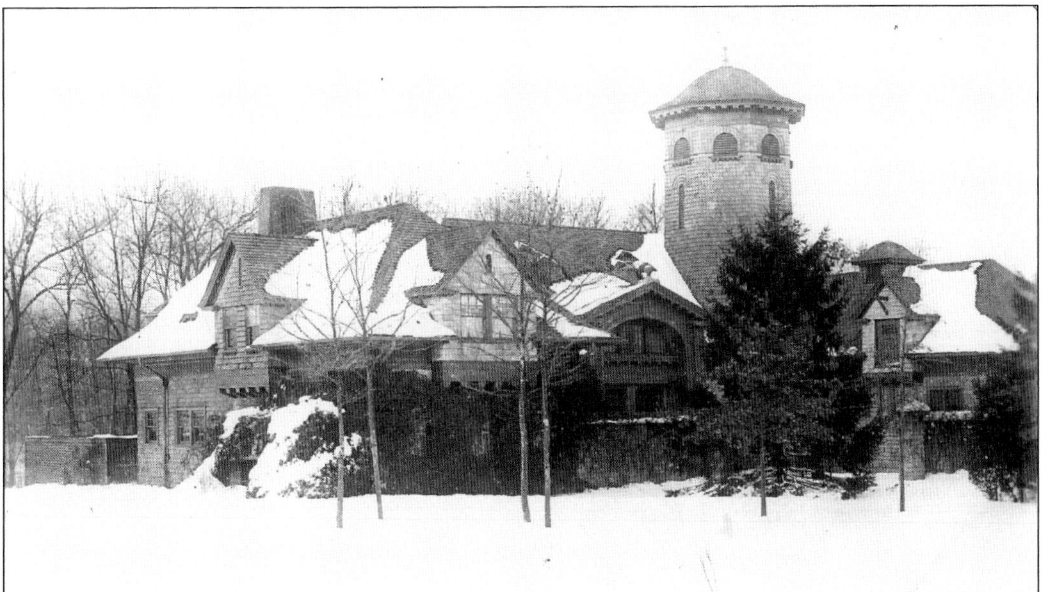

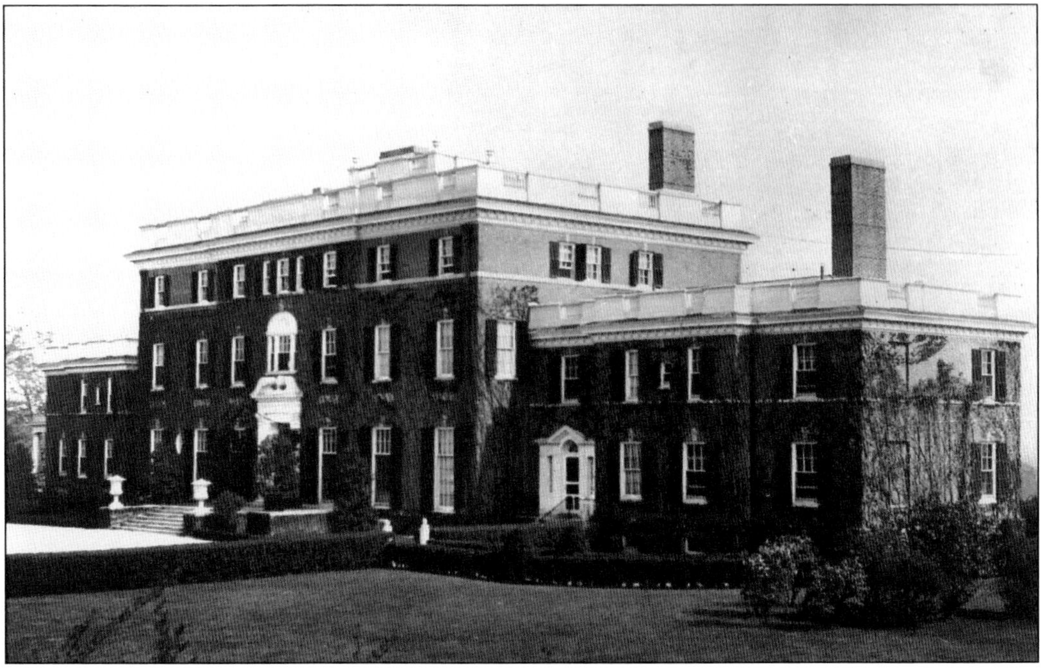

Cassleigh, above, designed by McKim, Mead and White in 1902, belonged to yachtsman Augustus Cass Canfield. It opened onto terraces and sloping lawns designed by Olmsted Brothers. Canfield died as his Georgian Revival house was completed, but his widow and children lived here until 1916. The next owner was mining executive John D. Ryan, who renamed it Derrymore. The house was demolished in 1950, and 100 acres was later acquired by Nassau County for Christopher Morley Park. The William L. Stow house (below) was designed by John Russell Pope in the Renaissance style in 1901. In 1906, Henry Carnegie Phipps bought the estate and renamed it Spring Hill. In 2004 the estate was subdivided for development. (Above, courtesy of the Nassau County Museum Collection, Long Island Studies Institute; below, courtesy of RLS.)

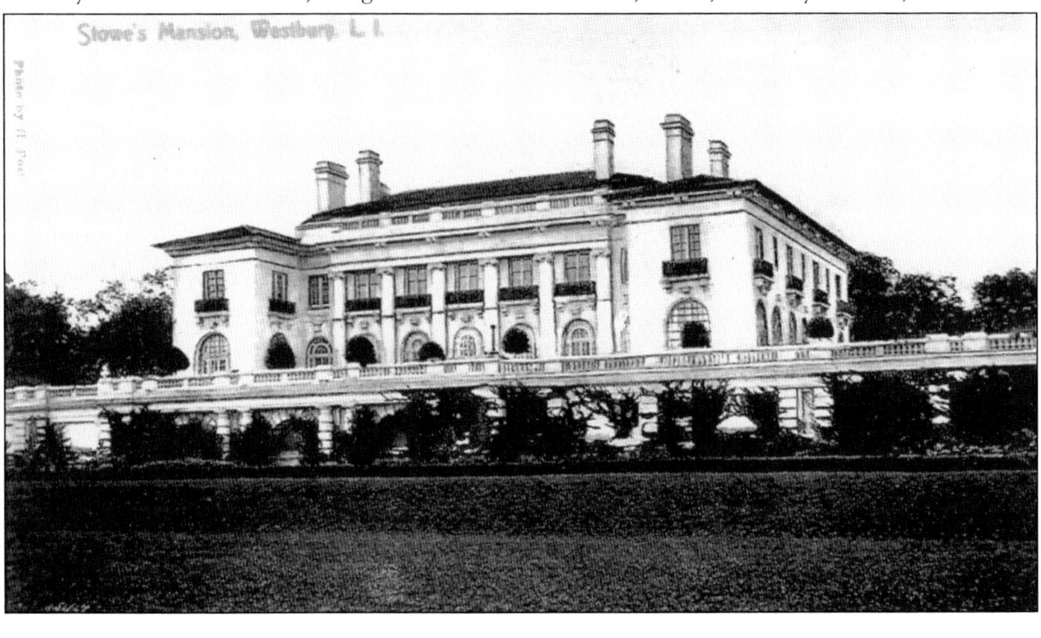

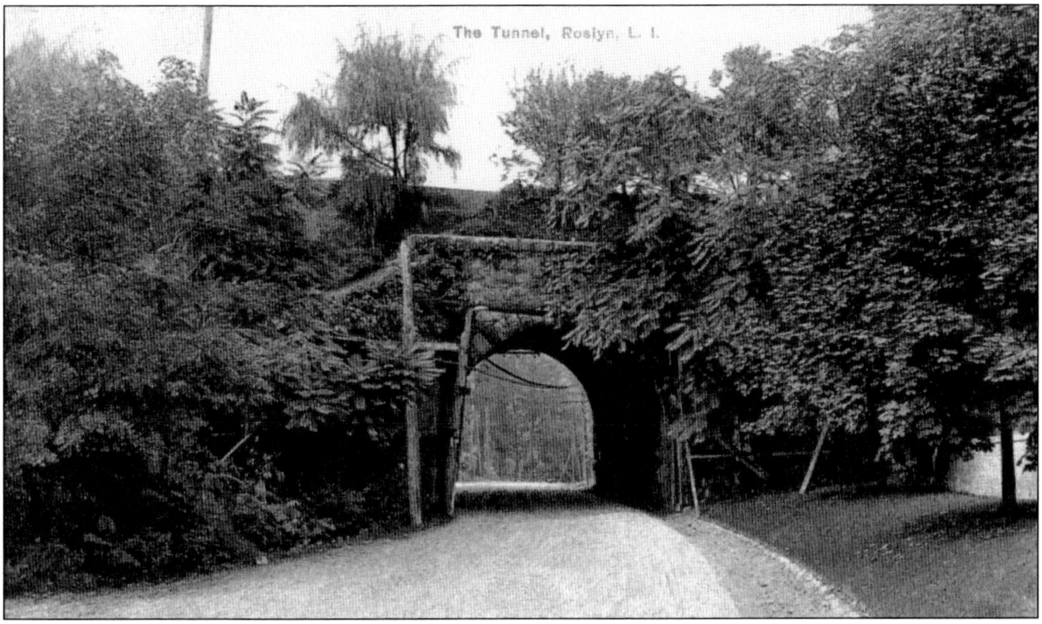

In 1865, Roslyn stonemason Samuel Dugan built the overpass (above) that allowed the Glen Cove branch of the Long Island Railroad to provide a link to New York City via the Hunters Point ferry. Roslyn's first passenger depot was built in 1864, replaced in 1887 by what the newspaper called "the handsomest station on the branch," seen below. The village Roslyn Heights began with the rowdy Bunker Hill neighborhood around the railroad station. Bunker Hill had many good Irish Catholic families, who had to travel to Manhasset for church. Around 1865, wharfmaster Thomas Boyle petitioned the diocese for local services. St. Mary's Church was the result because Boyle got the Protestant employers of local Catholics to add their signatures to his list. (Courtesy of John and Michelle Santos.)

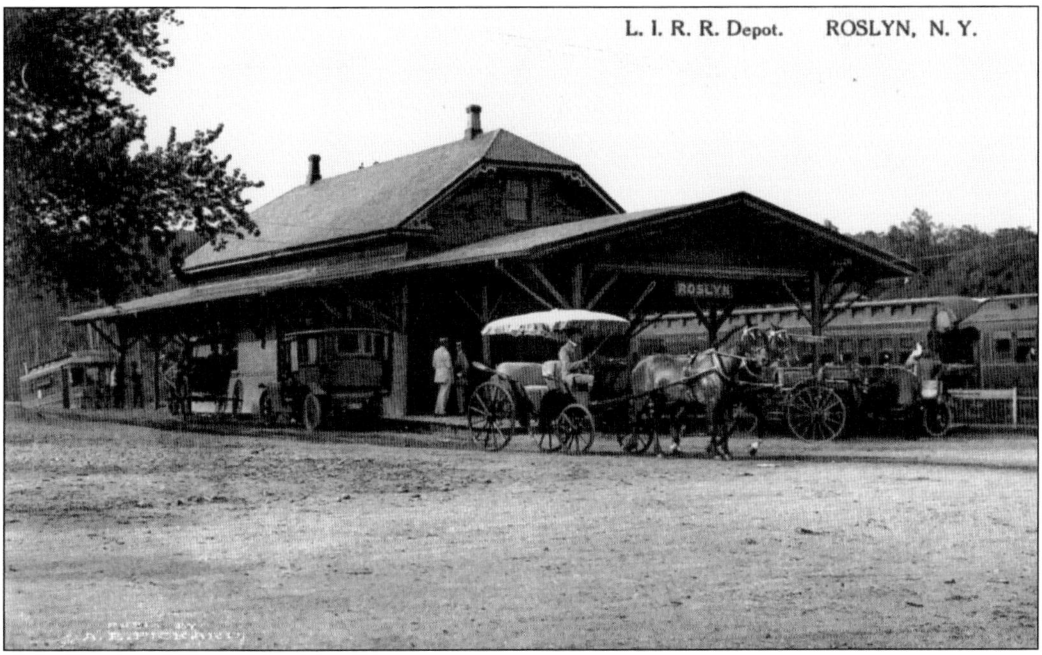

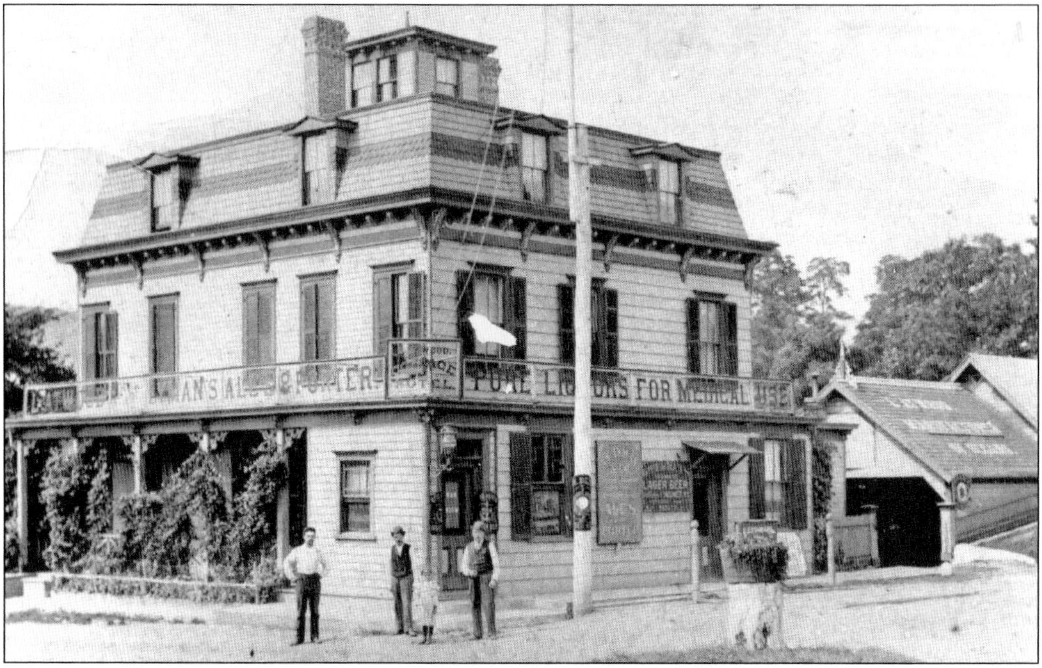

The Cottage Hotel, also called Speedling's, built around 1865, stood at Garden Street along the railroad, by the station. Seen here around 1900, the hotel offers ale and porter, as well as "pure liquors for medical use." On November 16, 1907, after the gala maiden run of the trolley to Mineola, guests were treated to a luncheon here. The building stands on Station Plaza today. (Courtesy of RLS.)

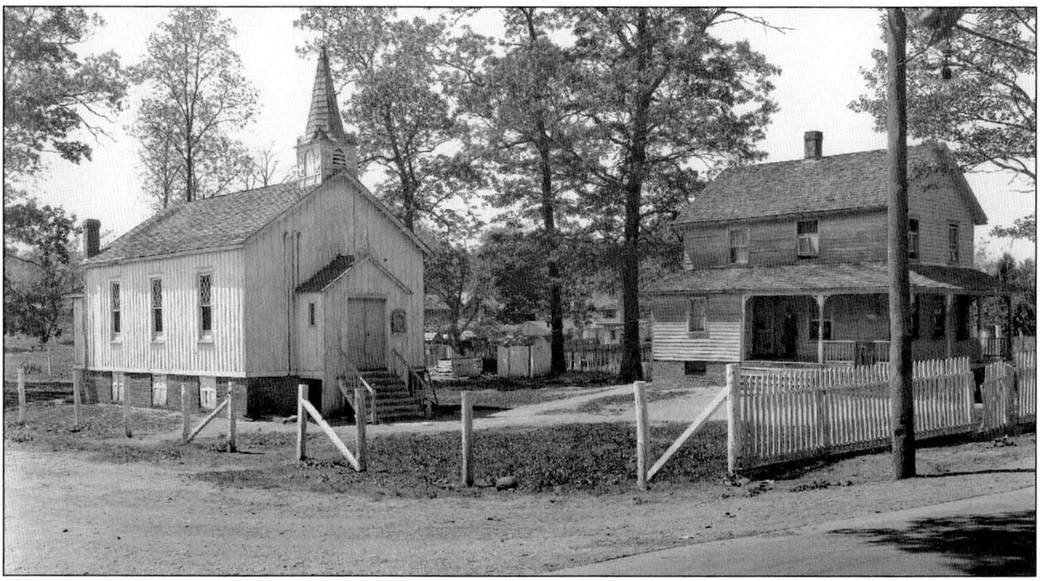

The Salem African Methodist Episcopal Church, established in 1867, was Roslyn's third-oldest religious community. The little board-and-batten chapel with its octagonal belfry cap appears to have been built around that time, although the two-and-a-half story parsonage may have followed some years later. The buildings still stand at the corner of Church Street and Roslyn Road. (Courtesy of the Queens Borough Public Library, Long Island Division, Joseph Burt Photographs.)

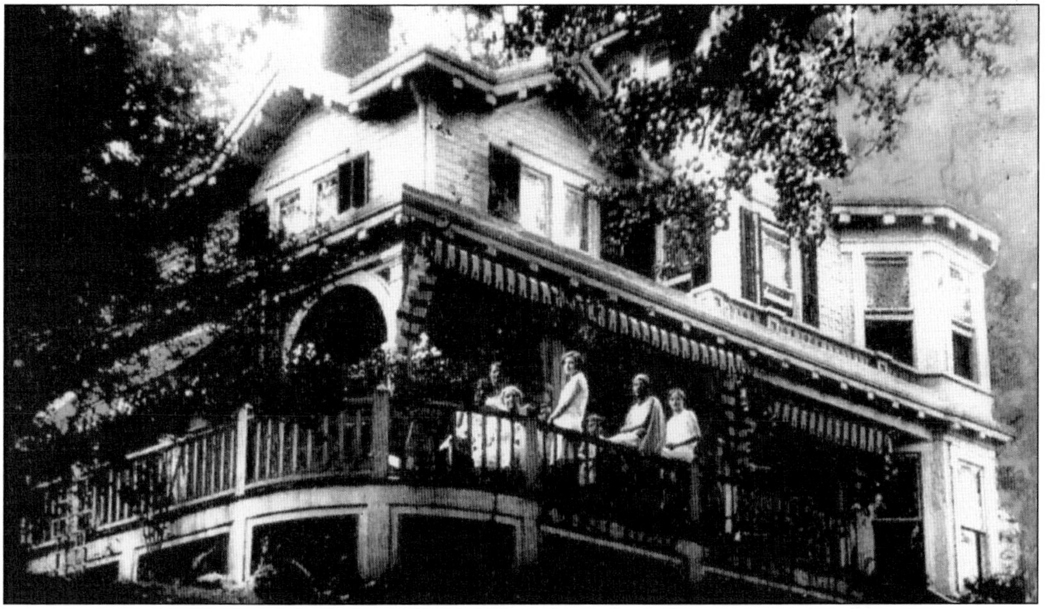

Flower Hill on the west side of Hempstead Harbor grew around the 1907 trolley line to Port Washington. It had several large estates, including this house built by carpenter John Dugan in 1875 for lawyer George Washington Denton. In 1919, the year William Pickering took this photograph, the house was purchased by Allene, Princess Henry XXXIII of Reuss, a small German principality. She owned the house until 1930. (Courtesy of Ian Zwerdling.)

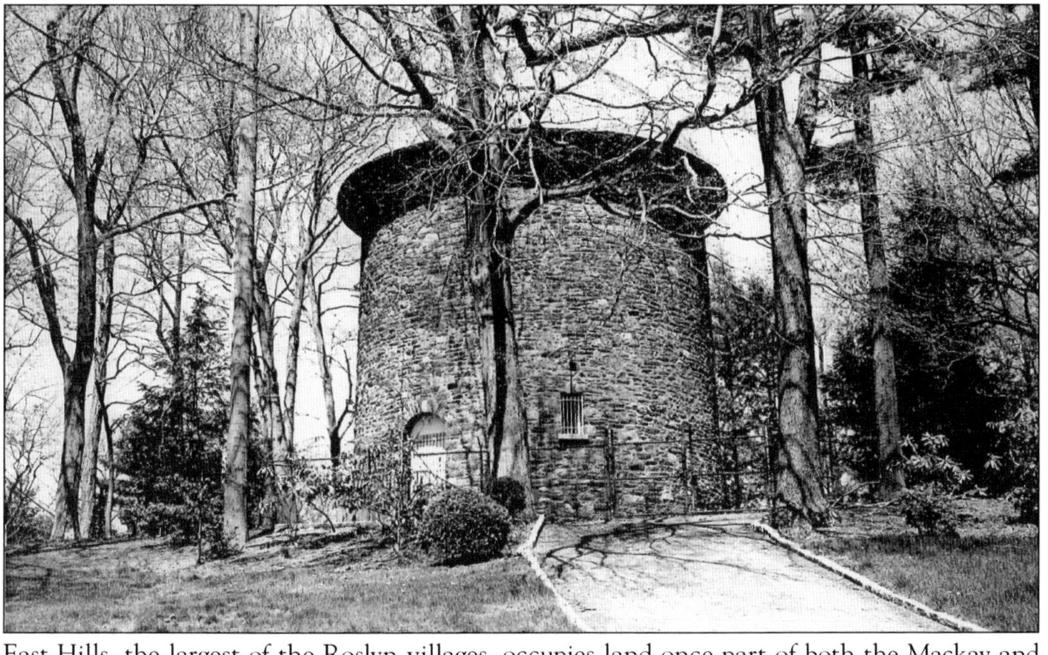

East Hills, the largest of the Roslyn villages, occupies land once part of both the Mackay and Taber properties, including Harbor Hill. Stanford White designed the Harbor Hill water tower shown here. The Mackays' water was piped more than a mile to the storage tank inside the circular stone tower. The tower, on Redwood Drive, is one of the few Mackay buildings standing today. (Photograph by Ray Jacobs, courtesy of RLS.)

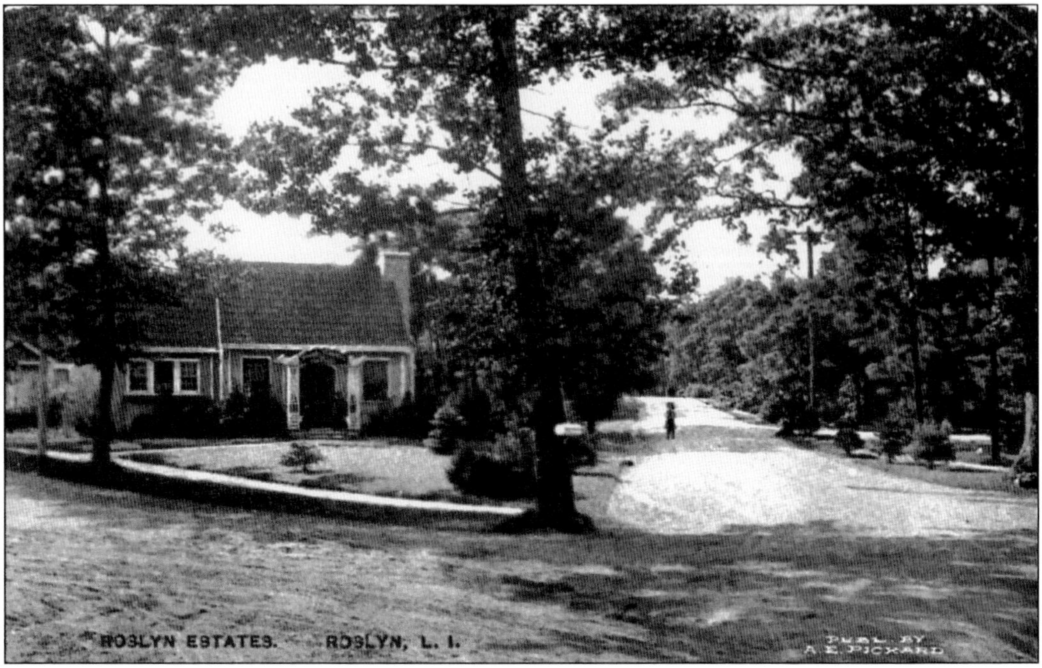

Roslyn Estates was designed as a garden community by developer Dean Alvord following his 1902 purchase of 263 acres of former farmland. Leaving many trees and natural landscape, Alvord laid out winding streets and ponds and built the first few houses. The cottage shown above, around 1912, was a sales office that Alvord later deeded to the property owners' association. The association leased it as a tearoom and restaurant, which for many years was the Wee Tappee Inn. Today it is the kosher Persian Kolbeh. Below, an original Alvord house, first owned by John A. Badenoch, stands near the southern end of the Birches. (Above, courtesy of Ian Zwerdling; below, courtesy of John and Michelle Santos.)

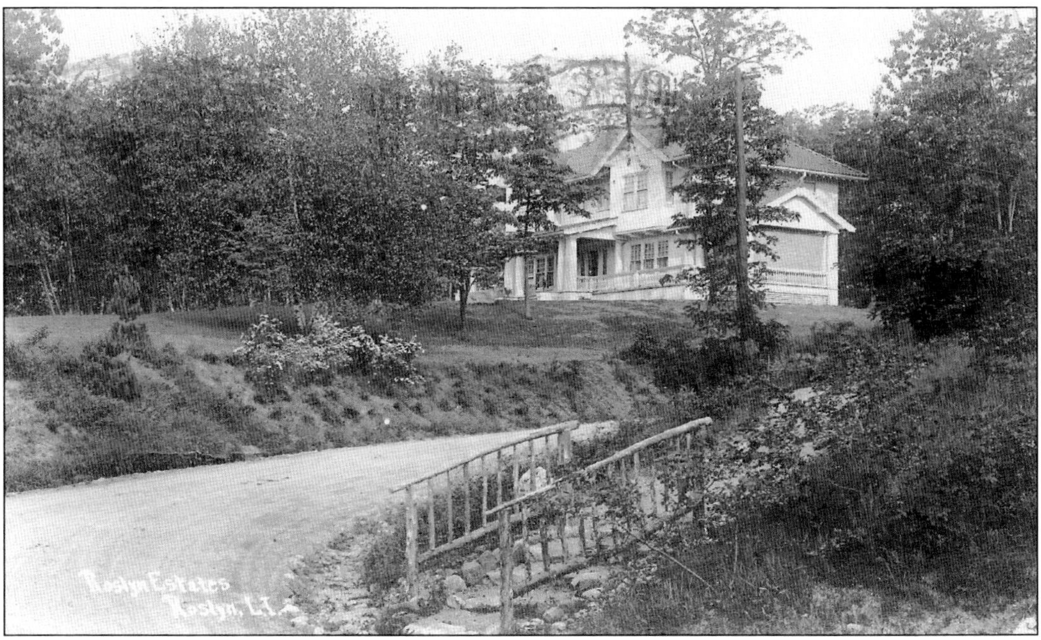

About the Roslyn Landmark Society

The Roslyn Landmark Society was founded in 1961 to preserve the history and historic resources of Roslyn and its neighboring villages along Long Island's north shore. The society presents regular programs and a historic house tour, as well as conducting historical and architectural research, publishing books, brochures, and other literature. It actively promotes historic preservation through the restoration of historic properties and by offering area residents expert advice, guidance, and knowledge on the restoration and renovation of historic buildings. The organization, in undertaking these efforts, accepts the responsibility to protect and preserve a vital legacy that exists for future generations.

Consistent with our mission to preserve history on a local level, this book was printed in South Carolina on American-made paper and manufactured entirely in the United States. Products carrying the accredited Forest Stewardship Council (FSC) label are printed on 100 percent FSC-certified paper.

MADE IN THE USA